travel

Asia
& India

Isabelle Young

LONELY PLANET PUBLICATIONS
Melbourne Oakland Paris London

Healthy Travel – Asia & India
1st edition

Published by
Lonely Planet Publications Pty Ltd ACN 005 607 983
192 Burwood Rd, Hawthorn, Victoria 3122, Australia

Lonely Planet Offices
Australia PO Box 617, Hawthorn, Victoria 3122
USA 150 Linden Street, Oakland, CA 94607
UK 10a Spring Place, London NW5 3BH
France 1 rue du Dahomey, 75011, Paris

Printed by
The Bookmaker Pty Ltd
Printed in China

Illustrations
Martin Harris & Kate Nolan

Published
February 2000

ISBN 1 86450 051 4

Contents

The external boundaries of India on this map have not been authenticated and may not be correct.

0   1000   2000 km

THE AUTHOR

ISABELLE YOUNG

Isabelle Young qualified as a doctor in Britain before deciding there must be more to life than bleeps and hospital coffee. She has travelled widely throughout the Middle East, Africa and India, which has provided plenty of opportunity for putting her training into practice.

MEDICAL ADVISERS

To ensure that the information included in this guide is as reliable as possible and in line with current practice, a team of expert medical advisers was on hand every step of the way.

TONY GHERARDIN

Overview, Before You Go, On the Move, Staying Healthy, Fever, Digestive System, Rarities, Older Travellers, Bites & Stings, Buying & Using Medicines, Medical Services

Dr Tony Gherardin is currently the national Medical Director of the Travellers Medical and Vaccination Centre (TMVC) group in Australia. He is a keen traveller and has spent several years living and working as a doctor overseas. When not travelling with his family, he now spends most of his time providing travel health advice to travellers heading in all directions around the globe.

CORINNE ELSE

Help ..., Respiratory System, Ears, Eyes & Teeth (Ears), Skin, Mental Wellbeing, Women Travellers, Men Travellers, First Aid (Wound Care), Buying & Using Medicines

Dr Corinne Else spends most of her time working as a general practitioner in the UK. Every now and again she manages to take time off to travel in Africa with her husband, helping him to research and write Lonely Planet guidebooks.

CHRISTOPHER VAN TILBERG
Climate, Altitude & Action, Water, First Aid

Dr Christopher Van Tilberg specialises in wilderness and emergency medicine. He is adventure sports editor for *Wilderness Medicine Letter* and active in mountain rescue and wilderness safety education. He is the author of *Backcountry Snowboarding* and *Canyoneering*, both published by The Mountaineers Books.

JOHN MASON
Babies & Children

Dr John Mason was a family physician for 13 years before becoming Clinical Director of the Preventative Healthcare Company. Part of his responsibility is to provide international travel care and advice to client company employees and their families, as well as managing their healthcare while abroad.

BRIAN MULHALL
HIV/AIDS & Sexual Health

Dr Brian Mulhall is a Clinical Senior Lecturer in the Department of Public Health and Community Medicine at the University of Sydney, Australia. He has travelled extensively and has written several texts on sex and travel. His contribution was sponsored by the New South Wales Health Department and the Commonwealth Department of Health as part of a sexual health promotion program for travellers.

LARRY & PAUL GOODYER
Medical Kit (Before You Go), Safe Drinking Water, Insect Bites (Staying Healthy)

Dr Larry Goodyer is the Chief Pharmacist for Nomad Travellers Store & Medical Centre, London, UK. He is also a senior lecturer in clinical pharmacy at King's College, London. His travels in India and Australia give him the first hand experience to produce medical kits for both tropical and developing world travel. Paul Goodyer is the managing director of Nomad Travellers Store & Medical Centre. His travels over the last 20 years include trips to Africa, Asia, South America and the Middle East. Getting ill on the road due to lack of knowledge led to the concept of a travellers medical centre.

SPECIAL THANKS

Special thanks go to St John Ambulance Australia for providing the information for the Emergency Resuscitation section on the inside backcover and the World Health Organization for permission to reproduce the maps between the first two chapters.

FROM THE AUTHOR

First, a big thank you to all the medical advisers, without whom this book would not have existed.

Thanks are also due to Graeme Johnson for the section on Eyes; Iain Corran for the section on Teeth; Chris Wheeler for the section on Feet; Michelle Sobel for the section on Diabetic Travellers; Bernadette Saulenier for the boxed text on Alternative First Aid for Travellers and Reiki; Leonie Englefield and Caz Price for the section on Lesbian Women's Health; and Glen Monks for the section on Gay Men's Health.

Many other people helped make this guide what it is through generously providing information, constructive comments and helpful suggestions. In no particular order, thanks go to Moya Tomlinson of Women's Health (London), and Christina Savage of the International Planned Parenthood Foundation for helpful advice and information for the Women Travellers chapter; Theresa Cannon and Christine Niven for helpful insights and pointers to information for the Traditional Asian Medicine chapter; Dr Michael Thomas of the Blood Care Foundation and Professor Neil Boyce of the Australian

Red Cross for their expert advice on blood transfusions; Dr John Putland of the Qantas Aviation Health Services Department and the British Airways Medical Service in Heathrow for providing heaps of background information on air travel for the On the Move chapter; the National Sports Information Centre (Australia) for great reference material on climatic extremes; John Nathan for helpful insights on older travellers; Peter Stroud of the Royal Melbourne Zoo for answering queries about dangerous animals; Roslyn Bullas of Lonely Planet's Pisces series for helpful advice on the Scuba Diving section; the staff at IAMAT for generously providing me with information on their organisation; Darren Elder of Lonely Planet's Cycling series for providing the safety tips for cyclists that appear in the Climate, Altitude & Action chapter; and Jenny Thorpe and Suzanne Harrison, travelling mothers extraordinaire, for invaluable insights into the rigours of travelling with little ones in tow.

Finally, in time-honoured tradition, thank you to my partner, David Petherbridge, for his help and unfailing support throughout this project – next time we'll climb mountains instead.

FROM THE PUBLISHER

This book was edited by Clay Lucas and proofed by Pete Cruttenden, with help from Graham Fricke. Maria Vallianos was responsible for design and layout of the book, with help from Design Manager Tamsin Wilson. Kirsty Hough and Anne Davey of Tanami Design came up with the original design concept for this book. Paul Piaia produced the maps; Martin Harris is responsible for all the illustrations in the book, except for Kate Nolan's cone shell illustration. David Kemp designed the cover. And special thanks is due to project manager Pete Cruttenden for putting up with so much for so long.

INTRODUCTION

Lonely Planet's aim has always been to enable adventurous travellers to get out there, to explore and better understand the world. Falling ill or getting injured on your travels prevents you from getting the most out of your travelling experience, which is why we decided to produce this *Healthy Travel* series.

Travelling can expose you to health risks you most probably would not have encountered had you stayed at home, but many of these risks are avoidable with good preparation beforehand and some common-sense measures while you are away. Even if you take all the recommended precautions, there's no guarantee that you won't fall ill at some stage on your travels, and concern about how to cope with illness in an unfamiliar setting is natural. Although this guide is not intended as a substitute for seeking medical help, we hope it will help alleviate those concerns by giving you enough background information to enable you to make informed decisions about what to do if you do fall ill or are injured.

Some chapters in this guide are designed to be read through in their entirety; the rest are there for you to dip into if the need arises. Before you leave, we suggest you take a look at the Overview chapter, which summarises the potential health risks of travel in the region, and read the Before You Go chapter, which gives you the complete lowdown on preparing for the trip. Travel medicine is an ever-changing topic, so we've given you plenty of guidance on where to get the most up-to-date information on specific health risks before you leave.

The Staying Healthy chapter gives you detailed advice on how to avoid illness and injury on your travels – essential reading for everyone. And when you return, it's a good idea to have a quick read of the When You Get Back chapter – this gives guidance on getting a checkup and signs and symptoms to look out for, as well as a discussion of that scourge of the returning traveller, post-travel blues.

The rest of the chapters are there in case you need them – and most travellers probably won't need to venture beyond the Diarrhoea section of the Digestive System chapter. If you get ill, turn to the Help ... chapter. This gives guidelines on how to go about finding medical help (use this in conjunction with the Medical Services appendix if necessary), as well as some basic measures for looking after yourself. In this chapter we've summarised the possible causes of some common symptoms, to help you work out what you may have. Alternatively, if you think you know what the problem is, you can turn straight to the relevant chapter later in the book, or you could look up your symptom in the index (symptoms are highlighted in colour in the index to make them easier to find).

We've aimed to group diseases and other medical problems into easily identifiable categories, as reflected in the chapter names. To cater for the differing needs of a wide range of travellers, we've included four chapters tailored to the needs of four major groups of travellers – women, men, babies and children, and older travellers. If something isn't in the chapter you think it should be in, it's always worth looking it up in the index.

Because accidents do happen, and help may not be as rapidly available as at home, we've included advice on basic first aid measures, including what to do in an emergency. Bear in mind, though, that first aid techniques can't be learnt just from a book. If you are going to be travelling in remote areas, it's definitely worth doing a first aid course before you go.

We hope that the advice in this guide helps ensure you have a healthy trip; if you do encounter problems, we hope it gives you greater confidence in dealing with them.

OVERVIEW

Health issues can loom large when you're planning a trip to Asia. Travellers tales of weird and wonderful infections, reports of disease outbreaks and grim portrayals of the state of health in some nations can make travel in parts of the region seem at best ridiculously foolhardy and at worst positively masochistic.

The reality, however, is much more mundane. Hundreds of thousands of travellers visit Asia every year, and healthwise most suffer nothing worse than a bout of diarrhoea. There *are* some potential health risks associated with travel in Asia that don't exist if you're travelling in places usually classified as low risk (Australia, New Zealand, North America and Western Europe), but if you're well informed about the potential risks, well prepared and take a few common-sense precautions, you'd be very unlucky *not* to stay healthy on your travels.

Admittedly, the health problems in some parts of the region (for example the subcontinent and parts of South-East Asia, especially countries affected by war) can seem daunting. In less-developed countries, lack of resources and under-investment in health care, compounded by overcrowding and low standards of living, mean that diseases that are practically unheard of now in the west (like dysentery and typhoid) are still common. In these countries, a large proportion of the population does not have access to clean water supplies or adequate sewage disposal facilities. Malnourishment is common in less-developed areas, and this increases people's susceptibility to infection and illness. In addition, many people do not have access to adequate and affordable health care. Before you become too alarmed, however, bear in mind that as a traveller in the region, you do not necessarily have the same health risks as the local population.

Asia is a politically and economically diverse region, however. Travel in Hong Kong, Japan, Singapore, South Korea and Taiwan, for example, is unlikely to involve any more risks (apart from general travel-related risks like accidents and sexually transmitted infections) than travel in the west.

Just be aware that because much of south and South-East Asia is within tropical and subtropical zones, this exposes you to some diseases (eg malaria and dengue fever) and health risks (eg sunburn and heat exhaustion) that don't exist if you're travelling in more temperate climates. Altitude is an important physical challenge to take into account if you are going to any of Asia's high places.

As well as your destination, the potential health risks you face depend on what sort of trip you're planning (five star, overlanding, adventure or activity trips expose you to different risks) and how long you are staying (longer generally means more chance of being exposed to a disease). If you're just plannning to stay at a major tourist resort in Thailand, for example, you're going to be exposed to fewer risks than if you're planning to backpack through India.

Wherever you're going, an important consideration is access to and availability of medical facilities. With the exception of Japan, Singapore, South Korea, Hong Kong and Taiwan, you will find that medical facilities are fairly limited, especially outside major cities and tourist resorts (see the Medical Services chapter for more details or consult your travel guidebook). This is a particularly important consideration if you suffer from any preexisting illness or have any special health needs.

Remember that even if adequate medical care is available in urban areas, it's generally not available in rural areas. In particular, emergency services are not the rapid response services you may be used to and, except in the more developed countries in the region, you can't rely on these. When medical help is available, it may not be of a standard you're used to.

The following section summarises the potential health risks of travel in the Asian region, together with recommended measures for minimising these risks. You might also want to refer to the maps at the end of this chapter, which show the distribution of some key diseases in the region. For a more detailed discussion of all these issues, see the Before You Go and Staying Healthy chapters later in this book. Note that because disease patterns alter and new outbreaks occur, you will need to get the latest information before you go – information sources are listed in the Before You Go chapter.

IMMUNISATIONS (p30)

Infectious diseases are common throughout China, South-East Asia and the subcontinent. Immunisations can help protect you from some of these diseases. Ideally you should get your immunisations organised at least six weeks before you go, although it's always worth seeking advice up to the last minute if necessary.

- Everybody needs to be up to date with routine immunisations like **tetanus, polio** and other **childhood illnesses** (including measles, mumps and rubella).
- **Hepatitis A** is strongly recommended for all destinations in Asia, except Japan.
- Other immunisations you may need, depending on your travel plans, include **typhoid, meningococcal meningitis, Japanese B encephalitis, rabies** and **hepatitis B**.
- Note that if you are coming to Asia from a yellow-fever-infected area (sub-Saharan Africa and some parts of South America) you may need an **immunisation certificate** for yellow fever as a condition of entry, depending on your destination.

MALARIA PILLS (p37)

Although malaria is not generally a major risk for travellers in the region, especially if you're planning to stick to the main tourist routes, there are some high-risk foci, so you should get up-to-date advice on risk areas and resistance patterns before you go. The map on p21 shows which areas are currently affected.

DISEASES CARRIED IN FOOD & WATER (p75)
Risk

Illnesses transmitted in this way include **diarrhoea, dysentery** and **hepatitis** (A and E), which are the commonest causes of illness in travellers to Asia, although you're at much less risk if you're travelling in countries with high standards of public hygiene, such as Japan, Singapore, South Korea and Taiwan. **Giardiasis** (a type of diarrhoea) is particularly common in travellers to the subcontinent. **Intestinal parasites** can also be transmitted through food and water, and are a risk mainly in rural areas. You should avoid eating some reef fish because of the risk of **poisoning**. Other diseases trasnmitted through food and water include **cholera, typhoid** and **polio**, but as a traveller you're generally at low risk of these. All of these diseases are more of a risk in the rainy season.

Prevention

To avoid getting sick:

- take care over what you eat and drink
- drink bottled, boiled or purified water
- wash your hands frequently, especially after you use the toilet and before you eat
- avoid eating raw fish and crustaceans (because of parasites transmitted in this way)

DISEASES CARRIED BY INSECTS (p83)
Risk

Dengue and **dengue haemorrhagic fever** (carried by mosquitoes) are currently a high risk to travellers in most tropical and subtropical parts of Asia, especially South-East Asia, but also Sri Lanka, Bangladesh, India and the Maldives.

There's a risk of **malaria** (also carried by mosquitoes) throughout tropical and subtropical parts of the region, although the risk varies between and within countries. There's currently no risk of malaria in Brunei, the Maldives or Singapore. The risk to travellers is generally low, although this depends on where you are going. Multidrug resistance is a major problem in parts of South-East Asia, and resistance to chloroquine is common throughout most of the region.

Other diseases carried by insects exist in the region (again commonest in tropical and subtropical zones) but they are generally of low risk to travellers. These include **Japanese B encephalitis** (spread by mosquitoes; risk highest in rural areas), **filariasis** (mosquitoes), **leishmaniasis** and **sandfly fever** (sandflies), **scrub typhus** (mites) and various **tick fevers** (lice and ticks). **Plague** (spread by fleas) exists in some countries in the region, including China, Mongolia, Myanmar and Vietnam but the risk to travellers is miniscule.

Prevention

It makes sense to take measures to prevent insect bites wherever you go in Asia. Currently, the only disease carried by insects that can be prevented by vaccination is Japanese B encephalitis. Cover up and use insect repellent.

OTHER DISEASES
Risk

Although **tuberculosis (TB)** (p128) is a major public health problem in Asia, especially the Indian subcontinent, the risk to short-term travellers is very low unless you will be living in close contact with members of the local population.

Schistosomiasis (p331) is a parasitic disease you can get from contact with fresh water (bathing, swimming or paddling) in some parts of Asia, mainly the Yangzi river basin in China, the Mekong Delta in Vietnam, the southern Philippines and central Sulawesi (Indonesia).

Outbreaks of **meningococcal meningitis** (p126) occur periodically in northern India, Pakistan, Nepal and Mongolia, although the risk to travellers is generally low.

Rabies (p345) exists in all countries in the region apart from Japan and Taiwan, and is a considerable public health problem in some nations, including India and Thailand. Bites and scratches from dogs and monkeys are probably the greatest risk to you. Pretravel immunisation may be advisable in some circumstances.

Intestinal parasites (p149) like **hookworm** are common in tropical, rural areas in Asia and you can get them by going barefoot, as well as through contaminated food and water.

Prevention
These risks are avoidable with the following precautions:

▶ if necessary, get immunised against meningitis, rabies and TB
▶ don't swim or paddle in fresh water in schistosomiasis risk areas
▶ avoid contact with animals to prevent potentially rabid bites
▶ don't walk barefoot or in sandals

HIV/AIDS & SEXUALLY TRANSMITTED INFECTIONS (p203)
Risk
You're at risk of these infections anywhere if you don't take measures to protect yourself. HIV/AIDS is a growing public health problem in some parts of the region and transmission here is mainly through heterosexual contact. In some areas there are high levels of infection among injecting drug users. Hepatitis B is common throughout the region but generally poses a small risk for most travellers, although expatriates and long-term travellers are at higher risk. All the 'traditional' STIs (like gonorrhoea, syphilis etc) also occur.

Prevention
Wherever you go, it makes sense to take precautions:

▶ always use a latex condom if you have sex with a new partner while you are away
▶ as a general rule, avoid injections and anything that involves skin-piercing
▶ in most countries in the region, avoid any unnecessary medical or dental procedures
▶ take steps to minimise your risk of injury through accidents

▶ consider taking a kit containing sterile needles and syringes in case of an emergency (and carry it on you)

▶ never share needles

BLOOD TRANSFUSIONS (p93)

Risk

In most countries in Asia, with the exception of Japan, blood supplies in general use are not thought to be as safe from diseases like HIV/AIDS and hepatitis B as they are in Australia, New Zealand, North America and Western Europe.

Prevention

Minimise your risks by taking steps to avoid injury and by not travelling in less developed countries if you have a condition that makes blood transfusion a possibility. If transfusion is unavoidable for medical reasons, make sure you find a source of safe blood.

ENVIRONMENTAL HAZARDS

Risk

Sunburn (p72) is a considerable risk in most parts of tropical and subtropical Asia. Coping with the heat (p71) can be a challenge if you are going to tropical or subtropical parts of Asia. Hot, humid conditions, as well as poor environmental cleanliness, make infection (p195) of cuts and scratches more likely when you're travelling in many parts of Asia. Cold (p296) can be a significant risk in high areas and in the more temperate parts of Asia. With some of the highest mountains in the world, you need to be aware of the effects of altitude (p300) on your health in some destinations in Asia, notably the Himalaya and the Karakoram.

Prevention

You can take measures to minimise the impact of environmental challenges:

▶ allow yourself time to acclimatise to the heat and take steps to avoid dehydration

▶ take care to protect your skin from the effects of the sun
▶ look after all cuts and scratches to prevent infection
▶ always be prepared for climatic extremes, especially if you are trekking or walking at high altitudes
▶ make sure you are informed about the effects of altitude on your health and follow the rules for safe ascent

ACCIDENTS & INJURY (p86)
Risk
Accidents *do* happen, and they're a common cause of injury (and the main cause of death) in travellers. Road traffic accidents are a notoriously high risk for travellers to most parts of Asia, especially motorbike or moped accidents.

Prevention
If you are aware of the potential risk, and use a bit of common sense, this should help you to avoid accidents and injury.

OTHER HAZARDS
Risk
Fleas (p339), lice (p197) and scabies (p196) are potential hazards in most places, especially if you're staying in budget accommodation, but don't generally cause serious illness. Ticks (p337) and mites are a hazard if you are trekking in rural areas, especially scrubland, and can transmit a nasty disease, scrub typhus, although this is very uncommon in travellers. Leeches (p335) are common in damp, forested areas throughout the region but don't carry any disease.

Wild animals (p345), snakes (p343), scorpions (p342), crocodiles (p319) and marine creatures (p318) are other hazards to be aware of in some areas, but generally pose a very small risk to you.

Prevention
You can avoid these hazards fairly easily:

▶ cover up and use insect repellents
▶ give all creatures a wide berth – look but don't touch

MALARIA

Map data supplied by
World Health Organization

Areas with no malaria

Areas with limited risk

Areas with malaria

Areas not covered by
this guide

0   1000   2000 km

*The external boundaries of
India on this map have not
been authenticated and
may not be correct.*

DENGUE FEVER

Map data supplied by World Health Organization

Areas with no dengue fever

Areas with dengue fever

Areas not covered by this guide

0   1000   2000 km

The external boundaries of India on this map have not been authenticated and may not be correct.

LYMPHATIC FILARIASIS

Map data supplied by World Health Organization

Areas with no lymphatic filariasis

Areas with lymphatic filariasis

Areas not covered by this guide

0   1000   2000 km

The external boundaries of India on this map have not been authenticated and may not be correct.

SCHISTOSOMIASIS (BILHARZIA)

Map data supplied by
World Health Organization

Areas with no schistosomiasis

Areas with schistosomiasis

Areas not covered by
this guide

The external boundaries of
India on this map have not
been authenticated and
may not be correct.

0   1000   2000 km

BEFORE YOU GO ─────────────

Staying healthy on your travels in most parts of Asia does require a bit of pretravel effort. It may seem like a chore now, but it could save you much hassle later – after all, you don't want to waste the trip of your lifetime languishing in your room, worrying if you've contracted an awful disease you could have been immunised against (but never got around to before you left), or trailing around looking for a doctor when the only foreign phrase you know is 'Hello, I'm from Australia'.

It's tempting to leave all this preparatory stuff to the last minute – don't! You'll have a hundred and one other things to do just before you go, and you don't want to be doing them with a sore arm. It's best to start thinking about the health issues of your trip as early as possible, and certainly at least six weeks in advance. But if things don't work out as planned, it's always worth visiting your doctor or travel health clinic for advice and immunisations, however late you've left it.

INFORMATION SOURCES ─────────

Part of your pretravel preparations is to find out about the health risks of your destination, and this has never been easier. You can get up-to-date information and advice on your travel health risks from your family doctor, travel health clinics, and national and state health departments. Even handier, you've got a great information source at your fingertips – the internet. For general information on a variety of travel health issues, you could try some of the many publications available – we've listed a selection under Books at the end of this chapter.

TRAVEL HEALTH CLINICS & INFORMATION LINES

Specialist travel health clinics are probably the best places to visit for immunisations and travel health advice, although they are often more expensive than going to your local health department or family doctor. If you have an ongoing medical

condition, or any general health concerns, you may prefer to
go to your usual doctor. Some travel health clinics provide
specific travel health briefs (usually for a fee) by mail, phone
or fax, which you can then take to your doctor. Most clinics
sell travellers essentials like insect repellents, mosquito nets
and 'sterile' kits.

UK

As you'd expect, there's no shortage of travel health clinics
and information lines. Here's a selection to get you started.

British Airways Travel Clinics – countrywide network of clinics
(plus three in South Africa) and you don't need to be travelling on
British Airways to use them. Phone ☎ 01276-685040 or check out
their web site (www.britishairways.com/travelqa/fyi/health/) for
your nearest clinic.

Hospital for Tropical Diseases Travel Clinic (☎ 020-7388 9600),
Mortimer Market Centre, Capper St, London WC1E; ring their
travel health information line ☎ 0839-337733 for advice.

Liverpool School of Tropical Medicine Travel Clinic (☎ 0151-708
9393), Pembroke Place, Liverpool L3 5QA; ring their travel
health advice line ☎ 0906-708 8807 for destination-specific
advice on immunisations and other travel health issues.

Malaria Health Line (☎ 0891-600350) – recorded information on
malaria risks from the Malaria Reference Laboratory at the
London School of Hygiene & Tropical Medicine.

MASTA (Medical Advisory Services for Travellers; ☎ 020-7631
4408) at the London School of Hygiene & Tropical Medicine,
Keppel St, London WC1E 7BR – no travel clinic but provides
information and travel health products; ring ☎ 0906-8 224100
for detailed health information on your destination.

Nomad Travellers Store & Medical Centre (☎ 020-8889 7014,
travel health line ☎ 09068-633414, nomad.travstore@virgin.net)
3-4 Wellington Terrace, Turnpike Lane, London N8 0PX– they
have a travel clinic and sell a wide range of travel equipment, as
well as health-related products.

The booklet *Health Advice for Travellers* published by the
Department of Health (☎ 0800-555777 to order a copy) has

basic advice and details of reciprocal health care agreements, however, it's of limited use if you're going to Asia, as this doesn't include any countries in Asia or the subcontinent.

North America

To find a travel health clinic in your area, you could call your state health department, or you could try one of the following.

Centers for Disease Control and Prevention – based in Atlanta, Georgia, the CDC is the central source of travel health information in North America. The CDC has phone (☎ 888-232-3228) and fax (☎ 888-232-3299) travel health information lines, and can also advise you on travel medicine providers in your area.

American Society of Tropical Medicine & Hygiene (☎ 847-480-9592, fax 847-480-9282, www.astmh.org), 60 Revere Drive, Suite 500, Northbrook, IL 60062, can provide you with a comprehensive list of travel health providers in your area.

International Society of Travel Medicine (☎ 770-736-7060, www.istm.org), PO Box 871089, Stone Mountain, GA 30087; contact the ISTM for a list of ISTM member clinics.

The CDC publishes an excellent booklet, *Health Information for International Travel* – call ☎ 202-512-1800 or order it from the Superintendent of Documents, US Government Printing Office, Washington DC.

The US State Department Citizen's Emergency Center has travel advisories on a recording, and can also provide you with access to medical advice and assistance over the phone if you are in an emergency situation overseas. Remember to take a record of the number (☎ 202-647-5225) with you.

Australia & New Zealand

The Travellers Medical and Vaccination Centre has a network of clinics in most major cities – use the phone book to find your nearest clinic or check out their web site (www.tmvc.com.au). TMVC also has clinics in Bangkok and Singapore. They can provide an online personalised travel health report (for a fee) via their web site. The Australian Department of Human

Services and Health publishes a booklet, *Health Information for International Travel*, but it's a bit out of date (1993) and probably not worth the trouble.

TRAVEL HEALTH WEB SITES

These are a great source of information, both before you go and when you are on the road. Two authoritative web sites are the first point of call for the latest on travel health issues.

WHO (**www.who.ch**) – the World Health Organization's official site, this has all the information you'll ever need on the state of the world's health, including disease distribution maps and the latest health recommendations for international travel. The section at www.who.int/emc is probably going to be most useful to you – it has disease outbreak news and travel health advice.

CDC (**www.cdc.gov**) – the official site of the US Centers for Disease Control and Prevention, this has loads of useful information, including disease outbreak news and disease risks according to destination.

Other sites worth checking out include the following.

MASTA (**www.masta.org**) – this highly recommended site of the Medical Advisory Services for Travellers (see earlier) is easy to use and provides concise readable information on all the important issues. It also has useful links, including to the Foreign and Commonwealth Office for advice on safe travel.

Medical College of Wisconsin Travelers Clinic (**www.intmed.mcw/travel.html**) – this site has useful information on all the usual travel health issues, and an impressively comprehensive list of links to a variety of other travel health information sites. Browse till you drop.

Shorelands (**www.tripprep.com**) – this well-organised site is easy to navigate and has lots of good travel health information, as well as a comprehensive directory of travel medicine providers around the world and handy country profiles that include US State Department travel advisory information.

Travel Health Information Service (**www.travelhealth.com**) – this chatty site, run by US-based Dr Stephen Blythe, is easy to navigate and has loads of good information and links.

Travellers Medical and Vaccination Centre (**www.tmvc.com.au**) –
   this Australian-based site has lots of useful information, including disease outbreak news and good sections on travelling while
   pregnant and with children.

There are also authoritative sites providing information on
more specialist areas like diving medicine and altitude – these
are listed in the relevant sections.

USEFUL ORGANISATIONS

The International Association for Medical Assistance to
Travelers (IAMAT) is a nonprofit foundation that can provide
you with a list of English-speaking doctors worldwide, as
well as travel health information. Doctors affiliated to
IAMAT charge a fixed fee. Membership is free, but the foundation welcomes a donation. Contact IAMAT (www.sentex.
net) in Canada (☎ 519-836-0102, fax 519-836-3412) at 40
Regal Rd, Guelph, Ontario N1K 1B5; in the USA (☎ 716-
754-4883) at 417 Center Street, Lewiston, NY 14092; in
Switzerland at 57 Voirets, 1212 Grand-Lancy-Geneva; or in
New Zealand at PO Box 5049, Christchurch 5.

MedicAlert Foundation International (☎ 800-432-5378),
2323 Colorado Ave, Turlock, CA 95380-1009, USA, is a nonprofit organisation providing (for a membership fee) medical
identification bracelets or tags with details of drug allergies or
important medical conditions you have, plus a call collect
number for their 24-hour Emergency Response Center. It's
worth considering this if you have asthma, diabetes or severe
allergy, or if you're taking steroids or blood-thinning medicine. Non-US residents can contact affiliate offices locally,
including in the UK ☎ 020-7833 3034; check out MedicAlert's
web site (www.medicalert.org) for a complete list.

AEA/SOS International (☎ 800-523-8930, PO Box 11568,
Philadelphia, PA 31685) is a travel insurance provider who
can provide US-based members with details of health risks
and English-speaking doctors in key Asian cities.

IMMUNISATIONS

Immunisations help protect you from some of the diseases you may be at risk of getting on your travels. Unfortunately, there are many more diseases (such as diarrhoea, malaria and dengue fever) you may encounter while travelling in Asia that can't be prevented by in this way.

Yellow fever is the only immunisation you might need to show a certificate for as a condition of entry into some countries – see the boxed text for more details. However, wherever you're going, it's a good idea to make sure your immunisations are recorded on an official certificate – your doctor or travel health centre will usually issue you with a record. This way you'll know what you're protected against and when you're due for a top-up, and if necessary, you'll be able to show it to any doctor treating you.

Be wary of advice on immunisations and other health issues given to you by embassies or travel agents, especially

Homoeopathic Immunisations

You may want to consider these if you've left your immunisations to the last minute – you could boost protection with a homoeopathic immunisation for a week or so until the protective effect of the injection kicks in: They may also be useful is if you can't have the conventional injections for some reason. Just bear in mind that the effectiveness of homoeopathic immunisations has not been fully explored, especially under travel conditions.

To find out more about homoeopathic immunisations, contact a registered homoeopathic practitioner or your national organisation of homoeopaths. In addition, you could try some of the publications on homoeopathic medicine listed under Books, most of which cover this topic. The UK-based Society of Homoeopaths (☎ 01604 621400, societyofhomoeopaths @btinternet.com, 2 Artizan Rd, Northampton NN1 4HU, UK) produces a helpful leaflet *Homoeopathy and Foreign Travel.*

Yellow Fever

If you're travelling to Asia, you only need this immunisation if you're coming from a yellow-fever-infected area (sub-Saharan Africa and parts of South America). Yellow fever doesn't exist in Asia, but mosquitoes capable of transmitting it do. This means it could exist if travellers from infected areas bring the disease with them. Asian countries protect themselves from this risk by requiring any traveller from an infected area to have a certificate proving they have been vaccinated against yellow fever. Most countries in Asia currently have this requirement; exceptions are Japan, Mongolia and Korea.

if they say that 'no immunisations are needed'. What they mean is that you won't be asked for any vaccination certificates when you roll up at the border, not that you don't need the jabs for your own protection.

SPECIAL CONSIDERATIONS

Just bear in mind that immunisations are not suitable for everyone. If you're pregnant, for example, there are some immunisations that are best avoided – see p254 for more details. Babies and children are also a special case – we discuss this in more detail in the section on Immunisations (p263) in the Babies & Children chapter later in this book.

Other special considerations include any serious reactions you may have had to immunisations in the past, or if your immunity is lowered for some reason (eg you're taking steroids or you're HIV-positive). In this situation, some immunisations are best avoided – you'll need to discuss this with your doctor well in advance of travelling. For more details see the Travellers with Special Needs section on p49.

TIMING

Ideally, you need to get your immunisations organised about six to eight weeks before you travel. This is because usually you need to wait one to two weeks after a booster or the last dose of an immunisation course before you're fully protected, and some courses may need to be given over a period of several weeks. Although there's no medical reason why you can't have all your injections together, it's a bit masochistic and it may make side effects like fever or sore arm worse. Generally, if you've had a full course of an immunisation before, you will only need a booster injection.

Don't panic if you have left it to the last minute. Immunisation schedules can be rushed if necessary, and most vaccinations you'll need for Asia can be given together two weeks, or even one week, before you leave. Just bear in mind that you won't be as well protected for the first week or two of your trip. Note that a full course of rabies vaccine takes a month, as does Japanese B encephalitis. Cholera and yellow fever need to be separated by at least three weeks, but you're very unlikely to be having these for a trip to Asia alone.

WHICH ONES?

Working out which immunisations you need doesn't just depend on your destination, your doctor will also take the following into account: the length of your trip; whether you're going to be travelling in rural areas or sticking to the resorts; whether you're planning to work; which immunisations you've had in the past; any medications you're on; and any allergies you have. So while we can give you some idea of the immunisations you're *likely* to need, for a definitive list you'll need to discuss your requirements with your doctor.

Whatever your travel plans, it's a good idea to be up to date with all your routine immunisations, including:

■ tetanus (often given together with diphtheria)
■ polio
■ 'childhood' illnesses (measles, mumps and rubella)

In addition, you'll generally need some specific travel-related immunisations.

vaccine	full course	booster	comments
tetanus, usually given with diphtheria	three doses given at four-week intervals	every 10 years	full course is usually given in childhood
polio	three doses given at four-week intervals	every 10 years; usually given orally	full course is usually given in childhood
hepatitis A vaccine	single dose plus booster at six to 12 months	gives good protection for at least 12 months	with booster, it protects for more than 10 years
hepatitis A immunoglobulin	single injection; needs to be given as close to travel as possible	N/A	gives protection only for a limited length of time (two to six months, depending on dose)
typhoid	single injection OR three or four oral doses	injection: every three years; oral: one to five years	oral typhoid vaccine needs to be completed one week before you start malaria pills
meningococcal meningitis	one dose	N/A	protection lasts three years
hepatitis B	two doses one month apart plus a third dose six months later	three to five years	more rapid courses are available if necessary
rabies (pre-exposure)	three doses over one month	two years	if you're planning to take antimalarials, you may need to have a different type of injection
Japanese B encephalitis	three doses over a month	three years	protection lasts for two to three years
BCG (for tuberculosis)	single dose	protection lasts for life	often given in childhood, so you may already be protected

Cholera

Note that immunisation against cholera is no longer generally recommended, except in special circumstances, as it provides short-lived and poor protection. In any case, as a traveller you're at very low risk of cholera.

Hepatitis A

All travellers to Asia (unless you're just travelling to Japan) should be protected against this common disease (figures suggest that up to 20 travellers out of every 1000 get hepatitis A). Hepatitis A vaccine gives good protection for at least a year (longer if you have a booster). Alternatively, you can have immunoglobulin, which protects you for a limited time only and carries a theoretical though miniscule risk (in western countries) of blood-borne diseases like HIV. A combined hepatitis A and typhoid vaccine has recently become available, which should cut down the number of jabs you need to have.

Hepatitis B

This immunisation is recommended for long-term travellers to hepatitis B hot spots like China, South-East Asia and the Indian subcontinent. Other situations in which it's recommended are if you're going to be working as a medic or nurse, or if you're at risk from needle sharing or sexual contact at your destination. This immunisation is given in childhood in some countries, including Australia and the USA. A combined hepatitis A and B vaccine is available if you need to have both.

Japanese B Encephalitis

You may need this if you're planning to spend more than a month in rural areas of the Indian subcontinent, China, Japan, South-East Asia or the Philippines.

Meningococcal Meningitis

Check with your doctor or travel health clinic for the latest information on outbreaks, but this immunisation is currently recommended for Nepal and long-term travel in northern Pakistan, northern India, Mongolia and a few areas of Vietnam.

Rabies

With rabies, you have the choice of having the immunisation either before you go (called preexposure) or just if you're unlucky enough to get bitten (postexposure). Preexposure vaccination involves receiving a course of three injections over a period of a month before you leave. This primes your system against rabies, giving you some, but not complete, protection against it. If you then get bitten by a suspect animal, you will need to have two boosters to prevent rabies developing.

If you didn't have preexposure vaccination, you will need the full course of rabies vaccination (five injections over a month) as well as an immediate injection of rabies antibodies (also called human rabies immunoglobulin; RIG). RIG can be made from horse or human blood, but human-derived RIG can be difficult to obtain in many countries in Asia; even if it is available, it's probably best to avoid human blood products in these countries. RIG is very expensive and both types tend to be in short supply and difficult to obtain in many places.

Consider having preexposure rabies vaccination if you're going to be travelling through Asia for more than three months or if you're going to be handling animals. Children are at particular risk of being bitten, so may need to be vaccinated even if you're going for only a short time – discuss with your doctor or a travel health clinic. Wherever you go, it's worth taking precautions to avoid getting bitten by potentially rabid animals.

Finally, if you've heard of the old rabies injections which were given into the stomach and were extremely uncomfortable, be reassured. The modern rabies vaccine is usually given in your arm and has few side effects. However, the older vaccine is still used in many less developed areas.

Tuberculosis

You may have been immunised against this as a child, but even if you weren't, you probably won't need to be unless you're going to be living with local people for three months or more in most parts of Asia (except Japan).

Typhoid

You'll need this if you're going for more than a couple of weeks to most parts of Asia (except Japan), especially the Indian subcontinent. The oral typhoid vaccine can sometimes give you a tummy upset. If you were unlucky enough to have had the old injectable typhoid vaccine, you'll know that it can produce some pretty unpleasant reactions (fever, aches and pains), but the new one causes very few effects.

SIDE EFFECTS

Immunisations are like any other medication in that they can have unwanted effects. These are generally unpleasant rather than dangerous, although very occasionally serious allergic reactions can occur. There's no evidence that immunisations damage your immune system in any way.

If you tend to faint after injections, plan to sit quietly for 10 minutes or so after having your shots. The most common reactions are soreness around the injection site, sometimes with redness and swelling, and maybe a slight fever or a general feeling of being unwell. Tetanus, for example, commonly gives you a sore arm, while the hepatitis A vaccine can occasionally give you a fever in the evening. These reactions generally settle quickly with painkillers and rest, and an ice pack on your arm can help soothe any soreness.

! If you get more serious reactions that don't settle overnight, contact the clinic where you had your injections.

Very occasionally immunisations can provoke allergic reactions due to substances they may contain, like albumin from eggs, which is why you sometimes have to stay at the clinic for half an hour after the injection. Allergic reactions are a possibility with any immunisation, but some immunisations are more likely to cause this than others (eg Japanese B encephalitis). These reactions are more likely if you know you are allergic to eggs or if you have multiple allergies, especially to bee stings; discuss this with your doctor.

MALARIA PILLS

If you're going to a malarial area in Asia (see map p21), you'll need to take measures to avoid getting this serious, potentially fatal disease.

Although you're generally less at risk of getting malaria in Asia than in the more infamous malarial zones of sub-Saharan Africa and South America, there are some high-risk foci in Asia. Also, malaria in many parts of South-East Asia – especially areas of eastern Thailand and western Cambodia – is

Malaria Facts

Here are some facts you need to be aware of about this infamous disease:

- malaria is spread by mosquitoes
- malaria is a potentially fatal disease
- malaria is becoming more common and more difficult to treat because of drug resistance
- most cases of malaria in travellers occur in people who didn't take antimalarials or who didn't take them properly
- most malaria deaths in travellers occur because the diagnosis is delayed or missed
- malaria is particularly dangerous in children and pregnant women
- malaria can be transmitted by transfusion of blood and other blood products, by needle sharing among injecting drug users and from mother to fetus

resistant to most of the drugs commonly used in the prevention and treatment of malaria.

You can't rely on just taking preventive drugs for protection against malaria, especially with the rise in resistance of the malarial parasite to commonly used antimalarial drugs, you also need to take all necessary precautions to prevent insect bites (see the section on Insect Bites in the Staying Healthy chapter for the complete lowdown on this).

Malaria can be rapidly fatal, so you need to know what to do if you think you have it – see the section on Malaria in the Fever chapter for detailed guidance on diagnosing and treating malaria.

For some low-risk malarial areas, you may not need to take malaria pills, but instead you may be advised to carry with you emergency treatment for malaria to use if necessary. If you do, you need to be absolutely clear about when to take it and what to do – see Emergency Standby Treatment later in this section for more details.

MALARIA INFORMATION SOURCES

Preventing illness and death from malaria has become more complicated in recent years with the rise in resistance of the malarial parasite to old favourites like chloroquine. Because it's such a complex and rapidly changing issue, it's not a good idea to rely on advice from friends or other travellers, however well intentioned or knowledgeable they are.

Up-to-date and reliable information about malaria risks and prevention, is readily available from travel health clinics, information lines and via the web – see Information Sources earlier in this chapter. For information on malaria risks in selected countries in the region, you could check out www.actmalaria.org (although this is not aimed primarily at travellers). For more general information on all aspects of malaria, the Malaria Foundation web site (www.malaria.org) is an excellent resource.

MALARIA RISK

Malarial mosquitoes bite at night and tend to like rural areas, so if you are in rural areas during the hours of darkness in a malaria zone, you'll generally be at higher risk than if you're planning to spend all your time in urban areas. Mosquitoes breed in stagnant water, and the risk of malaria is seasonal to a certain extent, with a higher risk just after the rainy season. You're generally safe from malarial mosquitoes at altitudes above about 2500m. Areas in the same country can have different risks of malaria (for example, there's a very low risk of malaria in the coastal resorts in Thailand, but inland the risk is much greater) and different areas may have different levels of resistance to antimalarial drugs.

The following commonly visited areas in Asia currently have low malarial risk and no malaria pills are recommended – but these may change so make sure you get the latest information before you leave:

- all main cities in South-East Asia
- Singapore, Hong Kong and peninsular Malaysia
- most resorts and mainstream tourist areas in Indonesia, Philippines, Thailand and Vietnam
- Kathmandu and mountain trekking areas in Nepal
- most of China (excluding Yunnan and Hainan Island)

WHICH PILLS?

Preventive drugs against malaria work by killing off the malarial parasites before they can cause the disease. Which drug you're offered will depend on where you're going, as resistance of the parasites to the various malaria pills varies from region to region. Just to confuse the issue, there is a lack of consensus internationally about the most appropriate prevention. For example, if you're in the US, you generally won't be offered the option to take chloroquine plus proguanil, a widely used combination in travellers from Western Europe; you're likely to be offered mefloquine (Lariam) instead.

You need to start taking malaria pills before you leave to give them a chance to reach maximum protective levels in your body before you meet any malarial mosquitoes. This also gives any side effects a chance to show up before you go, in case you need to change medication.

- Chloroquine (with or without proguanil) needs to be started at least one week in advance.
- It's best to start mefloquine two to three weeks before you go – see the boxed text on mefloquine over the page for more details.
- Doxycycline needs to be started two days before you leave.

Don't be tempted to stop taking your malaria pills as soon as you leave or you may get malaria from parasites you picked up in the last few days of your trip.

All malaria pills need to be continued for four weeks after you return home.

It's best to take your malaria pills after food as this makes side effects like nausea and stomach upset less likely. For the best protection, you need to take malaria pills regularly.

Long-Haul Travellers

If you're planning on travelling in a malarial area for six months or more, you may be wondering what to do about protection against malaria. You've got two main options: you can either continue to take your usual malaria prevention pills or you can decide not to take them. If you do decide to stop them (discuss this with your doctor before you go), you need to be extremely vigilant at avoiding mosquito bites, and you need to be very clear about where your nearest doctor is and when to take emergency standby treatment.

Taking malaria pills for more than six months can work out quite expensive, and, unless you're really conscientious, it can be easy to forget to take your pills. Note that you don't build up immunity to malaria with time, so you're still at risk of getting it, even if you've been in a risk area for a long time.

As far as possible, it's best to take with you all the malaria pills you think you will need, as some malaria pills may not be available in some parts of Asia and you may not be able to get exactly what you want. Discuss the alternatives with your doctor or travel health clinic before you go. If you do end up needing to buy malaria pills when you are away, make sure you get expert advice on this.

The Great Malaria Pill Debate

Which malaria pills to take, and whether to take them at all, tends to be a hot topic of conversation among travellers, especially as Asia doesn't have the uniformly high risk of malaria that sub-Saharan Africa has, for example. In high-risk malarial areas, the bottom line is that the risk of death or severe illness is much greater if you don't take malaria pills. However, many of the usual traveller destinations in Asia don't have a high malarial risk (see Malaria Risk earlier in this section). With some malaria pills, there's been debate about whether the benefits of taking them outweigh the risks in all situations. And if travellers are so concerned about potential side effects that they're not taking their malaria pills, they're clearly not an effective preventive. You'll need to decide for yourself on this one, but bear in mind that if you can't or would prefer not to take a particular malaria pill, there are other possibilities that may be better than taking nothing at all.

It's true that you can still get malaria even if you take your malaria pills regularly (one reason is drug resistance, which can vary immensely from area to area), but bear in mind that if you do get malaria, the illness is likely to be less severe if you were taking antimalarials.

Drug resistance is a problem that currently vexes whole departments of experts worldwide. The answer to the problem is generally believed to lie in controlling the mosquitoes that spread the disease. There are hopes of a malarial vaccine, but there's still a long way to go before this becomes a reality.

DOSES & SIDE EFFECTS

! Minor side effects are common with all the drugs but if you get major side effects that make you unsure about continuing the drug, seek advice about changing to a medication that suits you better.

Mefloquine (Lariam)

This drug is taken weekly. It was developed as an alternative to chloroquine when it became clear that chloroquine resistance had become widespread. It is currently the most effective malarial, although resistance to mefloquine has now appeared and is on the increase. Currently, areas where mefloquine resistance is established include Thailand (in the border

---

Should I take Mefloquine (Lariam)?

As you're probably aware, this controversial malaria drug has attracted quite a bit of media attention, and it's a frequent talking point in travellers circles.

No one doubts that mefloquine is currently the most effective drug at preventing malaria; the issue is side effects. Mefloquine commonly causes 'minor' side effects like nausea and diarrhoea, as do the other antimalarials, but it can also have more disturbing side effects. These range from weird dreams, dizziness and anxiety to panic attacks, depression and even fits (seizures). Some travellers claim to be permanently affected by mefloquine. Equally, a large proportion of travellers take mefloquine and have no problems.

Experts disagree on how common the disabling side effects are. Figures from studies range from one in 10,000 (about the same number as for travellers taking chloroquine and proguanil) to much higher rates (one in 140 in a recent study by the London School of Hygiene & Tropical Medicine).

Some experts point out that, purely on a statistical basis, many millions of people take mefloquine at any one time, so some people are bound to develop symptoms even though they may be totally unrelated to taking the drug. Several studies have shown that most people get used to the side effects with time.

---

regions with Cambodia and Myanmar) and western Cambodia. This is likely to change, so check with a travel health clinic or the CDC and WHO web sites mentioned under Information Sources earlier for the latest recommendations.

See the boxed text on this page for a discussion of the possible side effects of mefloquine. If side effects do occur, it's usually after the first two to three doses. Starting mefloquine two to three weeks before you leave gives you time to change to an alternative if necessary.

Mefloquine is not suitable for everyone: you should not take it if you have epilepsy (fits) or if you have had severe depression or other major mind problems in the past, or if you are on medicines (for example beta blockers) for a heart condition – check with your doctor. Mefloquine is best avoided

As a result of the controversy, the British guidelines for the use of mefloquine were thoroughly reviewed in 1997, and it was agreed that because of the risk of side effects, mefloquine should only be used when the risk of resistant malaria is high.

We suggest you find out for yourself what different people have to say about mefloquine and then make up your own mind. In high-risk areas in South-East Asia, mefloquine resistance has appeared, and doxycycline is usually the recommended preventive.

You can get information on mefloquine from any travel health clinic, your doctor, a pharmacist or any of the web sites listed earlier in this chapter. For more specific information about the mefloquine issue, you could check out the Lariam Action USA web site (www.suggskelly.com/lariam), which has good links to other resources on mefloquine, or the excellent 'Lariam or not to Lariam' on www.geocities.com/The Tropics/6913/lariam.htm, which has an incredibly comprehensive list of links, including one to Roche, the manufacturer of Lariam. Lariam Action USA (☎ 510-663-5168) can also be contacted at 1563 Solano Avenue #248, Berkeley, CA 94707.

Whatever you decide, remember malaria is a potentially fatal disease and it's vital you take precautions against it in risk areas.

in the first three months of pregnancy and in small children, although it can be taken by older children and in the final six months of pregnancy if absolutely necessary.

! *Note that because of the risk of dizziness and fits, mefloquine is best avoided if you're going to be doing precision tasks like scuba diving or flying a plane, or if you are going to high altitude (it could mask signs of altitude sickness).*

Chloroquine plus Proguanil

This regimen involves taking a weekly chloroquine tablet plus daily proguanil. Proguanil is not available in the USA, but is widely available in Europe or Canada. Advantages are that both agents are relatively safe, and there's long experience of use. The problem is that resistance is now widespread to both agents worldwide, especially in most of South-East Asia, but this is a useful combination in areas where mild to moderate chloroquine resistance exists.

Minor side effects are quite common and include headaches, nausea, diarrhoea and indigestion. Itching may be a problem, especially if you're dark-skinned. Chloroquine can cause temporary blurred vision; prolonged use of chloroquine (usually more than five years) can result in more serious eye problems, but this tends to be of more concern for expatriates than travellers. Proguanil is very safe, but can cause mouth ulcers.

This combination is safe in pregnancy (you may need to take a folate supplement with proguanil) and for children. Chloroquine isn't suitable for everyone: you shouldn't take it if you have epilepsy or are taking medication for epilepsy.

Doxycycline

This tetracycline antibiotic is a relatively new option for malaria, although it's been used for treatment of other infections for some time. It needs to be taken daily. Drug resistance hasn't been reported yet, but it's probably only a matter of time. It's useful where mefloquine-resistant malaria is present or if you can't or would prefer not to take mefloquine.

Side effects include diarrhoea, sensitivity to sunlight and vaginal thrush, and it may make the oral contraceptive pill less effective, so you should seek advice on this if necessary. It can cause irritation in your gullet, so you should always swallow it with plenty of water. Doxycycline is best avoided in pregnancy and is not suitable for children under eight years.

EMERGENCY STANDBY TREATMENT

If you're going to be in a high-risk malarial area without ready access to medical care, you will need to take with you treatment drugs for malaria for use in an emergency. If you can get hold of one, it's a good idea to take a malaria diagnostic test kit (eg MalaQuick) with you too. These kits have recently become available, and are accurate and easy to use. You can get them from selected travel health clinics (including TMVC in Australia and New Zealand and Nomad Travellers Store & Medical Centre in the UK) or check out www.med-diagnostics.com/index.html for more details. You can use the kits to confirm the diagnosis if you suspect you have malaria (even if you were taking malaria pills). They usually contain two tests and you should keep them as cool as possible, as this prolongs their lifespan.

Discuss the issue of emergency treatment for malaria with your doctor when you're getting your malaria pills sorted out. It's not just a question of popping the pills; you also need to be clear about when to use it and what to do if problems arise. You need to use a different medication from the one you used for prevention. For more guidelines on emergency treatment of malaria, see the Malaria section in the Fever chapter.

TRAVEL HEALTH INSURANCE

However lucky (or poor) you're feeling, it's vital you have adequate travel health insurance to cover your whole trip, usually as part of a general travel insurance covering loss of belongings, flight cancellations etc. Even if the costs of medical care in some countries are low, the costs of evacuation are always phenomenal. If you have medical insurance in your home country, remember that it may not cover you for travel in Asia.

Travel insurance policies are available from a variety of sources, including credit or charge card companies, travel agents and travel health clinics, as well as from insurance brokers. Insurance plans vary in the details of the services they provide, so it's worth shopping around to find exactly what you want. Always check the small print to be clear what the policy covers. Many insurance providers have a 24-hour hotline you can ring for assistance in an emergency, and they can provide you with names of English-speaking doctors, arrange referral to a hospital and guarantee payment if you need to pay upfront (as is usual in most Asian countries). Most insurance policies will cover you for medical evacuation if necessary.

You will need to inform the insurance providers of any medical condition you have, as this may increase the premium you have to pay. Once you're over a certain age (usually 65 years) your premium automatically increases. Note that routine health problems and preexisting conditions are not usually covered by travel health insurance policies.

Check if your policy covers the following:

- the total cost of any medical or surgical treatment you might need
- any additional costs you might incur if you were delayed by illness or injury or had to travel when injured
- emergency evacuation – without insurance this can cost thousands of dollars, which you would need to provide upfront
- provision of safe blood supplies
- dental treatment
- travel while pregnant
- adventure sports eg altitude, trekking, scuba diving – consider getting special insurance to cover these activities if necessary

Note that you will generally have to pay cash upfront for medical treatment and be reimbursed later, so it's a good idea to have an emergency stash just in case. Always keep any receipts from treatment in case you need to present them later to be reimbursed.

If you're going somewhere remote, you could consider registering with a local air ambulance service so you can be rescued by air in the event of an emergency, although this may be covered by your insurance policy – check before you go.

GETTING ORGANISED

MEDICAL CHECKUP

Not everyone needs a medical checkup before going on a trip, but in some situations it's a good idea.

If you're going to be away for more than about six months or you're going to remote areas, a medical checkup is a good idea to make sure there are no problems waiting to happen. now is the time to sort out any niggling problems. If you're going to be doing something strenuous like trekking at altitude and you're on the good side of 40, it's probably a good idea to have a fitness check before you go.

Arrange to get a plentiful supply of any prescription medicines from your doctor before you go, as well as a written record of your prescription (generic and brand name). If you are going to be travelling to remote areas, discuss whether you should take emergency treatment for diarrhoea or chest infections with you, which you will need to get on prescription.

Women Travellers

Travel can present problems for some contraceptive methods (like the oral contraceptive pill), so you may want to discuss this with your doctor before you go. If you think you may need to start contraception while you are away, it's a good idea to have this sorted out before you leave. If you're considering the possibility of stopping your periods temporarily (eg if you're going to be away trekking in a remote area at an inappropriate moment), this is something you need to discuss with your doctor as early as possible. If you know you're prone to getting bladder infections or thrush, it's a good idea to talk to your doctor about the possibility of taking treatment with you; treatment for thrush may be available over the counter in some western countries.

If you're planning on travelling when pregnant, see the section on Pregnant Travellers in the Women Travellers chapter.

Babies & Children

If you're travelling with babies or young children, it might be reassuring to discuss with your doctor tactics for dealing with any problems you might come up against while you are away. For a more details on preparing for travel with children, see the Babies & Children chapter later in this book.

DENTAL CHECKUP

You know it makes sense ... you don't want to find you need a filling when you're travelling in a remote area far from the nearest painkilling injection. It's definitely worth making time for this before you go, especially if you haven't been for a while. Your teeth can get quite a battering when you're travelling: you often end up drinking large quantities of sweet drinks, and inadequate water supplies may mean that you have to take a break from your usual dental health routine. For guidelines on keeping your teeth healthy while you are away, see the Teeth section of the Ears, Eyes & Teeth chapter.

EYES

If you wear contact lenses, it's a good idea to talk to your optometrist about hygiene and other issues on the road; take a plentiful supply of any cleaning solutions you use. If you wear glasses, take a replacement pair just in case, and your prescription – in many Asian countries you can have prescription lenses made up for you, often much more cheaply than at home. See also the Eyes section of the Ears, Eyes & Teeth chapter later in this book.

TRAVELLERS WITH SPECIAL NEEDS

You don't have to be able bodied or in perfect health to travel, but make sure you know what to expect and be prepared to take extra precautions. A short trip to a tourist centre or a developed country like Japan, Singapore or Taiwan may not present you with any major difficulties, but you may want to think more carefully about longer trips, especially to areas with higher risk to travellers (such as the Indian subcontinent and South-East Asia) or to remote areas (trekking in Nepal). It's not all bad news, however. If you are going to tropical Asia you may find that some conditions like arthritis and lung problems actually improve while you are away.

Whatever your plans, you'll need to get advice from your doctor or specialist before you go, so you're clear about problems you may encounter when you're travelling and what to do about them. It's a good idea to take with you a written summary of your medical problems and treatment you've had – ask your doctor for this before you go.

Check that your travel health insurance covers you for complications arising from preexisting illnesses. Remember that medical facilities in most countries in Asia – except for Japan, South Korea, Taiwan, Singapore and some major cities in the region – are very different from what you may be used to. If you are going to remote areas, it may be difficult to access any facilities at all.

Travellers with disabilities may find there are practical difficulties involved in travelling in Asia, as generally facilities lag well behind those in most western countries.

Although you may be able to replace some medicines while you are away, it's best to take a plentiful supply with you, as well as any equipment you need like syringes, needles, blood or urine tests and any arthritis aids or inhalant devices you need.

Crossing time zones can be problematic for the timing of

medications, especially for diabetics, so it's a good idea to work out a schedule with your doctor before you go.

Make sure you let the airline know well in advance of any special requirements you may have. Check with your doctor or the medical department of the airline you are travelling with for advice on potential health hazards flying may involve. For example, the lower oxygen availability in aircraft cabins may be a problem if you suffer from severe heart or lung problems.

Travelling can be very physically demanding, so make sure your itinerary is realistic and has the flexibility to allow for rest days, sick days and any unexpected difficulties.

Support Groups & Information Sources

If you have any special health needs, most major national or state disease foundations or support groups will be able to provide you with information and advice on travelling.

Travellers with heart conditions or stroke could try a national association like the American Heart Foundation (☎ 212-953-1900, www.ahf.org), 320 East 43rd St, New York, NY 10017, USA; the British Heart Foundation (☎ 020-7935 0185), www.bhf.org.uk, 14 Fitzharding St, London W1H 4DH, UK; or in Australia, you could ring the Heartline information service on ☎ 1300-362 787.

Travellers needing dialysis could get a copy of a directory of dialysis centers worldwide from Creative Age Publications ☎ 800-442-5667, 6728 Densmore Ave, Van Nuys, CA 91406.

In the USA, the Arthritis Foundation produces an excellent, extremely comprehensive guide to travel with arthritis, *Travel and Arthritis*; phone ☎ 800-542-0295 or 206-547-2707 for a copy or access it online (www.orthop.washington.edu).

US-based travellers with disabilities could contact one of the following organisations: Mobility International USA (☎ 541-343-1284, www.miusa.org), PO Box 10767, Eugene, OR 97440; Access Foundation (☎ 516-887-5798), PO Box 356, Malverne, NY 11565; and the Society for the Advancement of

Travel for the Handicapped (SATH; ☎ 718-858-5483, sath.org/index.html), 26 Court St, Brooklyn, NY 11242.

In the UK, the Royal Association for Disability & Rehabilitation (RADAR; ☎ 020-7250 3222, fax 250 0212, www.radar.org.uk), 12 City Forum, 250 City Rd, London EC1V 8AF, produces three holiday fact packs (costing UK£2 each) which cover planning and insurance, as well as useful organisations, transport and equipment, and specialised accommodation for travellers with disabilities.

Australians and New Zealanders can contact the National Information Communication Awareness Network (NICAN; ☎ 02-6285 3713, fax 6285 3714, www.nican.com.au), PO Box 407, Curtin, ACT 2605.

The Global Access web site (www.geocities.com/Paris/1052) has lots of information for travellers with disabilities, as well as links to related sites.

HIV-Positive Travellers

If you are HIV-positive, travelling poses some special problems, although this depends to a certain extent on your CD4 count. It's essential you get specialist advice on this before you travel (from your doctor, specialist physician or travel health clinic).

As a rule, live vaccines (eg oral polio, oral typhoid, measles, mumps and rubella and yellow fever) need to be avoided. You are generally at greater risk of travel-related illnesses; if you do get ill, it may have a greater impact on you. It's even more important to take great care over what you eat and drink, and you may want to consider taking antibiotics to prevent diarrhoea – discuss this before you go. You are at greater risk than other travellers of tuberculosis, hepatitis A and leishmaniasis if you travel to Asia, although you are not at any increased risk of malaria.

Just bear in mind that attitudes towards HIV infection may be very different in Asian countries from what you are used to. Consider hiding any obvious clues to your condition (like medications etc) or at least making it as inconspicuous as possible when you are crossing borders. Although some countries in Asia ask for HIV testing for work permits and long stays, you're unlikely to be asked for this if you're going for a short holiday.

You should be able to get more information on all these issues from your national HIV/AIDS organisation, or you could check out the following web resources: www.travel health.com/aids.htm, www.cdc.gov/travel/hivtrav, or aegis .com, which has loads of good links on a variety of HIV-related topics. In the UK, you could contact the Terrence Higgins Trust (☎ 020-7242 1010, www.tht.org.uk), 52-54 Grays Inn Rd, London WC1X 8JU.

Diabetic Travellers

This section was written by Michelle Sobel, a Type 1 diabetic who never lets her condition get in the way of her travels.

Preventive self-care is your aim, wherever you travel. If you are prepared and in good diabetic control, you're in the best position to enjoy your experiences abroad. Before you go, discuss with your doctor or specialist physician what to do if you get sick, dosage adjustments, immunisations and other travel-related health issues.

You'll find that the level and type of care offered to diabetics varies from country to country. It's a good idea to find out before you go what to expect at your destination. National diabetic associations are usually the best resource for information on local diabetic care. The International Diabetes Federation (www.idf.org), 1 rue Defacqz, B-1000 Brussels, Belgium, maintains a listing of diabetic associations in different countries in the world. You could also try your national diabetes organisation for information before you go, such as the American Diabetes Association (www.diabetes.org) or the British Diabetic Association (www.diabetes.org/bda.htm; BDA Careline ☎ 020-7636 6112) or Diabetes Australia (www.diabetes.org.au) for general information on travelling with diabetes. The British Diabetic Association produces a useful leaflet for diabetic travellers, as well as a number of specific country guides. Alternatively, you could check out www.diabeticresource .com (click on 'Travel'). A useful publication you could consider getting is the *Diabetic Traveller's Companion* (Nerida Nichol, RandomHouse NZ).

Insulin & Other Diabetic Supplies Before you leave, call the relevant manufacturer to get information on the availability abroad of diabetic supplies like test strips, medication (oral and insulin) and glucose meters. Consumer-friendly meter and pump manufacturers will advise you on repair, replacement, and delivery policies if your equipment malfunctions or is lost abroad.

Note that most nations measure blood glucose in mmol/L; the US, however, primarily uses mg/dL. Different meters report glucose readings using either or both of these standards. To convert mmol/L to mg/dL, multiply the glucose reading by 18. To convert mg/dL, divide the glucose by 18 (ie 4mmol/L = 72 mg/dL).

Take two to three times the medical supplies you expect to use (in carry-on, waterproof packs), to protect against loss or damage. On day trips, I carry two half bottles (instead of one or two full bottles) of insulin, so there's backup in case of breakage. To reduce bulk, try insulin pens over syringes. However, note that that at room temperature some insulin pen cartridges (particularly those with slow-acting and premixed insulin) may have shorter lives (as short as seven or 14 days) than vials (which last about a month). Some diabetic care providers suggest reusing sharps. Consult your physician about reusing and ask for advice on sterilising needles and syringes if necessary. Always discard needles and lancets appropriately when dull; never share sharps or meters.

You should be aware that insulin may be sold in different concentrations from country to country. If you run out and need to replenish abroad, use the appropriate syringe with the appropriate concentration. If you mix and match syringes and concentrations (eg you use U-40 insulin in a syringe marked 'for U-100 insulin only') you'll be at greater risk of over or under-injecting insulin. It's a good idea to retain generic-name prescriptions (even if invalid abroad) and medication inserts, as medications may have different brand names in Asia.

If you find you are running out of supplies in somewhere with limited resources (say, Laos), make sure you resupply in better-stocked neighbouring countries (eg Hong Kong). For extended travel and emergencies, consider preparing medical supplies for contacts to mail. Packaging is available to insulate insulin from heat and physical damage, in the mail. Note that in Asia syringes and meters occasionally prompt questions from officials, so make sure you have documentation from your doctor on you all the time.

On the Move Crossing time zones can be problematic, especially for Type 1 diabetics. Before you leave, take a copy of your itinerary to your diabetic care provider and ask for specific guidance on adjusting your individual protocol en route and as you acclimatise. As a rule, though, keep your watch on home time until the morning after you land. It's always necessary to check blood sugars frequently and to modify dosages, mealtimes and food choices as necessary. If you make adjustments based on how you feel – a very unreliable indicator at any time – hyper and hypoglycaemic reactions are almost inevitable. Remember that that jet lag can impair your ability to tell highs and lows.

Staying Healthy Unaccustomed physical activity, erratic sleep and meal times, unfamiliar foods, climate change, altitude sickness and stress are just some of the many variables that can aggravate control while you are away. The potential effects of unstable blood glucose (like disorientation, headaches and lethargy) are no fun, especially when you're away from home.

When you're travelling, Type 1 diabetics need to take particular care to prevent hyper and hypoglycaemic reactions. Ideally, monitor at least six times daily; if possible, bring two meters, as well as visual blood glucose strips as backup. Carry emergency food, foil-wrapped ketone strips and glucagon. In the event of a reaction, wearing a medical bracelet showing that you are a diabetic (see MedicAlert under Useful Organisations earlier in this chapter) can help prevent misdiagnosis (symptoms are often otherwise presumed to be induced by alcohol or illegal substances).

All diabetics should follow basic guidelines to prevent food-borne illness. If you do (or don't) take extra risks and end up ill, know what you need to do to prevent highs and lows related to illness. Wounds in hot, humid climates get infected easier and faster – always keep your feet dry, clean, and comfortable. Never walk barefoot, even on the beach. In hot or remote regions, take special care to stay hydrated. Pack extra supplies of medication, food, and water. Protect your skin from sunburn (severe sunburn can elevate blood sugars).

Keep insulin chilled in thermoses or insulated cool packs. Gels that freeze when shaken can protect insulin for a few hours. Make sure you don't freeze insulin, and don't place it directly against ice. Keep insulin out of direct sunlight. And ask hostels, friends etc to refrigerate your supplies when have the opportunity. Avoid travelling alone; solo travelers should check in with contacts. Cell phones are handy.

ACTIVITY & ADVENTURE TRIPS

If you're going to be spending time in remote areas more than a day or so away from medical help (eg if you're trekking), it's probably worth doing a first aid course before you leave. Contact your local first aid organisation for details of courses available. Consider doing a more specialist survival skills course, especially if you're going trekking in remote or isolated areas in harsh environmental conditions. Expeditioners can get specialist information from the Expedition Advisory

Centre at the Royal Geographical Society (☎ 020-7591 3030, www.rgs.org/ex), 1 Kensington Gore, London SW7 2AR.

If you're planning on doing any diving in Asia, remember to get a diving medical check before you leave, as (in theory) you will need a certificate of fitness before any dive centre will let you dive. Consider doing a diving course before you leave.

WHAT TO TAKE

MEDICAL KIT

It's a good idea to take at least a basic medical kit with you, although there's no need to go overboard on it. You'll probably be able to get most things, or at least something similar, in many countries in Asia, although it's more convenient to have your own supply of reliable and familiar basics with you. It saves you the hassle of having to decipher instructions written in another language and it's probably safer too, given

---

Drug Names

This is a confusing issue for everyone, medics included. All drugs have two names: a generic (official medical) name and the brand name (chosen by the manufacturer). Because brand names vary from country to country, we've used the official medical name for all drugs mentioned in this book. This may seem a bit frustrating to you if you're reading this at home, but it means that any doctor or pharmacist anywhere in the world will be able to recognise the generic name (or at least can look it up) and should be able to suggest brands available locally.

If you want to find out the generic name of a drug, look on the packet or leaflet accompanying the drug – the generic name should be there, usually in smaller type just below the brand name – or ask a pharmacist.

You'll find more information on all aspects of buying and using medicines while you are away in the appendix at the back of this book.

---

the very real concerns over the safety and quality of some medicines available in Asia (see the Buying & Using Medicines appendix for a more detailed discussion of this issue).

Be Prepared

Before you go, make sure you are clear about when and how to use any medication you have with you – side effects are more likely if medicines are taken inappropriately or in the wrong dose. Many medicines come with an information leaflet from the manufacturers giving safety information and guidance for use, so keep this and refer to if necessary.

If you take any medicine regularly (eg for a heart condition or the contraceptive pill), remember to take a written record as well as a prescription giving the generic name as well as the brand name and dose in case you need to replace it for any reason. If you're allergic to any drugs (for example penicillin), you should carry this information on you at all times. You can get engraved bracelets or tags with this information from specialist companies like MedicAlert (see Useful Organisations at the beginning of this chapter).

Customs

Customs officials can sometimes be suspicious of medications you may be carrying (there have been a few horror stories along the lines of 'Innocent Traveller Arrested for Carrying Painkillers') so it's best to keep medicines in their original packaging or container where possible, ideally with a prescription or doctor's letter showing what it is and why you need to take it. If you keep all your medications in an official-looking medical kit, you're less likely to have problems.

The Kit

You can make up your own kit, or prepacked kits are widely available from travel health clinics (see Information Sources earlier) and other travel equipment suppliers, saving you the trouble of having to think about what you might need. Better still, you can take a prepacked kit and add your own extras.

Resealable plastic bags are handy for keeping your medical supplies in, and it's best to keep the whole kit together in a waterproof and squash-proof container, such as a clear plastic box. 'Sterile kits' containing needles and syringes are usually easily recognised as such and shouldn't cause you problems at customs, but carrying loose syringes and needles is not a good idea. If you need to carry them on you for a medical reason, (if you're a diabetic, for example), get a letter from your doctor to say why you need them, and carry it on you at all times.

Try to keep medicines as cool as possible (stow them in the middle of your pack) and out of direct sunlight. Remember to keep all medicines out of reach of babies and children.

What to Include

This depends on where you're going and what you're planning to do. If you're planning to trek in remote areas of the Himalaya, you'll need to take a more comprehensive kit than if you're on a short holiday to a tourist resort in Bali (Indonesia), for example. Some suggestions on what to include in a basic medical kit are listed in this section; see also the boxed text 'Alternative First Aid for Travellers' and the following section on Alternative Travel Kits. If you're travelling with children, see the Medical Kits & Medications section in the Babies & Children chapter for tips on what to take.

Lotions, Potions & Pills Consider taking these for most destinations in Asia:

- any prescription medicines, including malaria pills if necessary
- paracetamol (acetaminophen) or aspirin (unless contraindicated) for pain and fever; consider also taking a stronger painkiller like co-codamol or an anti-inflammatory like ibuprofen
- antidiarrhoeals such as loperamide (probably the most useful and effective) or bismuth subsalicylate (Pepto-Bismol)
- oral rehydration sachets and measuring spoon

- 'indigestion' remedies such as antacid tablets or liquids
- antihistamine tablets for hay fever, itching and other allergies
- sting relief spray or hydrocortisone cream for insect bites
- emergency bee sting kit containing adrenaline (epinephrine) if you are allergic to stings
- antifungal cream for athlete's foot, crotch rot and thrush
- calamine cream or aloe vera for sunburn and other skin rashes
- sunscreen and lip salve (with sunblock)
- insect repellent (DEET or plant-based) and permethrin (for treating mosquito nets and clothes)
- anti-motion sickness remedies (eg promethazine or natural remedies; see boxed text 'Alternative First Aid for Travellers')
- water-purifying tablets or water filter/purifier
- over-the-counter cystitis treatment

In addition, you could consider taking:

- sugar-free chewing gum to keep your mouth moist in hot climates
- cough and cold remedies, sore throat lozenges
- eye drops for tired or dusty eyes
- multivitamins

First Aid Equipment We don't want to weigh you down, but you'll probably be glad to have at least some of these with you:

- thermometer
- scissors
- tweezers – to remove splinters and ticks
- sticking plasters (such as Band-Aids) of various sizes
- gauze swabs and adhesive tape
- bandages and safety pins to fasten them
- nonadhesive dressings (such as Melolin)
- antiseptic powder or solution (eg povidone-iodine), antiseptic wipes
- sterile kit, including needles, syringes, suture kit, cannula for giving a drip
- wound closure strips or butterfly closures (can sometimes be used instead of stitches)

Prescription Medicines Discuss with your doctor if you need to take any of the following with you:

- emergency treatment for malaria plus malaria diagnosis kit
- antibiotics for treating diarrhoea
- a course of antibiotics for chest, ear, skin etc infections, if you're going to be travelling in remote areas
- antibiotics to treat cystitis
- treatment for vaginal thrush (may be available without prescription in some countries)

Remote Areas Items you should consider taking with you if you are planning on trekking or travelling in remote areas or at high altitude in Asia include:

- sterile kit with an intravenous-fluid giving set, blood substitute solution and other intravenous fluids
- medicines to treat altitude sickness
- antibiotic eye and ear drops
- antibiotic cream or powder
- emergency inflatable splints
- blister kit
- elasticated support bandage
- triangular bandage for making an arm sling
- dental first aid kit

And Finally ...

If you have any medicines left over at the end of your trip, dispose of them carefully. You could consider giving them to a hospital or clinic, but don't be tempted to just leave them in your hotel room for the cleaner because medicines are only effective if used appropriately and can actually be harmful otherwise.

ALTERNATIVE TRAVEL KITS

You can make up your own alternative travel kit with tried and tested favourites, or you can buy a kit already made up. Unless you're planning to take just a few familiar remedies, you're probably best getting advice on what to take from your practitioner or local homoeopathic or naturopathic pharmacy. Alternatively, we give some guidance on homoeopathic and naturopathic remedies in the boxed text on the following page. Some of the publications on alternative therapies listed under Books later in this chapter have more suggestions for what you could include in a travel kit.

For the complete lowdown on aromatherapy options for travellers, try Valerie Ann Worwood's authoritative, comprehensive and very readable 'encyclopaedia' of aromatherapy, *The Fragrant Pharmacy*, which has lots of general advice for travellers and a suggested travel kit. Recommendations include a recipe for after-sun oil containing lavender, chamomile, bergamot and geranium essential oils. Enjoy ...

In the UK, Neal's Yard Remedies (☎ 0161-831 7875), catalogue from Unit 1, St James's Square, John Dalton Street, Manchester M2 6DS is a well-respected supplier of natural remedies. They have a variety of deliciously tempting mini-kits, as well as a Travel Roll, which you can either fill with your own remedies or get ready-packed with first aid remedies.

Also in the UK, Helios Homoeopathic Pharmacy (☎ 01892-537254, fax 546850, pharmacy@helios.co.uk) has a compact and incredibly comprehensive homoeopathic travel kit containing 36 remedies for travel-related problems (everything from drowning to fear of flying), together with a helpful leaflet giving guidance on what to use when. This is probably suitable for someone with prior experience of homoeopathy. Check out their web site (www.helios.co.uk) for more information.

You can order plant-based remedies like echinacea and Sweet Anne (good for digestive upsets) from Joanne Alexander at Snow Mountain Botanicals (☎ 888-743-2642, fax 707-743-2642, www.pacific.net/~smb).

A search on the web brings up more alternative kit possibilities, including the following: Adventure Medical Kits (www.adventure-medicalkits.com), Mountaintop Herbs (www.crisiskit.com), and Dr Christopher's kits (www.drchristopher.com/special/outdoor.html).

Alternative First Aid for Travellers

Bernadette Saulenier is a naturopath and Reiki practitioner who travels regularly between Australia and Europe. She has the following tips on homoeopathic/naturopathic first aid for travellers . Note that the remedies mentioned here are not likely to be available where you're going, so you will need to bring what you need with you. Remember that as a general rule, these remedies are best used for non-serious conditions and are not intended to replace medical diagnosis and treatment in serious cases.

Diarrhoea can ruin even the best-planned holiday and, as with anything else, prevention is better than cure. Treat water with tea-tree oil, a natural antiseptic: use two drops of tea-tree oil in 1L of water and let it stand overnight. Another preventive is to take slippery elm capsules orally before each meal – the powder coats and protects the delicate lining of the intestines against inflammation. If you get diarrhoea, homoeopathic remedies include arsenicum album, carbo vegetalis, podophyllum, ipecac or nux vomica – what to take depends on the characteristics of your illness. Ask your practitioner for guidance on this before you leave.

Constipation is also common when you're travelling: try pear or prune juice, or a tablespoon of linseeds/psyllium husks sprinkled on your food. Remember to drink plenty of water. If you are really desperate, you could try taking a mixture of cascara, senna and chelidonium herbs.

If you're hopping in and out of buses carrying heavy luggage, you're quite likely to get a few bruises. Arnica cream is a great remedy, applied on the bruise immediately (but avoid using it on open wounds and cuts). For bleeding wounds, take arnica 30c under your tongue.

Cocculus drops or ginger tablets are good remedies for preventing motion sickness, and homoeopathic melatonin drops are excellent for jet lag. Gelsemium drops or tablets will alleviate the aches and pains of sore muscles, and taking any form of antioxidant such as grapeseed extract or vitamin A, C or E will help your body to cope with fatigue, stress and lack of fresh air – all common on a long journey.

Mosquitoes hate the smell of geranium, so avoid getting bitten by putting a few drops of geranium oil on your skin. If you get bitten in spite of all your precautions, a drop of lavender oil will soothe the itch. For other bites and stings (spiders, bees, wasps or fleas) a few drops of ledum 30c under your tongue is beneficial.

For sunburn, try a few drops of soothing hypericum oil, which also promotes healing, or comfrey cream. If you're feeling the heat, take the tissue salt of calcium sulphate (Calc. Sulph 6x) every 15 minutes until you feel refreshed, or try Dr Bach's Rescue Remedy.

For irritant skin rashes and minor burns, try soothing calendula or comfrey cream. Lycopodium in a homoeopathic form will help fungal infections at the constitutional level, but you may find tea-tree oil, thuja and comfrey creams helpful applied to the rash.

Colds and flu seem to be common wherever you go. Echinacea tablets or vitamin C will boost your immune system and help you avoid illness. If you are stricken, combination 'Q' of tissue salts will help with sinus and throat infections, and herbal tea of thyme or sage will alleviate sore throat and feverish symptoms. Gelsemium is good for muscular aches and pains; allium cepa for runny nose and watery eyes.

For stress or panic attacks, Dr Bach's Rescue Remedy is invaluable. A few drops under the tongue every 15 minutes works wonders. If sleep eludes you, a tincture or tablet of combined valerian, scullcap and passionflower (or any of these herbs alone) is the best cure. Hops is another herb with soothing effect. If you can't find herbs, try taking tissue salts of magnesium phosphate (Mag. Phos. 6x) before bed.

BOOKS

If you're looking for more information, or perhaps just some bedtime reading, here's a small selection of the many books available on travel health and related issues. Some more specialist publications are listed in relevant sections later in this book. Books are published in different editions by different publishers in different countries, but a bookshop or library should be able to track down the following recommendations from the author or title.

GENERAL REFERENCE

For an authoritative, comprehensive and earnest reference source on travel health risks, try *Travellers' Health* by Dr Richard Dawood. *Where There is No Doctor* by David Werner is an excellent 'how-to-do-it' manual for the medically naive, aimed at people going to live in remote areas of developing countries. There's a companion text (only for the brave, surely), *Where There Is No Dentist*.

For a chatty, entertaining and comprehensive guide aimed at travellers and expatriates, try Dr Jane Wilson-Howarth's wonderfully titled *Bugs, Bites & Bowels*. A similar, very detailed guide aimed at travelling parents is *Your Child's Health Abroad* by Dr Jane Wilson-Howarth and Dr Matthew Ellis. *Staying Healthy in Asia, Africa & Latin America* by Dirk Schroeder is a good, well-organised, no-nonsense health guide for travellers. The *International Travel Health Guide* by Stuart R Rose is updated annually, and is a good source of general information.

If you're looking for a first aid manual, get hold of the authorised manual of your national primary care organisation such as the Red Cross or St John Ambulance Society.

ALTERNATIVE THERAPIES

For something a bit different, try *The Traveller's Guide to Homoeopathy* by Phyllis Speight or *The World Travellers'*

Manual of Homoeopathy by Dr Colin Lessel, which is incredibly comprehensive, full of fascinating detail – a work of love. *A Handbook of Homoeopathic Alternatives to Immunisation* by Susan Curtis makes interesting reading and is available by mail order from Neal's Yard Remedies (for contact details, see the Alternative Travel Kits section earlier in this chapter).

CLIMATE, ALTITUDE & ACTION

If you're planning on trekking or doing other adventure activities in Asia, you may want to read up on some health and safety issues before you go. For a comprehensive overview of health, safety and general outdoor survival issues, Tim Macartney-Snape's, *Being Outside,* is hard to beat. *Hiking & Backpacking, A Complete Guide* by Karen Bergen is an excellent, easy to read and practical guide to all aspects of walking in the wilderness, with a North American slant.

Medicine for Mountaineering (edited by J Wilkerson) is a classic reference for travellers likely to be more than 24 hours from medical care, or try the very readable *The High Altitude Medicine Handbook* by Andrew J Pollard and David R Murdoch (although it's aimed primarily at medical practitioners). There are a couple of good pocket guides for trekkers, including *Altitude Illness – Prevention & Treatment* by Stephen Bezruchka and *Mountain Sickness – Prevention, Recognition & Treatment* by Peter H Hackett.

If you want to make yourself really paranoid, try the surprisingly readable *Bites & Stings, The World of Venomous Animals* by John Nichol. You can find out all about the hazards of the deep in *Dangerous Marine Creatures* by Dr Carl Edmonds or Lonely Planet's *Pisces Guide to Venomous and Toxic Marine Life of the World.*

If you've ever wondered what to do if a volcano erupts at your feet or how to improvise a cooking pot from a length of bamboo, you'll find all the answers and much much more in the *SAS Survival Guide.*

ON THE MOVE

Getting there is half the fun they say … If you don't enjoy the moving experience (and many travellers don't), you'll want to read this chapter before you leave terra firma. Or bounce over it.

FIT TO FLY?

If you're fit and healthy, flying shouldn't be a problem for you beyond the stresses involved in any form of travelling. However, there are certain situations when you need to check with your doctor or the airline before flying:

- if you have a bad cold, sinus infection or a middle ear infection, it's best to avoid flying until you're better, as you're at risk of severe ear pain and possibly a burst eardrum – see the Ears section of the Ears, Eyes & Teeth chapter for more details
- if you've been scuba diving, you shouldn't fly for 12 hours after any dive and for 24 hours after a dive requiring decompression stops; note that you will need medical clearance before you fly if you required recompression treatment
- if you've got preexisting heart or lung problems, the lack of oxygen at altitude may be a problem, although as a general rule you shouldn't need extra oxygen if you can climb a flight of stairs
- if you've had an operation within 10 days of flying, check with the airline if you are able to fly
- if you've had blood clots in your blood vessels in the past, as sitting immobile for long periods of time during the flight may make further clots likely
- if you're more than 36 weeks pregnant

TRAVELLING WELL

If you're flying, the low cabin air humidity is great for minimising the odoriferous effects of squashing 300 or so stressed people into a closed space for eight or more hours, but it does dry you out. You'll feel better if you drink lots of (nonalcoholic) fluids; use mineral water aerosol sprays and moisturisers; and avoid tea, coffee and alcohol, as they can all increase fluid loss.

Fear of Flying?

If even the thought of flying reduces you to a quivering wreck, you may not be reading this book. If you are, you might like to know that help is at hand. Courses are available to cure you of your trembles, usually involving behavioural therapy – you're exposed to the situation under controlled conditions eg in a flight simulator, and in this way learn to combat your fears.

Considerable success is reported, and improvement can last up to five years after the course. Ask your airline or travel health provider for details of courses available to you. Or you could try a virtual reality therapy clinic – for details of one US-based clinic, check out www.virtuallybetter.com.

At cruising altitude, the volume of enclosed gases (eg in your ears and abdomen) expands by about a third. This shouldn't cause a problem if you can pop your ears (try swallowing or holding your nose and puffing out your cheeks), although you may find your abdomen swells up – so steer clear of the bubbly.

On any form of transport, aromatherapy is a great for soothing and relaxing you – try a few drops of rosemary or lavender in a tissue or handkerchief, and waft it under your nose every so often. Sitting inactive for long periods of time on any form of transport, especially in hot climates, makes your feet and ankles swell up, and may make blood clotting in your leg veins more likely, especially if you are prone to these, or if you're pregnant. Wriggle your toes and flex your calves while you're sitting or, if you can, get up and walk around. If you are prone to blood clotting, you may want to discuss this with your doctor before you leave, as you may need to take low-dose aspirin or an injection of a blood thinner.

Remember to keep any as-needed medications (eg for asthma or angina) readily at hand during any journey; keep it in your hand luggage if you're flying.

JET LAG
If you're going to be flying across three or more time zones, you may experience jet lag. This term describes a syndrome that you're probably familiar with, in various degrees of severity, if you have ever done a long-haul flight: tiredness, problems sleeping at the new night-time, headache, irritability, difficulty concentrating, and loss of appetite and other gastro upsets. Some of these effects are due to the physical stresses of the flight, like dehydration and immobility, but others are the result of having to reset your body clock.

Over a 24-hour period, your body shows rhythmical changes in various natural functions (such as levels of hormones, body temperature and blood pressure), which are designed to prime it to be active during the daytime and to sleep during the night. The trouble is that your internal clock takes time to adjust to a new routine, and when you fly directly to a new time, there's a temporary mismatch between your internal clock and the new external environment, which you experience as jet lag.

Jet lag can make you feel below par for the first week, depending on how many time zones you've crossed, so if you're on a short trip, it's worth taking a few steps to minimise the effects. Jet lag tends to be more of a problem if you're older and if you're flying west to east. You might want to consider having a stopover as this can help.

Unfortunately, there's no wonder pill for jet lag. Instead, you can speed up the adjustment process by helping out the *zeitgebers* (don't you love it? It's German for 'timegivers'). These are external influences that impact on your internal rhythms, the most important ones being meal times, sleep times and exposure to bright light. Here are some guidelines for minimising the effect of jet lag:

▸ recognise that jet lag may be a problem in the first few days and adjust your itinerary accordingly
▸ on the plane, set your watch to the new destination time and adjust your schedule to this time

- if it's daytime on arrival, get active and don't give yourself the chance to doze off
- eating is a potent time-setter, so try to take all your meals at the appropriate new time
- it can be torture, but try to stay awake until at least a reasonable bed time when you first arrive
- if you just can't keep your eyelids open, take a short nap – but beware ... set your alarm or get someone to wake you
- the first night's sleep may be a bit fragile, but after that things should improve

Drug remedies you could consider to help your body clock to adjust include sleeping tablets and melatonin. Sleeping tablets can help by enabling you to sleep at the appropriate time, but they can make you feel 'hungover' the next day and are not suitable for everyone.

There's been much excitement about melatonin, a naturally occurring hormone which influences body rhythms. Although melatonin is widely available from naturopathic suppliers, you should be aware that it's not as yet officially sanctioned (which means that it hasn't been fully studied for safety and possible side effects, and the optimum dose hasn't been determined), so it's not available on a medical prescription. If you decide to try it, follow the dosing instructions on the packaging. Melatonin needs to be taken at an appropriate time before sleep (usually about 8 pm at the new time).

Other less practical options (for the desperate only, surely) include mind-bogglingly complicated fasting/food regimens (check out *Overcoming Jetlag* by Dr Charles F Ehret and Lynne Waller Scanlon – said to be used by the US Army Rapid Deployment Forces) and bright light exposure via special light bulbs (but try carrying those in your pack).

MOTION SICKNESS

There are plenty of narrow winding roads, choppy seas, swaying camels, diesel fumes, phlegm puddles and various less than sweet odours to get you chundering when you're on the move in Asia, so be prepared with a supply of your favourite motion sickness remedies. Children and pregnant women are most likely to get motion sickness, but it can strike anyone.

In case you're fortunate enough not to know, early signs of an impending puke include headache, dizziness and clammy skin. This is the time to take action. Put this book down ...

If you can, fix your eyes firmly on the horizon and keep your head still (for example, brace it against a headrest). If you're below deck on a ship, lie down and close your eyes. Try eating something bland like a dry biscuit; alternatively, tasting and smelling a lemon is said to help. Cigarette smoke spells disaster – try to avoid it if you can.

Place yourself in the most stable part of the vehicle: this is between the wings on a plane, in the middle of a boat or in the front seat of a car.

Eating lightly before the journey may help. You'll find a variety of anti-sickness remedies on the market. Preparations containing ginger or mint (including mint sweets) are helpful, and don't need to be taken in advance. Other remedies need to be taken before you travel.

Hyoscine (as tablets or skin patches) is effective for short journeys, but has side effects like dry mouth and blurred vision, and is not suitable for everyone. It's best avoided by children, older people and pregnant women. Hyoscine skin patches are known as Scopoderm in the UK and Transderm-Scop in the US.

Antihistamines (eg cinnarizine, cyclizine, dimenhydrinate or promethazine – various brand names) are longer-lasting and have fewer side effects. They're generally available without prescription. Some antihistamines may make you drowsy, which can be an advantage on a long journey, but you should avoid driving and alcohol if you take them.

Alternatively, you could try something a bit different: special elasticated wristbands are available that work by applying pressure to acupuncture points, or there's a considerably more expensive battery-operated version.

STAYING HEALTHY

If you thought staying healthy on your travels was just about getting the right immunisations and perhaps a supply of malaria pills, you'll need to think again. Only a few travel-related illnesses, and none of the common problems such as sunburn, diarrhoea and infected cuts are preventable by immunisation. The good news is that you don't need a degree in medical science to stay healthy, just an awareness of the likely problems and some common sense.

○ Healthy mind, healthy body – for tips on cutting down on the mental stresses of travelling, see the Mental Wellbeing chapter.
○ Planning to let your hair down? For some safety tips on alcohol and drugs, see p230.

ACCLIMATISATION

○ For the complete lowdown on coping with cold conditions and altitude, see those sections in the Climate, Altitude & Action chapter.

Don't plan on hitting the ground running, especially if you're on a long trip. It's worth allowing yourself time to adjust physically and mentally to your new environment and lifestyle, especially in the first week. Factor in some time to take a breather, recover from jet lag and catch up on sleep.

If you've gone from a cool, temperate climate back home to a hot tropical one in Asia, you're likely to feel uncomfortably hot and easily exhausted for at least the first week. Your body has an amazing capacity to adjust to temperature changes, but it doesn't happen overnight. After about a week, your body will have acclimatised and you'll find you feel the heat less and your capacity for activity is back to normal. Don't underestimate the dangers of the heat – these are covered in detail in the Heat section of the Climate, Altitude & Activity chapter. Children and older travellers in particular may find it harder to adjust to hot climates.

You'll probably find you sweat heavily in the heat. Drink plenty of fluids to replace the amount you're sweating out, especially if the heat has made you lose your appetite too. Cool bottled, boiled or purified water is best, but any not-too-sweet soft drinks, fruit juice or green coconut milk are OK.

- Always have a supply of safe drinking water with you and remind yourself to sip from it regularly while you're out – or stop at lots of drinks stalls.
- Go easy on tea, coffee and alcohol, as all these make you lose fluid inappropriately (ie they are diuretics).
- Avoid overexerting yourself or eating a big meal during the hottest part of the day – it's the perfect time for a siesta or for reading that airport novel.

Physical activity generates heat, which means your body has to work even harder to stay cool. If you're planning an activity-packed holiday, try to take it easy during the first week, and build up to maximal activity as you acclimatise.

Wear loose, light-coloured clothing (dark colours absorb the heat more) made of natural fibres like cotton to help protect your skin from the sun without preventing heat loss. Prickly heat and fungal skin rashes are common in hot climates but if you wash regularly with water (avoid soap) and dry all your nooks and crannies carefully, you can help prevent these.

Remember to take steps to prevent sunburn – see Safe Sun later in this section

You'll probably find that your feet and ankles swell in the heat, especially at first, so it's a good idea to take footwear that is going to accommodate this.

SAFE SUN

Asia has some of the finest beaches in the world, and it can be hard to resist the temptation to stretch out in the sun and make that pearly shade of whiteness just a bad dream. However, unless you've been in a media blackout zone for the last decade or so, you'll know that there's no such thing as a safe suntan. Before you settle in for some serious sun worshipping, take a few steps to limit the potential damage. Remember: the bronzed Adonis of today is the Beijing duck of tomorrow ...

It's not only beachlovers who need to take care – if you're doing any outdoor activities, especially if you're near water or at altitude, you're at risk from the rays.

So what makes sunlight so deadly? Sunlight or solar energy is made up of radiation of many different wavelengths. It's the rays in the ultraviolet (UV) part of the spectrum that are the bad guys. In the short term, they can cause sunburn (and snow

Sunscreen

Sunscreens increase the length of time you can stay in the sun before you burn by reducing the amount of harmful radiation that penetrates the skin. The SPF (sun protection factor) rating is a rough guide to how long you can stay in the sun without burning, but don't rely too much on it. Laboratory conditions are no match for the realities of beach life. It's probably best to start with the highest SPF you can find (ideally 30+). Check that it blocks out both UVA and UVB (usually labelled as 'broad spectrum').

A suntan is a layer of skin pigment called melanin formed by your skin in defence against the sun. Although it can protect against sunburn, but it doesn't protect against the ageing effects of the sun. It takes two to three weeks before a suntan can provide good protection against sunburn.

If you do decide you want to tan, make sure you allow your skin to tan slowly without burning, starting with 15 or 20 minutes exposure a day, increasing this gradually. If your skin starts to feel sore or look red, head for the shade.

Remember that freckles may be cute, but they're also a sign that you've had too much sun.

blindness if you're somewhere snowy). This is bad news, but the long-term effects are even scarier:

- skin ageing: wrinkles, crow's feet, liver spots, warty rough areas (solar keratoses), broken veins
- skin cancer, including malignant melanoma (the nastiest type)
- eye problems: cataracts and malignant melanoma of the back of the eye

Sun intensity is affected by many factors, including obvious things like latitude (greater around the equator), time of the year (summer) and time of the day (midday). Sun intensity is also increased at altitude and by reflection off sea, snow and buildings. And we're doing our best to destroy the one thing that protects us from the harmful rays: the ozone layer.

Stay pale and interesting by covering up with clothes and wearing a hat. These provide by far the best protection from harmful rays (much better than any sun lotion). A wide-brimmed hat or a legionnaire-style cap with a neck protector (so flattering) keeps damaging rays off those easily forgotten bits: nose, ears, back of the neck, bald patch. Protect your eyes with sunglasses that block out UV rays. Avoid the sun when it's at its fiercest, usually between 11 am and 3 pm – follow the local example and rest in the shade or indoors.

!Remember to protect yourself from the sun during any outdoor activity, including sightseeing, riding in the backs of open pick-ups or lorries or on top of buses.

Note the following traps for the unwary:

- sunscreen needs to be applied 20 to 30 minutes before going into the sun and you should reapply it frequently after that, especially after swimming
- you can get sunburnt through water (eg when snorkelling), so take care to cover up and use plenty of water-resistant sunscreen
- how hot it is doesn't make any difference to whether you'll burn – you can still get burnt on a cold day if the sun is shining
- you can burn on a cloudy day because clouds still let through

some UV radiation; and you can burn in the shade from reflected light, especially off water

SAFE FOOD

○ Staying healthy is not just about eating safely, it's also about good nutrition – for a full discussion of this important issue see the Eating for Health section at the end of this chapter.

It's generally agreed that food, not water, is the most common source of gut troubles in travellers. The impressive line-up of diseases you can get in this way includes most forms of diarrhoea, dysentery, hepatitis A and E, all of which are common causes of illness in travellers in Asia. Typhoid is also transmitted in this way and although it's uncommon in travellers generally, it's relatively more comon in travellers to the Indian subcontinent.

The fact is that you can get sick from food anywhere, but travelling makes it more likely. Where sewage disposal systems are inadequate or nonexistent (most less developed countries in Asia), especially when there are high levels of disease in the population, there's much more chance that food, utensils and hands are going to be contaminated with disease-causing microorganisms ('germs'), mainly from faeces. For example, if a fly lands on your food in many western countries, it probably hasn't had a chance to wipe its feet on a pile of faeces beforehand, but this isn't true in many Asian countries.

Travelling usually means you're 'eating out' three meals a day for perhaps weeks on end, relying on other people to prepare your food safely. Most countries in Asia don't have enforceable food safety standards (but even in countries with supposedly high food safety standards, like Australia, outbreaks of food poisoning occur with alarming regularity). Disease-causing microorganisms love hot humid climates, and multiply gleefully in food left sitting around in these conditions, especially if power shortages mean refrigeration is inadequate. In addition, some types of food present specific hazards;

for example, raw fish in Thailand is a potential source of liver flukes parasites – see the Digestive System chapter for more details.

You can build up immunity to some diarrhoeal diseases, but you can't build up immunity to many of the more serious diseases (like dysentery or food poisoning) or to parasites (like liver flukes), so it's worth taking some basic precautions to minimise your risks. Having said that, standard advice on eating safely can often seem unrealistic at best and ludicrous at worst. Examine the cook's fingernails before wolfing down your banana pancake? Throw away your noodles because a fly landed on them? Get real ...

We can't tell you exactly what to avoid in every situation in every country because there are so many variables, but we can give you some guidelines to help you decide what's likely to be less safe and therefore better avoided. It's down to common sense basically, plus a little background knowledge.

- How food is prepared is more important than where it's prepared – a plate of noodles cooked in a steaming hot wok in front of you at a street stall is probably safer than food left out on display in an upmarket hotel buffet.
- Heating kills germs, so food that's served piping hot is likely to be safer than lukewarm or cold food, especially food that's been sitting around; note that freezing doesn't kill germs.
- Fruit and vegetables are difficult to clean (and may be contaminated where they are grown), but they should be safe if they're peeled or cooked.
- Well-cooked meat and seafood should be OK; raw or lightly cooked meat and seafood can be a source of parasites.
- Tinned food or milk, or powdered milk, is usually safe (check 'best before' dates if necessary).
- You'll be delighted to know that all forms of bread and cakes are usually safe, although it's best to avoid cream-filled goodies if you can, as microorganisms such as salmonella love cream.
- Popular eating places have an incentive to provide safe food to keep the customers coming.
- Your stomach's natural defences (mainly acid) can cope with

small amounts of contaminated foods – if you're not sure about something, don't pig out on it!

And here are a few cautions to bear in mind.

- The more food has been handled (peeled, sliced, arranged), the more likely it may have been contaminated by unwashed hands.

Diarrhoea-Prevention Remedies

There are two mainstream possibilities in this category: antibiotics or bismuth subsalicylate (Pepto Bismol). Although some antibiotics have been shown to be effective in preventing diarrhoea in travellers, there are concerns over side effects and the possibility that this may make antibiotic resistance more likely to develop. This means that taking preventive antibiotics isn't an option for most travellers and in any case it's just not practical for long term travellers. Preventive antibiotics may be advisable in some situations, for example if you have a preexisting condition (such as HIV infection or inflammatory bowel disease) that makes it particularly important for you to avoid illness, or if you're a businessperson on a short trip and you can't afford to lose a day with illness.

Bismuth subsalicylate is probably better known as an 'indigestion' remedy. In diarrhoea, it works by reducing the amount of fluid your gut produces in response to toxins from microorganisms. It comes in liquid form (60ml four times daily) but tablets (take two tablets four times daily) are more practical if your on the road. It's a possibility to consider (discuss with your doctor first) if you are on a short trip, although it's not suitable for everyone – see the section on Antidiarrhoeal Remedies on p142 for more details.

Alternative remedies that have been recommended for prevention of diarrhoea in travellers include lactobacillus (the bacteria in live natural yoghurt) or slippery elm capsules, or you could try general measures to increase your resistance to illness such as taking an 'immune-booster' like echinacea.

- Good food can be contaminated by dirty dishes or cutlery; blenders used for making fruit juices or lassi are often suspect.
- Food that looks and smells delicious can still be seething with microorganisms.
- Hot spices don't make food safe, just more palatable.
- Salads are best avoided because they are hard to clean adequately and they are often contaminated with bug-containing dirt.
- Fruit juices and other drinks (eg the Nepali brew *chhang*) may be diluted with unsafe water.
- Unpasteurised and unboiled milk and dairy products should be avoided (more likely in rural areas) as unpasteurised milk can transmit diseases (including TB, brucellosis and salmonella); boiling unpasteurised milk makes it safe to drink.
- Be wary of food, including ice cream, that has been kept frozen, especially if power cuts are a feature.
- Avoid raw fish, meat and seafood because of the risk of parasites.

Consider carrying your own utensils for eating street food. In the chopstick-using nations, consider carrying a pair of chopsticks with you or use disposable ones.

CLEAN HANDS

Before you skip over this uninspiringly titled but surprisingly important section, we're talking about washing your hands before you eat. Obvious perhaps, but in western countries we've been able to become complacent about this because we have efficient waste disposal systems and (usually) safe and plentiful water supplies.

Many of diseases you associate with tropical countries (for example, dysentery, typhoid and hepatitis) are actually diseases of poor hygiene rather than 'tropical' diseases. So it's worth reminding yourself to follow local custom and wash your hands before you eat (there's usually a basin or jug for this in most restaurants) and always after using the toilet. This is particularly important in areas like the Indian subcontinent where eating with your hands is the norm. Short fingernails are easier to keep clean than long ones.

Try to remember to keep your hands away from your mouth and eyes, especially on public transport, as you can introduce infection in this way.

It's tempting to assume that because environmental hygiene is poor due to lack of infrastructure and resources, personal cleanliness will also be poor. But it's worth observing local customs and perhaps adopting them yourself if they make sense to you, for example not letting your mouth touch a shared drinking vessel (pour the water into your mouth). The widespread custom in Asia of using one hand (usually the left) for toilet duty and the other for eating is a sensible habit to adopt. You might want to practise both these at home first.

SAFE DRINKING WATER

The problem with water is that not only can you not live without it, but neither can all sorts of disease-causing microorganisms. Although contaminated food is generally the most important source of gut infections when you're travelling in Asia, contaminated water is also a major source of illness, including diarrhoea, dysentery, hepatitis and typhoid.

In countries with good infrastructure and resources, communal water supplies are generally safe from contamination, but you can't rely on this in most countries in Asia (notable exceptions are Japan and Singapore). There's often contamination of the water supply at some point, usually by human or animal sewage. Unless you're sure that the water supply is safe, it's best not to take any chances.

For most of Asia, this means not drinking tap water and not brushing your teeth in it. Ice is obviously only as safe as the water it's made from, so it's best to avoid this too. If you're desperate for a cool drink, seal the ice in a plastic bag before putting it in your drink … but make sure the bag is clean first. Alcohol has some disinfectant properties, but at drinking strength it won't make water safe to drink. Consider carrying your own cup with you, as the cups you drink from are often a source of infection in themselves.

Don't Drink the Water ...

It's not just microbes you need to watch out for, chemical pollution is a serious problem in some areas, particularly in parts of India and Bangladesh. Groundwater often contains concentrations of nickel, lead, mercury and zinc above safe levels, and it may also contain DDT and other nasties. Well water has traditionally been thought of as a source of pure water, but there are disturbing reports from West Bengal (India) and northern and western Bangladesh about the level of arsenic in this water. Thousands of people in these areas are showing signs of arsenic poisoning. You'd be wise to avoid well water in these areas and to stick to boiling or purifying water from surface sources.

And if you're thinking bottled water is the safest alternative, be aware that when India's Consumer Education & Research Society tested the country's leading brands of bottled water, they found only three samples that met all health and safety standards. Ten out of the 13 brands contained unidentified floating objects and two had higher than permitted levels of toxic heavy metals.

How you deal with the water issue depends on where you are and what sort of trip you're on. Drinking bottled water is one obvious option, and it's widely available throughout Asia. However, bear in mind that it's not always fail-safe – the quality of some local brands can be little better than tap water, and plastic bottles can be refilled with any old water and sold to unsuspecting travellers. As a general rule, it's best to stick to major brands of bottled water, preferably with serrated tops – check the seal carefully. The cost of bottled water can add up over a long trip, especially if you're travelling in hot climates, and there's a very real concern over the environmental – and aesthetic – effect of millions of discarded and unrecycled plastic bottles. If you're trekking or travelling off the beaten track, bottled water is a less practical option anyway.

Boiling

The simplest and most effective way of making water safe to drink is to boil it, which kills all disease-causing bugs. You just need to bring it to a rolling boil for a minute or two and then let it cool – prolonged boiling is not necessary. Water boils at lower temperatures at high altitude; this is not likely to be a problem at the altitudes you're going to be reaching, but to be absolutely sure you could let it boil for about five minutes in these circumstances.

In many countries in Asia, such as China and Indonesia, boiled water is often provided routinely either for drinking on its own or for making up into tea, so it's always worth asking about this. Alternatively, you could use a small immersion heating coil in a heat-proof cup – these are widely available from hardware stores in places like India, or you could take one with you (but this relies on you having a power supply in your room and the correct plug type for the country).

Chemical Disinfectants

If boiling doesn't sound like a practical option, it's easy to disinfect clear water with chemicals. Chlorine and iodine are the chemicals most widely used. Both are available in tablet form, and iodine is also available as a liquid (add five drops of 2% tincture of iodine to every litre of water) or as crystals you can make up into a liquid. If you're dealing with *Giardia* (likely in most parts of Asia), a higher concentration is required. Follow the manufacturer's instructions and remember that you need to leave the water for about 20 minutes before it's safe to drink, or longer (an hour or two) if the water is really cold. Chlorine is generally less reliable than iodine as it is more likely to be affected by factors such as water alkalinity.

Note that iodine can cause thyroid problems if used continuously over a long time (more than six weeks), and you should avoid it altogether if you're pregnant or have thyroid problems. It's not suitable for children under 12 years. Neither iodine nor chlorine will kill *Cryptosporidia*, a recently identified cause of persistent diarrhoea in travellers to Nepal and some other parts of Asia. Silver tablets are also available, but they are not effective against parasite cysts so they shouldn't be used without filtering the water first.

The taste of chemically treated water can be a major turn-off, but there are ways of neutralising this. Charcoal resins or a carbon filter can remove the taste and smell of chemicals, or you can add ascorbic acid (vitamin C) to the chemically-treated water. Remember only to add these after the treated water has been allowed to stand for the required length of time.

! If the water is cloudy, chemicals won't be effective because organic matter tends to neutralise the chemical – you'll need to filter the water first.

Water Filters & Purifiers

No, you don't need to be a rocket scientist to understand what these devices do, it's actually pretty straightforward. Any travel equipment supplier (see Travel Health Clinics under Information Sources earlier in this chapter) worth their salt will be able to tell you all you need to know about the products they supply, but it's worth having an idea beforehand what you're looking for.

Not sure about the terminology? Simple filters are just sieves or strainers and their effectiveness depends on how fine they are. Generally they don't make water safe to drink without further treatment (boiling or disinfectant chemicals), as they don't remove the smallest disease-causing bugs (viruses and some bacteria), although fine-pore ceramic filters are exceptions. Purifiers are dual action: they filter water and disinfect it (eg with an iodine resin).

Filters and purifiers can be gravity or pump action. Pump action is probably the more realistic option unless you have plenty of time on your hands, but can be hard work. Water purifiers often contain a carbon filter to remove traces of chemicals used to disinfect the water. Before you buy one, check the following.

- What does it claim to remove? Does it make water totally safe to drink?
- What do you want to use it for? Some devices are suitable for occasional or emergency use, whereas others are good for continuous use over a long period of time.
- What's the flow rate like? You don't want to pump for two hours for a sip of water.
- How portable/breakable is it? Ceramic filters are very effective, but need a bit of care as they can crack.
- How often does the filter need to be replaced? Filters can get clogged and there's a risk of bacterial growth occurring in them, so they usually need to be cleaned or replaced after a certain length of time.
- How easy is it to take apart and clean if it becomes clogged?
- Is it endorsed by an independent organisation?

Even if you're using a water purifier, try to choose the cleanest water source possible, and never drink water from rivers, lakes or wells without purifying it first.

!Make sure you have more than one means of purifying water in case one method fails (eg take some iodine as well as a pump action purifier).

INSECT BITES

Small bloodsuckers tend to rate highly in travellers hate lists. The itch and discomfort from their bites can be sanity-challenging in itself, but to add insult to injury, some insects are responsible for transmitting a variety of serious (and not quite so serious) diseases. In Asia, these include:

mosquitoes	malaria, dengue fever, filariasis, Japanese B encephalitis
ticks	typhus, relapsing fever and other fevers
mites	typhus
lice	typhus
fleas	plague
sandflies	leishmaniasis, sandfly fever

The risk of meeting a disease-carrying insect vary to a certain extent with where you're headed for, but it obviously makes sense wherever you go to make sure you don't get bitten by any of these bloodsuckers. In Asia, Japanese B encephalitis is the only one of these diseases you can be immunised against. Remember: don't get bitten and you won't get these diseases.

Use chemical repellents and physical barriers (clothes, nets, screening) to minimise your chances of getting bitten. Biting insects are attracted by the most surprising things, including body heat, chemicals in your sweat, perfumes, soap and types of clothing. Most mosquitoes are night-biters, but some (such as the mosquito that transmits dengue) bite mainly during the day.

Beat the bloodsuckers with the following measures:

▶ cover up with long-sleeved tops and long trousers or a skirt; light-coloured clothing is thought to be less attractive to mosquitoes than dark colours

▶ use insect repellents on any exposed areas; if you're using sunscreen or other lotions, apply insect repellent last, and reapply after swimming if necessary; note that insect repellent may reduce the protection of a sunscreen

▶ sleep in a screened room or, if this is not possible (quite likely), sleep under a treated mosquito net. Always cover children's beds or cots with treated mosquito nets; air-conditioned rooms are usually insect-free zones

▶ remember day-biting mosquitoes, and avoid shady conditions in the late afternoon or taking an afternoon siesta without the protection of a mosquito net

▶ spray your room or tent with an insect spray before you retire for the night to get rid of any lurking insects

▶ consider using electric insecticide vaporisers or burn mosquito coils – both are widely available in Asia, but you need a power socket for a vaporiser, and both are less effective if you have a fan going

There are many insect repellent products on the market, but the most effective are those containing the compound DEET (diethyltoluamide) – check the label or ask your pharmacist to tell you which brands contain DEET. Some widely available brands include Rid, Doom, Jungle Formula, Repel and Autan.

DEET is very effective against mosquitoes, midges, ticks, bedbugs and leeches, and slightly less effective against flies. One application should last up to four hours, although if it's very humid or you're very sweaty, it may not last as long as this. Basically, the higher the concentration, the longer it will last, with around 50% being optimal, although there are some longer acting formulations which have lower strengths of DEET. Remember to try a test dose before you leave to check for allergy or skin irritation.

If you're worried about the safety of DEET, be reassured: it's generally agreed that safety concerns over DEET are largely unfounded. However, for children, it's probably best to err on the cautious side, and choose a lower strength long-acting cream.

You may prefer to use one of the new lemon eucalyptus-based natural products, which have been shown to be an effective alternative to DEET, with similar action times (although DEET is probably still your best bet in high-risk areas). Other natural repellents include citronella and pyrethrum, but these tend to be less effective and have a short action (up to an hour), making them less practical to use.

Cotton bands soaked in insect repellent and worn on your wrist and ankles (ankles are a prime target for mosquitoes) are useful as the repellent doesn't rub off as easily.

Taking vitamin B1 (thiamine), garlic or brewer's yeast have all been advocated as making you less attractive to insects (but be aware that they haven't been shown to work in trials). They may be worth a try, in conjunction with insect repellents on exposed areas. Electronic buzzing devices have not been shown to be effective.

Permethrin is an effective insecticide that can be applied to clothes and mosquito nets. It repels and kills mosquitoes, fleas, ticks, mites, bedbugs, cockroaches and flies. If you're planning on trekking through tick-infested areas (rainforests, scrubland, pastures), consider treating your clothes (especially trousers and socks) with permethrin before you go.

!*Wearing permethrin-treated clothes and applying DEET to your skin is considered to give the best level of protection against mosquitoes.*

The quality of screening and nets provided by accommodation in Asia tends to be very variable, and there always seems to be at least one mosquito-sized hole in any net or screen. It's worth considering taking a mosquito net with you, especially one that has been soaked in permethrin. Most travel equipment suppliers have a wide variety of mosquito nets to suit your individual needs, and most nets are very light and don't take up much room in a pack. If you don't want to bother with finding ways to put your net up, consider taking a stand-alone version (Long Road is one supplier; contact them on ☎ 800-359-6040 in the USA or via their web site www.longroad.com).

ACCIDENTS & INJURY

It's time to mention the 'D' word. It might come as a surprise to you, but the commonest cause of death in younger travellers is accidents, not nasty tropical illnesses (for older people it's preexisting illnesses like heart disease). Accidents are the main reason for needing a blood transfusion or other medical treatment, with all the potential for problems such as HIV and hepatitis B infection that this may entail.

When you're on holiday you tend to take all sorts of risks you probably would not dream of taking if you were at home – it's part of what makes travelling so good. But remember that you're not immune from danger just because you're on holiday. Accidents are, well, just that, and they can and do happen. It's not just a matter of fate – where they depend on your actions, they're preventable to a certain extent, especially if you're aware of the risks.

While we don't want to rain on your beach party, just be aware that alcohol and other mind-altering substances are major factors in accidents in travellers, from dignity-challenging falls to life-threatening road traffic accidents.

So now we've thoroughly depressed you, what steps can you take to ensure you come back in one piece? Accidents are preventable to a great extent, especially if you're aware of the potential risks, and a little common sense goes a long way towards preventing accidents.

Road Safety

Temple sculpture isn't the only riotously chaotic art form in Asia – some would say driving is too. If you're going to waste that return ticket, it's most likely to be because of a road traffic accident. Pedestrians, vehicle passengers, but most of all, motorcycle and moped riders are at risk. Just because there may be no laws governing road safety (or at least none that are enforceable) doesn't mean you should ignore common-sense safety precautions. These include:

- avoid alcohol if you're driving even if there are no laws to break
- wear a helmet and protective clothing if you're riding a motorcycle or moped; shorts and T shirt don't provide much protection against road rash if you come off
- use a seat belt if at all possible and resist the temptation to go as fast as the other lunatics
- check that your hire car has a minimum of safety features – like brakes, for example
- avoid travelling at night, which can be tricky in the best of conditions and downright dangerous in many parts of Asia

Public transport can be risky, especially in crowded urban areas, as lack of resources and the need to make a living often override any safety considerations. There are loads of examples we can cite of the dangers of public transport here: the sinking of a passenger ferry in Indonesia, the derailment of a passenger train in India, and the lamentable safety record of China's national carrier. However, it's all very well for us to advise you to choose the safest vehicle you can, but you often have no alternative.

Fire & Fixtures

Fire is another obvious hazard, particularly in countries where

Hazards of War

If you're sensible, you'll probably plan on avoiding areas affected by current conflicts, but in some countries you may come up against the legacy of past conflicts in the form of undetonated mines, mortars and bombs. In Asia, countries worst affected include Cambodia, Vietnam, Myanmar (probably, although exact figures are not available) and Laos (the Ho Chi Minh Trail especially). The figures for landmines are astonishing: worldwide there are approximately 120 million landmines buried in 71 countries (or about one for every 17 children in the world). Of these, about 6 million are in Cambodia and about 4 million in Vietnam. Mines are a major cause of death and disability in affected countries. You'll see many limbless people all over Cambodia, which has one of the highest per capita rates of amputees of any country in the world as a result of landmine injuries.

Landmines have an enormous socioeconomic and medical cost through their effects on use of arable land and restriction of movement, as well as the huge costs of treatment and rehabilitation of victims. Although mines are removed each year, this is more than made up for by planting of new mines. It has been estimated that at the current rate, assuming no new mines are laid, it will take 1100 years to clear the world of mines …

It's not all doom and gloom, however. In recognition of the urgent need to find a solution to this humanitarian problem, high-profile campaigns (including the International Committee of the Red Cross campaign launched in 1994, as well

smoking is a national pastime and heating and cooking relies
on gas or open fires. It's obvious, but just think of k.d. lang
and never smoke in bed.

Any self-respecting phobic will obviously work out well in
advance potential escape routes from a hotel room. Balconies
are a notable hazard for the unwary and the inebriated – stay
well away from the edge.

as organisations working at a national level) aimed at banning the use of mines have finally borne fruit. On 1 March
1999, the Ottawa Treaty came into force, banning the use of
landmines under international humanitarian law. Over 120
countries were signatories to the treaty; notable exceptions
include the USA, China and Israel. For more information,
contact the ICRC (☎ 22 734 6001, 19 avenue de la Paix, CH-
1202 Geneva, Switzerland or your national Red
Cross/Crescent Branch) or check out their web site
(www.icrc.org).

You're unlikely to wander through minefields if you stick
to usual tourist routes, but as mines were laid along paths
and in rice fields, it is possible if you are going off the beat-
en track in affected countries. Here are some basic rules to
follow in risk areas:

- never touch any war relics you may come across, especially if they look even remotely like a mine
- in high-risk countries (eg Cambodia) never stray from
  well-marked paths and stick to the main tourist attractions
- if you do plan to go off the usual tourist route, check with
  reliable sources (eg the local expat community or your
  embassy) about the possibility of mines
- if you accidentally wander into a mined area, retrace your
  steps if you can clearly see them; otherwise stay where
  you are and call for help
- don't rush in to help a mine victim as there may be other
  mines nearby; find someone who knows how to safely
  enter a mined area

!Travellers have died from carbon monoxide poisoning from fires in poorly ventilated rooms.

Beach & Water Safety

South-East Asia's fabulous beaches are a major drawcard for travellers. However, you should be aware that drowning is a surprisingly common cause of death, especially in children and young adults. Even strong swimmers get taken by unexpectedly strong currents or because of a lack of respect for the waves. Lifeguards and safety notices aren't part of the scene on most Asian beaches, so don't rely on these to keep you safe. In most places you'll be on your own if you get into trouble.

▶ Check locally for advice on currents and safe swimming spots – don't assume that there are no hazards just because there are no warning signs.
▶ If you're unused to surf or you're unsure of your swimming capabilities, play safe and avoid going in.
▶ Never run and dive in the water, even if you've checked the depth before.
▶ Don't swim straight after a meal, as this makes you more likely to get cramps.
▶ It's best not to swim if you've had alcohol or other mind-altering substances.
▶ Wear shoes to protect your feet from injury.
▶ Check the beach for sharp (and soft) objects before you sit down – some beaches (though less likely in tourist resorts) may double as dumping grounds and public toilets.

If you're swimming in fresh water in some parts of Asia you're at risk of a schistosomiasis (also called bilharzia), which is caused by a tiny worm – see the section on p331 for more details on where this is a risk and how to prevent it.

!For guidelines on diving and underwater safety, see the section on Scuba Diving in the Water chapter.

SEX & TRAVEL

It seems that not even the runs, rickety beds, paper thin walls, sunburn and sand can dampen the ardour of many travellers. Maybe it's the aphrodisiac properties of the heat, or the feeling of freedom travelling can give. Or is it just the cheap beer? Maybe sex is the reason you're going travelling. Whatever the reason, it makes sense to arm yourself with the facts about your risks of getting a sexually transmitted infection (STI) and a pack of condoms. STIs are a worldwide problem.

A sexual encounter with a new partner anywhere carries a risk of HIV or one of the other STIs, but it can be even riskier when you're travelling. This is partly because the countries you're travelling in may have higher infection rates for HIV and STIs than your own, but also because when you're travelling you're more likely to be in contact with people who are at greater risk of being infected. More worrying still, surveys have shown that, in spite of the risks, many travellers don't take precautions to protect themselves.

It's easy to think 'it could never happen to me', but it can and does (sex *and* STIs). Anyone who's having sex can get an STI, 'nice' girls and college boys included. You may think you're safe, for example, because you're not going to have sex with someone in a high-risk group or you're only going to have sex with fellow travellers. Think again. Who has your fellow traveller had sex with before you? Can you trust them to have been as careful or as aware of the risks as you?

Traditionally high-risk groups are men who have sex with men, people who inject drugs, sex workers, anybody who's had multiple partners and anybody who's had sex with people in these groups. You'll know if you're in the first group, and perhaps you'll recognise and be able to avoid the second and third groups, but are you sure you'd know if someone was in one of the last two groups? It's difficult to be sure of your new partner's sexual history and you may just be getting the edited highlights. 'Sex worker' is a pretty vague category anyway,

Corporate Hospitality

If you are doing business in Asia, just be aware that it's common practice in many countries for entertainment to include escorts, strippers and dancers – in some circumstances, it can be difficult to refuse services without seeming to be a party-pooper. If it seems likely that you'll face this situation, work out what you want to do (and how you'll do it) well in advance.

and starts to look even vaguer when you've included the guy who has sex with women travellers in return for free meals, drinks or status, or an unmarried woman in a country where most women are married or don't go out. You can be fairly sure that you're not going to be the first traveller they've had sex with.

In theory at least, STIs are simple to prevent – don't have sex. But … for many people risk reduction is a more realistic option. We're not suggesting you become a celibate saint, but keep your head out of the clouds – avoid obviously risky situations (use your common sense and don't believe everything your new partner may tell you) and always practise safer sex by using condoms with any new sexual partner. Check out the following safety tips:

▶ consider safer ways of having casual sex that don't involve intercourse
▶ if you have a regular partner, play fair by making sure you don't transmit an STI to them
▶ many STIs are passed in an alcoholic haze – try to avoid getting into situations where this might happen
▶ you never know when you might need a condom, so be prepared – it doesn't mean you have to have sex

If you do slip up while you're away, don't just pretend it never happened and perhaps put yourself and other partners at risk – arrange for a check up when you get home.

BLOOD TRANSFUSIONS

The emergence of AIDS worldwide has brought this issue into the limelight for travellers. Although blood transfusion can be lifesaving in certain situations, it's worth remembering that it's a risky procedure wherever you are – and this risk is increased in countries with limited resources or facilities for screening blood. Problems associated with blood transfusion include transmission of diseases such as HIV, malaria, hepatitis (B, C and D) and syphilis, as well as potentially serious serious reactions if the blood is not matched properly.

Reliable sources of blood are currently only available in some 40 to 50 countries in the world, which is obviously a hugely unsatisfactory – and unfair – situation. Efforts are being made to increase the provision of safe blood throughout the world, but there's a long way to go. Even when blood is screened for all the endemic diseases, there's still a risk that early infections will have been missed. In Asia, the only places you could expect blood to be routinely screened to a high standard are Hong Kong, Japan, Singapore and Thailand.

Before you get too paranoid, remember that the chance you will need a blood transfusion while you are away is small. One study estimated that in a two-week trip, about one in 10,000 travellers would need a blood transfusion. Your risk obviously increases the longer you are away, and if you are doing 'risky' activities like rock climbing or trekking. It's vital to have adequate medical insurance that covers emergency evacuation if necessary. For a summary of the currently accepted guidelines on blood transfusion for international travellers, you could check out www.armchair.com/info/bloodtrf.html.

Although it's probably down to fate in the end, you can do much to minimise your risk of needing a blood transfusion:

▶ take steps to avoid injury, especially road traffic accidents (the most likely reason for needing a blood transfusion if you're otherwise healthy) – see the Accidents & Injury section earlier for guidelines on this

▶ some diseases like malaria and dengue carry a risk of needing a blood transfusion, so take steps to avoid these by preventing insect bites and taking malaria preventives if appropriate

▶ avoid travelling in countries with unreliable blood supplies if you have a condition that might mean that you need a blood transfusion eg pregnancy or stomach ulcer

▶ remember that blood should be transfused only when absolutely necessary, and in many cases non-blood fluids can be safely used instead in the short term – in practice, however, you'll have to rely on someone else's opinion on this

▶ consider carrying sterile fluids for use in an emergency, although this is not likely to be a practical option unless you are in a very remote area away from medical help

If a blood transfusion is unavoidable, try to make sure it's from as reliable a source as possible – check with your embassy, your travel insurance company, clinics dealing with international travellers, the local Red Cross or Red Crescent Society or the local expatriate community for advice on safe local sources. It should be possible to find a source of adequately screened blood in most major cities.

Before you go, check what arrangements your travel insurance company has for providing safe blood in an emergency. Alternatively, you might want to consider joining the Blood Care Foundation. This charitable organisation has a global network of blood banks that claim to supply travellers with safe blood and sterile transfusion equipment within 12 hours anywhere in the world, for a membership fee. The Blood Care Foundation (☎ 01732-742 427, fax 451 199) can be contacted at 16 Lonsdale Gardens, Tunbridge Wells, Kent TN1 1NU, UK.

It's a good idea to find out what your blood group is and to keep a note of this on you while you are away, as it may be useful in an emergency situation. O rhesus-negative blood can be given to anyone, and is known as the universal donor. Note that rhesus-negative blood is hard to find in most countries in Asia. This might be a problem if you're a woman of child-bearing age who is rhesus negative. If you think this may be a problem for you, discuss with your doctor before you go.

your blood type	blood types you can receive
A	A, O
B	B, O
AB	A, B, AB, O
O	O
rhesus positive	rhesus positive, rhesus negative
rhesus negative	rhesus negative

INJECTIONS

Needles and other medical or dental equipment that may be contaminated with blood or body fluids can transmit HIV and hepatitis (B and C). Lack of resources and less rigorous sterilisation procedures in many less-developed Asian countries make this a real risk in these areas.

Carry a few sterile needles and syringes with you in your medical kit (with an official note to say why you are carrying them), but this is only any good if you remember to carry them on you at all times and are prepared to insist on them being used if necessary. Prepacked 'sterile kits' are available from most travel health clinics and travel equipment suppliers. If you do need an injection, make sure you see the sterile wrapping opened in front of you.

- Minimise your risks of needing medical or dental procedures while you are away by having medical and dental checkups before you go, and by taking good care of yourself while you are away.
- Any equipment used for a medical or dental procedure can be contaminated if it is not properly sterilised.
- Injections tend to be a popular method of administering medicines in Asia, so ask if there is a tablet you can take instead.
- Boiling needles for 20 minutes will inactivate HIV.
- Never share needles.
- Acupuncture, tattooing and ear, nose or body piercing all carry risks of infection if equipment is not sterilised between use.

EATING FOR HEALTH

'The foundation of life and tranquillity comes from food. Those who do not know how to eat properly do not deserve to live.'
(Tang dynasty medical scholar Sun Zi Miao, quoted in *Traditional Chinese Medicine* by Rey Tiquia, Choice Books.)

Eating well is all about making sure you get enough of the right nutrients to enable you to function at your best, mentally and physically, and it makes you less vulnerable to illness. When you're on the road, your diet may be very different from normal; in addition, a different lifestyle, stress and new activities may mean your nutritional requirements are increased. If you get sick, you need a good diet to give your body the best chance to combat the illness and for damaged tissues to repair themselves.

Being unfamiliar with local foods may make you less likely to vary your diet and you may be uncertain about their nutritional value. You may skip good things like fresh fruit and vegetables if you're worried about possible effects on your health. If you're on the move all the time, it may be difficult not to miss meals. It can all add up to you feeling below par and being more vulnerable to infection and other illnesses.

In general, making sure you have a balanced diet in most parts of Asia shouldn't be a problem. However, in some places (eg Tibet and Mongolia) and in some situations (eg if you're trekking in a remote area), this might not be so easy. And you can get the budgeting bug so bad that your diet suffers.

EATING THE RIGHT STUFF

Everybody needs six basics for life: water, carbohydrates, protein, fat, vitamins and minerals. Foods aren't a pure source of just of one type of nutrient, they contain various elements in different quantities, so the best way to make sure you get enough of the right things is to eat a varied diet. You shouldn't find this difficult in Asia, where most diets consist of a carbohydrate staple (rice, noodles, potatoes, bread) which you eat with a protein source (meat, fish, beans and pulses) and vegetables. Fresh fruit is widely available.

As a guide, you need to eat a variety of foods from each of five core groups:

- bread (roti, naan, chapatti, pizza base etc), other cereals (rice, noodles, pasta, pancakes etc) and potatoes – eat lots of these, they provide carbohydrate, fibre, some calcium and iron, and B vitamins
- fruit and vegetables – eat lots of these, they give you vitamin C, carotenes (vitamin A), folate, fibre and some carbohydrate
- milk and dairy products – eat moderate amounts for calcium, zinc, protein, vitamin B12, vitamin B2, vitamin A and vitamin D
- meat, fish, nuts, beans and pulses (lentils, dhal) – these provide iron, protein, B vitamins (especially B12; meat only), zinc and magnesium; eat in moderation
- fat and sugary foods (butter, oil, margarine, cakes, biscuits, sweets, soft drinks etc) – eat sparingly from this group, which mainly provides fat, including essential fatty acids, some vitamins and salt

Bear in mind that if you're sick, your requirements change and you may need to increase the amounts of some food groups to increase your intake of protein, vitamins and minerals, for example.

Vitamins & Minerals

These nutrients are essential for health. They're generally needed in small amounts for many of the processes carried out in your body. In many developed countries, common foods like bread and breakfast cereals are fortified with vitamins, but this is not the case in most Asian countries. Although stir-frying is great for keeping all the goodies in the vegetables, stewing and boiling vegetables in curries tends to leach out most of the useful vitamins.

Although most nutritionists would agree that it's best to get what you need by varying your diet, when you're travelling there are some situations when it may be a good idea to take multivitamin and mineral supplements. Many vitamins and minerals come from fresh fruit and vegetables, so supplements are a good idea if you think you'll be missing out on these for any reason (eg you're on a long trek or you're travelling somewhere these are likely to be in short supply). If you have heavy periods, especially if you've cut out animal products from your diet, you may need to take supplements containing iron to prevent anaemia. If you don't eat any foods of animal origin, you will need to take a vitamin B12 supplement. Finally, if you're recovering from illness, you could give your body a helping hand by taking multivitamin supplements.

Energy & Protein

Carbohydrates are the main source of food energy, and most Asian diets are constructed around a variety of starchy staples (officially known as complex carbohydrates) like bread, rice, noodles or potatoes. Simple sugars are good as instant energy suppliers, but complex carbohydrates are better for providing more sustained energy as they are broken down more slowly in the body.

You'll have no trouble getting sugary foods like sweets in Asia; other sources of simple sugars include fruit, jam, honey and milk. If you don't have enough carbs in your diet, more protein is used instead, making less available for growth and repair. If your blood sugar gets low, you may start to feel weak, wobbly and headachey, signalling that it's time for that sweet fix.

Protein is an important component of your diet, but healthy adults only need a small amount of protein daily. Protein is important for growth and repair, so it's vital that growing children get sufficient quantities. Protein can also help with wound healing, so try to increase the amount you are eating if you have been sick or injured. Good sources of animal protein include meat, fish, poultry, eggs and dairy foods (milk, cheese etc). Non-animal sources of protein include cereals (bread, rice, oats etc), nuts, seeds and pulses (beans, lentils etc).

Fat is the most concentrated source of energy, providing, weight for weight, just over twice as much as carbohydrate or protein. Foods rich in fat include all the obvious things like oil, butter, ghee and any foods cooked in these; meat; egg yolks; many processed and fast foods; and less obvious foods of plant origin like coconut milk, avocado and nuts. Dare we tell you that alcohol provides nearly as much energy as fat?

FADING AWAY?

Losing weight when you're travelling in Asia is pretty common. There are lots of reasons for this, including getting sick, having a change in diet and perhaps being more active. You may have a bit of padding to spare, but keep an eye on how much weight you're losing and don't allow yourself to lose too much, as this may put you at risk of illness, as well as draining you of energy.

If you find you're losing weight, remember that with a vegetarian diet you generally have to eat larger quantities of plant foods to get the same amount of energy. Increase your quota of energy-giving foods, including fats, and consider taking multivitamin supplements. If you're ill, you need to get treatment for this. If you have ongoing diarrhoea, you may not be absorbing nutrients properly.

VEGGING OUT

If you've somehow managed to close your eyes to the realities of meat production back home, you may find that wandering through a few Asian food markets brings it up close and personal. It depends where you're travelling and how strict a vegetarian you are, but overall, especially in main tourist areas, you shouldn't have any trouble getting a balanced vegetarian diet in Asia; India, for example, is a vegetarian's paradise.

If you've just turned vegetarian, be aware that your body takes a bit of time to adjust to getting some nutrients from plant sources, so it's worth taking a bit of care with your diet. Getting enough protein isn't generally a problem, especially if you eat dairy products or eggs. Note that proteins from plant sources often lack one or more amino acids (the building blocks of protein). Most traditionally vegetarian diets have dealt with this by basing meals around a combination of protein sources so that deficiencies are complemented. Examples of combinations include: pulses (beans, dhal) and rice, pulses and cereal (beans and bread), and nuts and cereal (nut butter on bread).

Because iron from plant sources is less well absorbed than iron from meat, iron-deficiency anaemia is a risk if you aren't careful, especially in menstruating women. Another vitamin you might not get enough of is vitamin B12 as it's only derived from animal sources. If you cut out all animal foods from your diet, you'll need to take a supplement to make up for this, although in many developed countries foods are often fortified with vitamins, including B12. Yeast extracts and fermented soybean substances like tempeh and miso contain a substance similar to B12 but it doesn't have the same effect in the body, so you'll still need B12 supplements. Good plant sources of nutrients include:

- protein – soya protein, pulses, bread, grains, seeds (eg sesame), potatoes
- calcium (for healthy bones) – tofu, seeds, green leafy vegetables, nuts, bread, dried fruit (eg apricots)
- iron – pulses, green vegetables, dried fruits, nuts; absorption of iron is increased by by consuming a source of vitamin C at the same time (fruit, fruit juice or vegetables); tea, coffee, and phytate and oxalates from plants will reduce the absorption of iron

ASIAN DIETS

In case you're wondering how traditional Asian diets shape up, the news is good ... well mostly. The widespread emphasis on foods of plant origin and seafood, together with healthy methods of cooking like steaming and stir frying, makes

Asian cuisine one of the healthier cuisines of the world in terms of lower risk of heart disease and bowel cancer.

The benefits of stir-frying are supposed to include lower fat, less chance of nutrients being destroyed by cooking and higher fibre content. Soybeans are native to China and are eaten in a variety of forms throughout much of Asia. They have received a lot of attention, partly because they have the highest protein content of any plant food, but also because they contain a substance similar to oestrogen, which is thought to be one reason why Asian women have been found to have fewer menopausal problems.

The main problem with Asian cuisine for the health conscious is the high salt content in soy sauce and many other popular condiments like *nam pla* (Thai fish sauce) and *nuam cham* (Vietnamese fish sauce). Monosodium glutamate is another source of salt that you may want to avoid.

Coconut milk is widely used in the cuisines of Indonesia, Thailand and South India in particular. It's one of the few plant-derived sources of saturated fat, so if you're watching your cholesterol, you'll want to go easy on this.

FOOD FOR ACTION

Food is fuel, and if you're active you need lots of it. For example you can use up to 4000KCal a day if you're active in a temperate climate. You need more energy to keep warm in a cold climate, when you might need up to 5000KCal a day.

If you're going trekking and are planning to carry all your food with you, you'll need to balance up the energy-giving properties of available foodstuffs with their weight and bulk. Bear in mind that if you're going on a long-ish hike, you'll want to have some variety in what you eat. Tinned food and fresh fruit tend to be out for all but short trips. Take enough for three main meals a day plus lots of between meal snacks. On top of this, it's a good idea to have a bit extra with you in case of emergencies.

Food as Medicine

Food has a fascinating role in traditional Asian medicine, in keeping with the holistic nature of these systems. Foods are used not only to promote wellbeing, but also to treat ill health. Often an imbalance of energy (resulting in ill health) will be treated with foods first and herbs later. Herbal infusions and tonics are widely used to promote health and protect against disease. The link between medicinal herbs and food is obvious, and herbal medicine is used in all traditional Asian medical systems.

Many of the spices used in Asian cooking have medicinal effects. Garlic, for example, is widely used in Asian cooking and is said to have beneficial effects on blood pressure and cholesterol levels, and is also thought to help combat infection. Ginger is good for digestion, nausea and a sluggish circulation. Shiitake mushrooms are said to improve resistance to disease and are used to treat tiredness and viral infections. Cumin, widely used in Indian cooking, is said to ease indigestion and headaches. Cardamom helps digestion and is a breath freshener.

What you take with you depends on what's available locally and whether you are taking stuff from home. Dehydrated meals are a camping stalwart, if not exactly a favourite, but they may not be available in many areas. Good snack foods that you shouldn't have trouble finding include dried fruit (apricots or dates, which are good sources of vitamins and iron too), nuts, chocolate and biscuits. Good protein sources are pulses (such as nuts, dried chickpeas, lentils and beans), tinned meats and fish. Make sure you include plenty of starchy foods for energy.

HELP ...

○ It's always best to seek help as soon as possible if a child is ill – see the Babies & Children chapter for more advice.

○ Major and minor trauma is covered in the First Aid appendix starting on p397.

Being ill far from home is miserable, but it's even worse when you don't speak the language and the medical system is unfamiliar and likely to be less reliable than you are used to. Scarier still is the thought of all those nasty tropical diseases that everyone's been talking about and that you now think you must have.

Take heart: you're generally at pretty low risk of most 'tropical' diseases – you're much more likely to get diarrhoea, an infected insect bite or a cold. Don't forget that your body has an enormous potential to fight off infection, and most minor illnesses respond to simple, nondrug treatments (discussed later in this chapter), so it's always worth trying these first.

As a general rule you should only self-medicate if there is no alternative (for example you're in a remote area far from medical help) and you are confident you know what you are doing. The treatment guidelines we give in this book are to help you make an informed decision about what to do in a given situation; they are not intended as a substitute for medical advice.

! You must see a doctor if you're seriously ill OR you've tried all the simple measures without any effect OR there's no improvement in your condition after a day or two.

If you're concerned about getting medical help when you are away, remember that doctors in touristed areas will be used to treating common travellers ailments. Also, doctors who work in tropical countries will have substantial experience in diagnosing and treating tropical diseases (like dengue and malaria) – much more than your doctor back home is likely to have.

It's best to avoid treating fellow travellers unless you know what you're doing as you probably won't be doing them any favours and you may need precious supplies of medicines yourself later.

HOW TO GET MEDICAL HELP

If you need to get help, there are various ways to go about it. Some key hospitals are listed at the end of this book in the Medical Services appendix, or you could try the telephone book or check your guidebook.

▸ Your embassy will generally be able to provide you with a list of local doctors.
▸ Ring your travel insurance hotline – they should be able to recommend a local doctor. Make sure you always carry this number on you while you are away.
▸ If you are a member of IAMAT (see Useful Organisations in the Before You Go chapter for more details), they will have supplied you with the names of local doctors – again, make sure you carry this information on you at all times.
▸ Upmarket hotels can often recommend a doctor and usually have a doctor attached to the staff.
▸ In an emergency, US citizens could try contacting the State Department's Citizen's Emergency Center (p27).
▸ You could try asking other travellers, members of the expat community or members of international aid organisations for the names of reliable doctors.
▸ Remember, you could always try contacting your doctor back home for advice, especially for exacerbations or complications arising from preexisting conditions.

See the Medical Services appendix for more details, but generally teaching hospitals in major towns are the most reliable. If you are in more remote areas, missionary hospitals or hospitals run by international organisations are a good bet. In rural areas, healthworkers can provide basic medical advice.

In many Asian countries, pharmacists and drugstore owners are a source of basic health advice for a large section of the local population. Bear in mind, though, that generally they are not medically qualified and their advice is no substitute for a proper medical consultation. They have been known to recommend inappropriate treatment (for example tuberculosis treatment for a simple cough), with potentially disastrous effects.

BASICS

WORKING OUT WHAT'S WRONG

Try to decide what your main problem is: do you feel feverish, have you got a headache, diarrhoea, a skin rash or a cough? If you think you know what's wrong, turn to the appropriate section later in this book; otherwise read on.

Ask yourself some simple questions:

- what diseases am I at risk for in this country or area? See the summary at the beginning of this book and the maps; if you're outside the danger zone, then these diseases are much less likely
- am I in a malaria zone? (see map p21 and check locally) If the answer is yes, read the section on malaria and seek medical advice as soon as possible (within eight hours)
- did I complete my vaccination courses properly before leaving? If yes, then these diseases are very unlikely, with the exception of cholera (you're unlikely to have been offered this vaccination anyway)
- have I been in any risk situations recently? Have I been bitten by insects (malaria, dengue etc), ticks (typhus, relapsing fever), had contact with animals (rabies), had any injections or transfusions (HIV, hepatitis B) or swum in rivers or lakes (schistosomiasis)?
- have any of my travelling companions been ill? If yes, you may be suffering from the same illness
- is a sexually transmitted infection a possibility? See HIV/AIDS & Sexual Health chapter later in this book for more guidelines

BASIC MEASURES

There are some simple things you can do when you're ill that will help you get better quicker.

▶ Stop travelling and rest up for a while.
▶ Make sure you're as comfortable as the circumstances allow: get a room with a fan if it's hot or get extra blankets if it's cold. It's probably worth spending a bit more on a decent room as you'll be surprised at the difference cheerful surroundings can make.
▶ Drink plenty of fluids (purified water, fruit juice, weak tea), especially if it's hot or you have a fever.
▶ If necessary, give yourself a break from alcohol, tobacco and strong tea or coffee.

Take your temperature and make a note of it. It's a good idea to do this regularly (eg four times a day) while you're ill, as it gives you an idea of how quickly you are improving or whether you need to try something different – see the section on Fever later in this chapter for more guidelines. You could get someone to take your pulse and to count your respiration rate (number of breaths per minute), but this is optional.

! Seek medical help if you don't improve after 48 hours (or
• before then if you get a lot worse).

Remember to make a note of any major symptoms you have (like a rash) and when it appeared, as well as any medication you take. This will make it easier to work out what's wrong if you need to see a doctor later.

TAKING A TEMPERATURE

There are three main types of thermometer: mercury, digital and liquid crystal ('fever strip'). Mercury ones are the most accurate, but they're also the most delicate and you can't take them with you in the cabin on a plane. Liquid crystal thermometers are the least accurate, but are convenient – follow the instructions on the packaging. The following instructions are for mercury and digital thermometers:

▶ wipe the thermometer with a small amount of antiseptic solution to make sure it's clean

- shake the thermometer so that the mercury is down in the bulb
- place the thermometer under the tongue OR if there is a chance that it may be bitten (eg a young child or if the person is very sick) place it in the armpit OR (for young babies) grease it slightly and slip it in the rectum
- leave the thermometer in place for two to three minutes (or follow the instructions on the packet) then remove it
- read and make a note of the temperature; temperatures are usually read in degrees Celsius, but may also be read in degrees Fahrenheit

PULSE & BREATHING RATE

Feeling the pulse and measuring the breathing rate are an important part of any medical assessment. Both can provide useful information, but only if you know what to look for and how these clues fit in with the rest of the picture. They're probably not going to be that useful in most common situations when you feel ill, although they are important to note in an emergency situation – for more guidance on how to deal with an emergency, see the inside backcover.

Temperature
- Normal temperature is 37°C or 98.6°F and up to 0.2°C above or 0.4°C below this.
- Fever is any temperature above this.
- Dangerously high fever is 40°C (104°C) and over – take measures immediately to bring the temperature down (see Fever later in this section).

Pulse & Breathing Rate

	pulse (beats/min)	breathing rate (breaths/min)
adults	60 to 80	12 to 20
children	80 to 100	up to 30
babies	100 to 140	40

Pulse Rate

To take your pulse, put two fingers on the inside of the wrist at the base of the thumb, and count how many beats there are to the minute; don't use your thumb because this has a pulse of its own, which may confuse things.

In an emergency situation, if you can't feel a pulse in the wrist try feeling the side of the neck beside the voice box (the Adam's apple in men) – see the inside backcover for an illustration of this. As well as counting the pulse, think about what it feels like: is it strong or weak? Is it regular or irregular?

Some abnormalities you may notice, and what they may mean if you are ill, are as follows. You need to seek medical advice urgently in all these situations:

- regular fast pulse (eg up to 120 or 140 bpm) – associated with high fever and serious illness
- weak, rapid pulse: shock (severe illness, major trauma etc) – be prepared to start emergency resuscitation (see inside backcover)
- irregular, very slow or very rapid pulse – heart problems
- slow pulse in spite of fever – could be typhoid (see p127)

Breathing Rate

Count the number of breaths per minute (get someone else to do this as it's impossible to get an accurate count on yourself). The breathing rate can be increased in many different situations, including lung problems (eg pneumonia) and fever.

OTHER SIGNS TO LOOK FOR

Other things you should check for and note include:

- any rashes, wounds, lumps or bumps
- yellow colour of the skin and whites of the eyes: jaundice
- pale lips and nails, pale inside of eye: anaemia
- blueness of the lips: may indicate a serious lung or heart problem
- unequal or otherwise abnormal pupils of the eyes
- abnormal drowsiness and/or confusion: this always indicates serious illness

SIGNS OF SERIOUS ILLNESS

You must seek medical attention if you experience any of the following problems. Remember that it's always best to seek help as soon as possible if a child is ill – see the Babies & Children chapter for more advice.

- any severe blood loss
- any severe continuous pain
- more than a day without passing any urine

Blood anywhere it shouldn't be:

- blood in urine
- blood in vomit – this may look like 'coffee grounds'; it won't always look bright red
- blood in faeces – may be bright red, more likely to be browny red and mixed in, or faeces may be black like tar (but remember that taking iron tablets can turn your faeces black)
- blood coughed up in spit
- any vaginal bleeding during pregnancy

Fever:

- high fever (more than 40°C or 104°F) that can't be brought down by the measures outlined under Fever (p112) later in this chapter
- fever without obvious cause that lasts more than two to three days

Problems with your digestive system:

- severe diarrhoea and vomiting
- abdominal pain and vomiting without being able to defecate
- severe vomiting where you can't take any fluids for over a day
- severe weight loss (more than a tenth of your normal body weight)

'Head' problems:

- convulsions
- severe headache with neck stiffness and sensitivity to light
- dizziness or extreme weakness, especially on standing

Lumps, bumps etc:

- any sores that won't go away
- any lumps that appear and grow
- any mole that bleeds or changes shape

SOME COMMON SIGNS & SYMPTOMS
FEVER

!Note that children can get very high temperatures very quick-
• ly and this can be dangerous if it causes convulsions (fits).
See the section on p277 for more details.

The term 'fever' means having a temperature higher than normal (see the boxed text on p112). It always means that there
is a disease process going on, and in travellers it's most likely to be a sign of infection. Producing a fever is thought to
help the body's natural defences to fight infection.

Having a fever usually makes you feel pretty rough. You
may feel intermittently hot and cold, with 'goose bumps' or
shivering, and you usually feel completely drained of energy.
The fever process itself causes muscular-type aches and pains
(often back ache) and headache.

You can feel hot even though your temperature measured on
a thermometer is not above normal, and sometimes you can
feel cold even though your temperature is raised, so it's always
worth taking your temperature with a thermometer to be sure.
(Touching your forehead with the back of your hand is a notoriously unreliable indicator of fever.) Take your temperature at
regular intervals (for example four times a day) and note what
it is – this way you can keep track of any improvement or
changes, and it gives you an idea of the pattern of the fever.

!Although the pattern of the fever can sometimes be helpful in
• determining the cause, in practice many diseases don't show
the textbook fever patterns, especially in travellers, so it's best
not to rely on this.

If you have a really high temperature, you can get rigors, unpleasant episodes of violent shivering and drenching sweating. They are always a sign of very serious illness, and you should seek medical advice as soon as possible, and immediately try simple measures to lower your temperature.

If you have a fever:

▶ take paracetamol (acetaminophen) or aspirin (avoid aspirin if you think you may have dengue fever) to lower your temperature and relieve any aches and pains
▶ dehydration is a particular risk with any fever, especially in hot climates, so drink plenty of fluids
▶ help your body to cool down – take cool showers or drape wet cloths or sponges over yourself and put the fan on
▶ make sure you don't get cold (but piling the blankets on to 'sweat it out' is not helpful)

Having a fever increases your metabolic rate and can make you lose weight – this is just the fever part of the illness, having diarrhoea and vomiting as well exacerbates the problem. Because of this, it's important to try to maintain a basic intake of food while you are sick and to make up for this as you start feeling better and your appetite increases. See the section on nutrition, Eating for Health, at the end of the Staying Healthy chapter for more guidelines.

These measures all treat the symptoms of the fever, not the underlying cause. In addition, you need to work out what's causing the fever.

Causes

Many fevers, as at home, are caused by viral illnesses, such as colds and flu (see the Respiratory System chapter), which can start suddenly and rarely last more than three to five days. With any fever, always check for any obvious causes, for example:

■ runny nose – cold (p163)
■ cough – bronchitis, chest infection (p170)

disease	page	associated symptoms/other clues
flu	p166	more common in cold months, may cause generalised aches and pains without any other symptoms
diarrhoea (various causes)	p132	see the Digestive System chapter later in the book for guidelines on diagnosing and treating diarrhoea
heatstroke	p294	headache, weakness, muscle cramps; more likely if you've been very active in unaccustomed heat
malaria	p118	fever often intermittent, joint aches, chills, headache; also possibly cough, abdominal pain, diarrhoea and jaundice (yellow skin)
dengue fever	p115	fever may seem to go, but comes back after a few days; headache, severe aches and pains, rash (possibly)
glandular fever-like illnesses	p169	sore throat, swollen neck glands, no energy
hepatitis	p158	nausea, vomiting, jaundice, dark urine, light faeces
meningitis	p126	fever, headache followed by neck stiffness, vomiting, sensitivity to light
typhoid (and related illnesses)	p127	often causes a persistent fever, diarrhoea may be a late symptom only
schistosomiasis (bilharzia)	p331	itching, wheezy cough and diarrhoea, but may cause no obvious symptoms
amoebic liver abscess	p148	pain in right upper part of abdomen
Japanese B encephalitis	p125	drowsiness, confusion, headache, fits
tuberculosis	p128	recurrent evening or night fever, usually with cough
typhus	p339	red rash, distinctive sore at site of tick bite, more likely if you've been trekking in rural areas

- sore throat (p168) – tonsillitis, glandular fever
- earache – ear infection (p173)
- facial or sinus pain – acute sinusitis (p164)
- abdominal pain – see following section
- bladder symptoms – cystitis (p239)
- pelvic infection (p245)
- boils or an infected cut (p195)
- toothache – tooth abscess (p185)

If you've ruled out all these, then you can start thinking about some other causes of fever, which we've summarised in the table on the previous page.

ABDOMINAL PAIN

It can be notoriously difficult to work out what's causing this – if the pain is severe, it's safer to seek medical advice as soon as possible. To give you some guidance, we've listed a few of the more common scenarios:

- with diarrhoea: usually crampy, comes in waves and may be relieved by passing wind or faeces; you may have a fever
- with constipation: spasms of pain in lower abdomen
- central abdominal pain: bladder infection, period pains, pelvic infection
- upper abdomen, just under rib cage, burning, worse after meals – heart burn, indigestion
- upper right abdomen, just under ribs – hepatitis (sometimes), liver abscess, gall stones
- appendicitis – see p158
- severe, colicky (comes and goes) pain that makes you writhe around that may go down into your pelvis (or testicles in men) could be a kidney stone, see p157

NAUSEA & VOMITING

When you're travelling you often get short episodes of nausea, sometimes with vomiting. They usually settle within a day without any specific treatment. They're usually due to viral infections, but there are many other causes:

- medicines eg malaria pills, antibiotics
- motion sickness (p69)
- food poisoning (p135)
- diarrhoeal illnesses (p132)
- dehydration or heatstroke (p294)
- meningitis (p126)
- migraine headache (p182)
- pregnancy (p251)

HEADACHE

Most fevers cause headache. Other possibilities are:

- dehydration, heatstroke (p294)
- migraine (p182)
- stress
- trapped nerve (sharp stabbing pains, intermittent)
- neck problems (eg arthritis)
- dengue fever (p115)
- malaria (p118)
- meningitis (p126)
- typhoid fever (p127)
- altitude sickness (p305)

RASH

There are many causes of rashes. See the Skin chapter later in this book for a more detailed discussion of skin problems, but causes of rashes include:

- viral illnesses
- measles & other childhood illnesses (p220)
- fungal infections (p193)
- allergic reactions, dermatitis (p191)
- dengue fever (p115)
- typhus (p339)
- cutaneous leishmaniasis (p216)
- schistosomiasis (p331)

FEVER

In this chapter we've grouped some infections that usually have fever as their main symptom – for a summary of the causes of fever, see p111.

○ For guidance on how to take a temperature see p106.

DENGUE & DENGUE HAEMORRHAGIC FEVER

This disease (see map on p22) is caused by a virus transmitted to humans via the bite of an infected mosquito. Dengue has spread rapidly in the last decade or so and is now one of the top public health problems in the tropical world. At the latest count, there were 50 million new cases occurring every year, and this is probably a conservative figure. Currently you're at greatest risk in South-East Asia, but dengue occurs in all tropical regions. For details on the latest outbreaks, check with a travel health clinic or the other information sources listed in the Before You Go chapter.

The Rise & Rise of Dengue

One of the reasons for the rise of dengue is that the mosquitoes responsible for transmitting the disease thrive in crowded urban areas, where they breed in any container that holds water, including discarded plastic wrapping and old tyres. Dengue mosquitoes are much less common in rural areas and are rarely found at altitudes above about 2000m. Poor living conditions and the rise in urban settlements with concomitant deforestation in many parts of Asia have encouraged the spread of dengue, and increasing resistance of dengue mosquitoes to insecticides have made control of the disease more difficult. At the same time, air travel has encouraged the spread of the disease throughout the tropics, most recently to Cuba, the Caribbean and South America. On a global scale, prevention of dengue depends on eradication of mosquito breeding grounds, improving urban living conditions and widespread use of insecticides – so don't hold your breath.

Note that there's currently no vaccine against dengue and none is likely in the near future. To avoid dengue, take steps to prevent mosquito bites, bearing in mind that the dengue mosquito mainly bites during the day. For the complete low-down on preventing mosquito bites, see the section on Insect Bites in the Staying Healthy chapter.

Symptoms

The illness usually starts quite suddenly with fever, headache, nausea and vomiting, and joint and muscle pains. The aches and pains can be severe, hence the old name 'breakbone fever'. The fever sometimes appears to settle after a few days, only to reappear a few days later ('saddleback fever'). Typically, you get a fine red rash, often around the third to fifth day. The illness can last anything from three to about 10 days, settling spontaneously without any specific treatment. However, many travellers report experiencing extreme tiredness with muscle wasting and lack of energy for several weeks or months after, which can be very debilitating, and may be a good reason to cut your trip short. On the other hand, symptoms can be very mild, and you may not realise that you've had it.

Rarely, you can get a more severe, potentially fatal form of dengue called dengue haemorrhagic fever (DHF), which is associated with uncontrolled bleeding and shock from loss of blood. Although DHF receives a lot of publicity and is very frightening, bear in mind that it is rare in travellers, and most deaths occur in children who are residents of the host country. DHF is thought to be due to infection with a second strain of the dengue virus within a certain period of time. You can get minor bleeding – nose bleeds, bleeding gums or bruising – with simple dengue.

Diagnosis & Treatment

A blood test can help diagnose dengue. There's no specific treatment, but if you think you have dengue fever:

▶ seek medical advice as soon as possible so that the diagnosis can be confirmed and other diagnoses, including malaria, can be ruled out
▶ rest and drink plenty of fluids
▶ take simple painkillers if necessary, but avoid aspirin as this can increase the likelihood of bleeding problems

You need to keep a look out for signs of DHF. Seek medical help urgently if you have any of the following (if they do occur, it's usually around the third day of illness):

▶ any worsening of your condition, especially if associated with any of the following symptoms
▶ spontaneous bruising of the skin, nose bleeds, bleeding from the gums, vomiting blood or abdominal pain
▶ signs of blood loss – thin, rapid pulse, restlessness, pale face and cold fingers and toes; this is a critical situation

DENGUE-LIKE FEVERS
Be aware that there are many dengue-like viruses that cause similar illnesses to dengue fever, all of which are transmitted by mosquitoes or sometimes ticks. They tend to occur in quite specific geographical areas, and doctors in those areas will know what to look for.

In Asia, you may hear Chikungunya infection or West Nile fever mentioned. There's no specific treatment for any of these and no vaccine. The most important message is prevention by avoiding insect and tick bites.

Dengue Again?
There are four different strains of the dengue virus. If you get dengue, you develop immunity against the infecting strain, but you'll still be vulnerable to the three remaining strains, so you could get it again. You're more likely to get a severe form of the disease second time around so if you've had dengue in the past, you should discuss the risks with your doctor before you go, and be extremely careful to avoid mosquito bites at all times.

MALARIA

!This section gives you guidelines on diagnosing and treating malaria; for the complete lowdown on preventing malaria see Malaria Pills (p37) and Insect Bites (p83) earlier in this book.

Malaria (see map p21) is caused by a parasite called *Plasmodium* which is carried by a type of night-biting mosquito present in most tropical and subtropical areas below about 2000m. When an infected female mosquito bites you, malarial parasites are injected into your bloodstream and get carried to your liver where they multiply. During this phase you don't get any symptoms.

Symptoms appear when the malarial parasites enter your bloodstream again, which occurs after a variable length of time depending on the type of malaria (usually about one to three weeks, but sometimes up to a year).

The malarial parasites enter and multiply in red blood cells, eventually destroying them. This can have effects on many organs in your body, including your guts (causing vomiting and diarrhoea), kidneys (causing kidney failure) and brain (cerebral malaria).

There are four different types of *Plasmodium* parasites, but the one of most concern is *P. falciparum*, which causes the most severe form of the disease and is responsible for most malaria deaths worldwide.

The others types, *P. vivax*, *P. ovale* and *P. malariae*, are less likely to cause severe complications so rapidly, but infection with any of these still needs to be treated promptly. *P. ovale* doesn't occur in Asia but the other two do, with *P. vivax* being quite common. *P. vivax* and *P. ovale* can remain inactive in the liver for some time, and can cause disease several weeks or months after you've left a risk area.

You can't tell the different forms of malaria apart on the basis of the early symptoms, so you have to assume that any malaria is due to *P. falciparum* unless proved otherwise (by a blood test).

Malaria can be effectively treated with drugs and the symptoms quickly disappear as the parasites are cleared from the blood. If malaria is treated appropriately, it won't recur. The picture you may have of recurring attacks of malaria is only true when the disease is not treated.

! The most important point to remember about malaria is that it can progress rapidly to severe complications (sometimes within 24 hours) so it's extremely important to seek medical help urgently if you get a fever in a malarial area.

Symptoms

Unfortunately, the symptoms of malaria are very variable and rather nonspecific, making it notoriously difficult to diagnose. The most important sign of malaria is having a fever (38°C or higher). In theory at least, you should notice three stages: a cold stage when you shiver and your temperature rockets up; followed by a hot stage when you feel hot, flushed and have a high temperature (this lasts for several hours); finally you get a wet stage when you become drenched in sweat, and your temperature falls. This is the textbook scenario – in reality the picture is likely to be much more vague, especially if you were taking malaria prevention pills.

Suspect malaria if you have a fever (38°C or higher) – it may just feel like an attack of flu – with or without any of the following symptoms:

- headache and aching muscles and joints
- nausea and vomiting, or diarrhoea (especially in children)
- cough
- abdominal discomfort and jaundice (yellowing of the skin and whites of the eyes)
- confusion, leading to coma (cerebral malaria)

! Remember that you can still get malaria even if you are taking malaria prevention pills.

Diagnosis & Treatment

It takes at least a week for malaria to appear after an infective bite, so a fever within the first week of your arrival in a malarial area is very unlikely to be malaria (unless you have come from a malarial area.

Malaria can be quickly and simply diagnosed from a sample of your blood, usually taken by pricking your finger. The test may need to be repeated if it's initially negative and you know malaria is likely. Most doctors and clinics in malarial areas will have facilities for doing a malaria blood test, or you can do a test yourself if you have a kit with you. You may be able to buy kits locally in some countries.

If you think you may have malaria:

▶ rest and take steps to bring down the fever – see p111 for guidelines on general measures you can take
▶ drink plenty of fluids
▶ seek medical help as soon as possible for a blood test to confirm the diagnosis
▶ once the diagnosis is confirmed, take the doctor's advice on treatment as they are likely to be experienced in treating malaria and will know what the most appropriate treatment is for the area you are in

If your symptoms continue or recur despite treatment, seek medical advice as you will need further treatment, or you may have another illness altogether that needs treating.

Don't forget that you will still need to take malaria pills after you recover – get medical advice on what would be most appropriate in your situation.

Remember that malaria can appear after you've left a malaria risk area – if you get a fever, seek medical help urgently and be sure to tell the doctor where you've been and which malaria pills you were taking, if any.

Emergency Self-treatment

Self-treatment of any serious disease isn't something to be undertaken lightly, and with malaria there are some special issues you need to be aware of.

First of all, it can be difficult to know when you have malaria as the symptoms are so nonspecific, and there's a worry that you might miss treating another potentially serious disease (although if you are carrying one of the new diagnosis kits, this is less of a problem – see p45 for more details).

Secondly, because of drug resistance, you need to be sure you are taking the appropriate treatment for the area you are in, especially as inadequately treated malaria can recur later.

Thirdly, most antimalarial treatments have a risk of significant side effects, and you are more likely to experience side effects at the doses used for treatment; in addition, they can interact with other drugs you may be taking. For these reasons:

- you should only consider self-treatment in an emergency ie if you do not have access to medical care within 24 hours of the start of symptoms
- emergency self-treatment is a first aid measure only – you still need to get yourself to medical help as soon as possible

When? If you are in a risk area, you must suspect malaria if you have an otherwise unexplained fever (over 38°C) that lasts more than eight hours without responding to simple fever-reducing measures.

Which Drugs? Although we give currently accepted guidelines here, recommendations change as resistance patterns vary and new facts come to light, so it's best to get the most up-to-date advice from your doctor or travel health clinic before you go, or to seek reliable local advice if necessary.

Treatment depends on what, if any, malaria prevention you were taking, as well as the presence of any malarial drug resistance. You need to take an antimalarial different from the one that you were taking as prevention. This is because the strain of malaria you have may be resistant to the antimalarial you were taking, and also because you are more likely to experience side effects if you take the same antimalarial for treatment.

In drug-resistant areas (ie all risk areas in Asia except low risk areas in China), options include:

- atovaquone-proguanil (Malarone) – this is good if you were taking mefloquine or doxycycline for prevention
- sulphadoxine/pyrimethamine (Fansidar) –this is good if you weren't taking any preventive antimalarials or you were taking chloroquine plus proguanil, unless you are in South-East Asia (especially Cambodia, Laos, Myanmar, Thailand and Vietnam) where resistance is high
- quinine sulphate – with this you will need to take another agent, usually one of the following: sulphadoxine/pyrimethamine (Fansidar) OR doxycycline OR tetracycline
- mefloquine – can be taken if you were taking doxycycline as prevention

In chloroquine-sensitive areas (ie only low risk areas in China, excluding Yunnan and Hainan Island), you could take either of the following:

- chloroquine – if you were not taking any prevention
- sulphadoxine/pyrimethamine (Fansidar) if you were taking chloroquine plus proguanil for prophylaxis

Side Effects & Cautions

○ For more details about mefloquine and chloroquine, see the section on Malaria Pills in the Before You Go chapter.

Atovaquone plus proguanil (Malarone) is highly effective against multidrug resistant strains of malaria. It's also safe and unlikely to cause you any adverse effects.

Sulphadoxine/pyrimethamine (Fansidar) has been widely used to treat malaria. It's no longer effective in most of South-East Asia because drug resistance has emerged, but it is currently

Malaria Standby Treatment – Doses & Schedules

Although we have done our best to ensure that these doses are correct at the time of going to print, there are many variables to take into account, so you should check these with your doctor before you leave. Note that although we give doses for children here, we do not recommend you take children to high risk malarial areas.

treatment	adult	child
atovaquone-proguanil (Malarone)	four tablets once daily for three days	11kg to 20kg one tablet once daily; 21kg to 30kg two tablets once daily; 31kg to 40kg three tablets once daily; over 40kg, as for adult
sulphadoxine/pyrimethamine (Fansidar)	single dose of three tablets	5kg to 10kg half tablet; 11 to 20kg one tablet; 21 to 30kg 1.5 tablets; 31 to 45kg two tablets; over 45kg three tablets
quinine sulphate PLUS-	two 300mg tablets three times daily for seven days	10mg/kg three times daily for seven days
sulphadoxine/pyrimethamine (Fansidar)	dose as above	dose as above
OR doxycycline	100mg once daily	over 8 years: 2mg/kg twice daily for seven days
OR tetracycline	250mg four times daily for seven days	over 8 years: 5mg/kg four times daily for seven days
mefloquine	two 250mg tablets and a further two six hours later	child 15kg or over: 15mg/kg single dose
chloroquine	four tablets (150mg base) each on days one and two, and two on day three (ie total of 10 tablets)	25mg base/kg over three days

effective in the Indian subcontinent and most of Indonesia. It's generally safe and effective at the doses used for treatment, but using it weekly for prevention is no longer recommended because serious skin reactions have occurred.

Side effects with **mefloquine** are common at the doses used for treatment, and include light-headedness, nausea, dizziness and vertigo; more serious side effects occur in about one in 100 people at this dose.

Quinine is the most effective drug against chloroquine-resistant malaria, but side effects are common. These include ringing in the ears, muffled hearing and sometimes dizziness, usually on the second or third day of treatment. These side effects usually go away once you stop taking it. Quinine can cause heart problems so you need medical supervision if you are on any heart medications, and these problems are more likely if you have been taking mefloquine for prevention. It can also cause your blood sugar to drop. Be aware that quinine is very toxic if taken at more than the recommended dose, and you should always keep it well out of reach of children. Because of these problems, it's not usually recommended as emergency standby treatment.

Other Treatments

You may hear talk of **artesunate** or **artemether** in connection with the treatment of malaria. These compounds are related to qinghaosu, and have been hailed as one of the most important developments in antimalarial therapy in recent years.

Qinghaosu has been used for over two millennia in traditional medical practice in China, but it's only been rediscovered and developed commercially over the last decade or so. It is unrelated to the other antimalarials, and appears to be safe and effective in the treatment of severe malaria (when it's sometimes used with mefloquine). It's not, however, suitable for use as a preventive. Its use is highly controlled at present, to prevent the emergence of resistance, and limited for the time being to areas with multidrug-resistant malaria such as in Thailand and Cambodia. It appears to have few side effects.

!*Note that halofantrine, which was commonly used in the emergency treatment of malaria, is no longer recommended because of possible side effects (heart rhythm problems) in susceptible people. These are more likely if you have been taking chloroquine, mefloquine or quinine. Although it is no longer recommended for standby treatment, it may still be available in some areas, and is better than nothing in an emergency.*

JAPANESE B ENCEPHALITIS

This viral illness is spread through the bite of an infected mosquito and epidemics occur sporadically throughout Asia and the Pacific. You're at risk of the disease if you're travelling in rural, rice-growing areas for any length of time, or during epidemics. An effective vaccine is available – see under Immunisations in the Before You Go chapter for more details.

The mosquito that carries the disease breeds in rice fields. Pigs, wading birds and even bats can be infected with the virus and act as reservoirs of infection, especially pigs as they often live in quite close proximity to people in rural areas. In an epidemic, the pig population is often slaughtered in an attempt to control spread of the disease.

Symptoms

These are a sudden onset of fever, with headache and vomiting. Sometimes you just get flu-like symptoms without any further problems, but in a proportion of cases, the infection progresses to involve the brain (this is what encephalitis means). Signs that the brain is involved include stiff neck and sensitivity to bright light, drowsiness, confusion, fits (especially in children), unsteadiness and other specific signs of brain involvement that the doctor will look for and recognise. This disease can be fatal and, even if you do recover, you can be left with intellectual impairment.

Treatment

There's no specific treatment. Seek medical advice as soon as possible if you think you have Japanese B encephalitis. In the meantime, rest, drink plenty of fluids and take simple painkillers if necessary. Prevention is by avoiding insect bites and getting vaccinated if necessary.

MENINGOCOCCAL MENINGITIS

○ See p114 for a list of common causes of headache.

Recurring epidemics of meningitis occur in parts of Asia. Currently, risk areas include Nepal, northern India, northern Pakistan and Mongolia, but epidemics have occurred elsewhere (eg in Vietnam) so you should check with your doctor or travel health clinic for the most up-to-date information on outbreaks. There is an effective vaccine available, which may be recommended for travel to these areas – for more details see the Immunisations section in the Before You Go chapter.

Generally, you're at pretty low risk of getting meningococcal meningitis, unless an epidemic is ongoing, but you should at least be aware of the risk because the disease can be rapidly fatal. It's transmitted by breathing in droplets coughed or sneezed into the air by sufferers or, more likely, by healthy carriers of the bacteria that causes this form of meningitis. You're obviously more at risk in crowded, poorly ventilated places, and epidemics are more likely to occur during the cooler months when people tend to crowd together. In Nepal, trekker's lodges are prime risk spots as people are crowded in together overnight.

Symptoms

Symptoms of meningitis are fever, severe headache, neck stiffness that prevents you from bending your head forward, nausea, vomiting, and sensitivity to light, which makes you you prefer to stay in darkness. You may get a widespread, blotchy purple rash before any other symptoms appear.

Meningitis

Meningitis is any infection of the lining of the brain and spinal cord. Lots of different infectious agents can cause meningitis, including bacteria and viruses. Viral meningitis usually settles without any treatment, whereas bacterial meningitis can rapidly cause death and is the one you're most likely to have heard of.

Treatment

Meningococcal meningitis is an extremely serious disease that can cause death within a few hours of you first feeling unwell. Seek medical help without delay if you have any of the symptoms listed above, especially if you are in a risk area.

Treatment is with large doses of penicillin (for example 1.2g of benzylpenicillin in adults; 600mg in children aged up to 10 years) given directly into the bloodstream or, if that's not possible, intramuscularly. If you're allergic to penicillin, an intramuscular injection of cefotaxime OR chloramphenicol are suitable alternatives.

If you've been in close contact with a sufferer, you can protect yourself from infection by taking antibiotics, usually rifampicin 500mg twice daily for two days (child 10mg/kg; under one year 5mg/kg) OR ciprofloxacin 500mg single dose (not suitable for children), but it's best to seek medical advice on this.

TYPHOID FEVER

Also known as enteric fever, typhoid occurs worldwide, but is most common where personal and environmental hygiene standards are low. It's caused by a type of salmonella bacteria, *Salmonella typhi*. Paratyphoid is similar, but causes a milder disease. There's an effective immunisation (see p36) against typhoid, and if you've been immunised you're very unlikely to get it.

Typhoid is transmitted via food and water; symptomless

carriers, especially when they're working as foodhandlers, are an important source of infection.

Symptoms

Symptoms vary, but you almost always get a fever and headache to start with – initially very similar to a cold or flu – with aches and pains, loss of appetite and generally feeling unwell. The fever gradually rises over the course of a week. Characteristically, your pulse is relatively slow compared with the fever (eg 80 beats per minute for an adult instead of perhaps 100), but this is something a medic will pick up on better than you, so don't agonise over it too much. Other symptoms include constipation or diarrhoea and stomach pains.

You may feel worse in the second week, with a constant fever and sometimes a red skin rash. Serious complications occur in about one in 10 cases – most commonly damage to the gut wall with subsequent leakage of the gut contents into the abdominal cavity causing peritonitis. Sometimes this is the first indication of an infection. Other symptoms include severe headache, sore throat and jaundice.

Diagnosis & Treatment

Diagnosis is by blood test. Early diagnosis is important – it may be difficult to diagnose typhoid yourself, but this is one reason why you should seek medical help for any fever that does not improve after 48 hours. Typhoid is a serious disease and is not something you should consider self-treating.

Rehydration therapy is important if diarrhoea has been a feature of the illness, but antibiotics are the mainstay of treatment. Chloramphenicol used to be the first line treatment, but resistance is widespread in Asia and India, so you will need to take ciprofloxacin 500mg twice daily.

TUBERCULOSIS (TB)

Called consumption in the old days because people just wasted away with it, TB is making a global comeback, especially in Asia. It's not likely to cause you an immediate problem like, say, malaria or dengue, but it's a risk you need to be aware of, especially if you're planning on staying with relatives or other any nationals of a host country which has high infection rates. There is a vaccination against TB which has a useful level of effectiveness, especially for children and young adults. You may already have had a routine TB vaccination as a teenager (but not in North America).

TB is caused by a bacterium and you get it by breathing in droplets expelled by infectious people through coughing, talking or sneezing. Your risk of being infected increases the

A Growing Problem

If you thought TB was on the way out, you'd be wrong. It appears set to be one of the biggest health threats of the 21st century – currently it kills more people worldwide than malaria and HIV combined. The World Health Organization (WHO) is so alarmed at the reemergence of this age-old killer that in 1993 it declared TB a global health emergency. It estimates that a third of the world's population is infected with TB, and Asia, especially South-East Asia, is the epicentre of this epidemic. Six countries in Asia account for more than 50% of the world's TB cases – India, China, Bangladesh, Pakistan, Indonesia and the Philippines.

The biggest worry currently is the emergence of treatment-resistant TB. Until 50 years ago, TB was incurable, but effective treatment was discovered in the middle of the 20th century. It takes several months of drug treatment to get rid of TB, even though people start to feel better after a few weeks. People often stop taking their treatment too early, either because they feel better or they can't afford to pay for treatment – one consequence is the rise of drug-resistant TB. So once again we are faced with the prospect of untreatable TB.

Find out all about TB before you go from the WHO's TB homepage (www.who.int/gtb).

Something in the Air?

Because TB is transmitted by droplets, and the air in plane cabins is recycled throughout the flight, there's been much concern in recent years about the possibility of transmission of TB during flights. A recent case illustrates the dangers – when a Ukrainian emigre with TB coughed his way through an eight-hour flight to New York, 13 of 40 passengers sitting near him were found to be infected. This case was made worse by the fact that the Ukrainian had drug-resistant TB (the former Russian states are a major source of this).

While you can't do much about who boards your flight, it's worth being aware of the risks. It's generally agreed that your risk is directly related to how close you are to the person, and it's only significant if you're close to them for a long time.

closer you are to the person and the longer you are exposed to them. You can also get a form of TB through drinking unpasteurised milk. Only about 15% of people who become infected go on to develop the disease or become infectious.

The TB bacteria may lie dormant for years until your resistance is lowered for some other reason, such as poor nutrition or another disease like HIV.

Symptoms

TB classically affects the lungs, but it can affect almost any other part of the body, including your joints, bones, brain and gut. Pulmonary (lung) TB is the most common way in which TB shows itself in adults. Symptoms develop slowly, often over the course of several months, and include weight loss, fever and night sweats, and a cough with blood-stained spit. Sometimes the disease can be much more severe, especially in children, presenting with symptoms of meningitis (headache, neck stiffness, sensitivity to light) and leading to coma.

Diagnosis & Treatment

Diagnosis is by laboratory test of your spit. TB is not something you're going to be self-treating, so seek specialist advice if you think you may be infected. Treatment is with a combination of antibiotics over a prolonged period of time (six to eight months; sometimes up to a year). Multidrug resistant TB is obviously a major headache to treat but it is possible, although treatment is very expensive.

Prevention

Prevention is by avoiding prolonged exposure to circumstances that make transmission more likely, such as sleeping in crowded communal dormitories or travelling on crowded public transport, especially if spitting is common (difficult, admittedly, in much of Asia). The majority of cases of TB imported to the UK, for example, are in young people visiting family in high risk areas, so if you're in this category, it's definitely worth discussing vaccination with your doctor.

You're more likely to get infected if your resistance is low, for example through ill health or bad diet, so it makes sense to look after yourself while you are on the road. Never drink unpasteurised milk or milk products – if you're in any doubt, boil it first.

DIGESTIVE SYSTEM

We've devoted quite a bit of space to this topic, in recognition of its high ranking in the league table of ailments afflicting travellers.

DIARRHOEA

○ See also the sections on preventing diarrhoea (p77) and diarrhoea in babies and children (p278).

However careful you are, you're likely to get at least one episode of diarrhoea while you're away. Diarrhoea (meaning passing loose, frequent faeces, often associated with vomiting) is the commonest travel-related illness, and Asia is one of the diarrhoea hot spots of the world. Figures suggest that about 50% of travellers to high risk areas in Asia get diarrhoea, so it's as well to be prepared. You're more likely to get it if you're young, especially if you're roughing it, and if you are on a long trip.

There are many different causes of diarrhoea in travellers, but the most common cause is toxin-producing bacteria.

Causes of Travellers Diarrhoea

About one-third of cases, usually mild, are due to nonspecific causes, including:

- stress
- jet lag
- new foods and a change in eating habits

The rest are divided up as follows:

- bacteria, the commonest cause
- viruses ('gastric flu')
- parasites (including *Giardia* and amoeba)
- food poisoning (eg from a toxin, often bacterial, in the food)

It's best to avoid getting diarrhoea in the first place. For the complete lowdown on avoiding diarrhoea, turn to the Staying Healthy chapter. If you understand how diarrhoea is passed from person to person, it'll help you avoid it. It sounds gross, but basically you get diarrhoea by eating other people's faeces – in food (mainly), water and other drinks, and from dirty utensils (plates, spoons, cups etc). Hands used to prepare food may not have been washed thoroughly after toilet duty, flies can transfer microbes via their feet, and a lack of environmental cleanliness means that dust and dirt is more likely to be contaminated with faeces.

You can also get diarrhoea from direct contact with an infected person (if you touch hands etc that haven't been washed adequately) or, more rarely, from swimming in contaminated water (by swallowing small amounts). Some infective agents such as *Giardia* can survive even in chlorinated water, and both fresh water and seawater may be contaminated with sewage.

Diarrhoea is a hot topic of conversation among travellers, and it can be hard to separate fact from fiction sometimes. Just remember:

- travellers diarrhoea is generally a short, mild illness, lasting on average about three to five days
- because of this, you don't usually need to get medical advice or have a test to find out what's causing your diarrhoea
- replacing lost fluids and salts is the most important part of treating any watery diarrhoea, whatever the cause
- you don't usually need antibiotic treatment for mild to moderate diarrhoea
- there are certain situations when antibiotics need to be used – in these situations it's best to get medical advice rather than self-treating

TYPES OF DIARRHOEAL ILLNESS

You'll probably find your illness fits into one of the following three patterns: mainly vomiting with some diarrhoea, watery

Quick Guide to Diarrhoeal Illnesses

Some characteristics of various diarrhoeal illnesses are summarised here, with their treatments, but remember that diarrhoeal illnesses are notoriously difficult to diagnose on the
basis of symptoms alone and the only way to be sure of the
diagnosis is through a laboratory test.

illness	timing	characteristics
food poisoning	usually comes on soon after eating	symptoms come on rapidly after eating the bad food; tends to cause vomiting predominantly; over in 24 to 48 hours
watery diarrhoea	usually strikes about the third day after you arrive	usually caused by bacteria less bloating and flatulence than with *Giardia*
shigella	two to three days	high temperature, blood in diarrhoea, abdominal cramps can be severe
giardiasis	two to six weeks	symptoms are variable but usually sudden onset explosive diarrhoea, associated typically with bloating, cramps and flatulence
amoebic dysentery	minimum one week, maybe as long as several weeks	bloody diarrhoea (not profuse like bacterial causes), cramps, tends to be prolonged
Cyclospora	two days to two weeks	prolonged diarrhoea with weight loss
irritable bowel syndrome	may start for the first time after an acute attack of travellers diarrhoea	may have alternating diarrhoea and constipation, abdominal pains, but no weight loss
tropical sprue	usually develops after an acute attack of diarrhoea	prolonged watery diarrhoea usually associated with profound weight loss

diarrhoea (the most common type of travellers diarrhoea) or diarrhoea with blood (dysentery) and fever.

Vomiting & Diarrhoea

! Remember that there are many causes of nausea and vomiting – for a summary of these, see p113.

If you suddenly get an attack of nausea and profuse vomiting soon after eating something dodgy, it's probably due to food poisoning. This is a worldwide problem that is more likely when you're eating food not prepared by yourself, especially where food preparation and storage procedures may be suspect. Vomiting is the main symptom, although you may get quite bad stomach cramps with it, and, later, some watery diarrhoea. The whole episode should be over in about 24 to 48 hours. You may have a suspicion that you've eaten something that wasn't fresh (seafood is a common culprit); another clue is if everyone else who ate it falls ill too.

No specific treatment is needed as a rule. You should rest, sip fluids if possible (see p139 for more details on this), and wait for it to settle down, which it should start doing in about 12 to 24 hours. It's best to avoid anti-vomiting medication as vomiting is your body's way of getting rid of the bad stuff.

! Note that if the illness doesn't settle down within 24 hours, if it gets much worse, if there's any blood in the vomit or diarrhoea, if you have a high fever, if you have very severe stomach pains or a severe headache, you should seek medical help urgently.

Watery Diarrhoea

This is the type of diarrhoea you're most likely to get when you are away. The cause varies with your destination, but it's usually bacterial, often a strain of a bacteria called *Escherichia coli*. This bacteria is part of the normal flora of your gut, but this strain has turned nasty. In Asia, another common bacterial cause is *Campylobacter jejuni*.

You're usually not that ill (up to six visits to the toilet a day) and the episode generally resolves itself in a few days (on average three to five). It rarely causes severe dehydration (although the potential is always there and this is a greater risk in children and older travellers).

If you get a fever with it, it's usually low (less than 38°C). You often get nausea and vomiting with it, at least to start with, but it's not a major feature of the illness – unlike with food poisoning (see Vomiting & Diarrhoea earlier). You commonly get stomach cramps, bloating and frequent gas. Sometimes the illness can progress to a bloody diarrhoea (dysentery) – see the following section for details.

The mainstay of treatment is replacing lost fluids and salts, which you should start doing straight away – see the following section on Dealing with Diarrhoea for more details. You don't usually need antibiotics for this type of diarrhoea.

Dysentery

Dysentery is any diarrhoea with blood in it. It can be more severe and protracted than the more common watery diarrhoea described earlier. Out of every 10 travellers stricken with diarrhoea, only about one will have dysentery. It's usually caused by bacteria, including various shigella and salmonella species, but it may be caused by a parasite, *Entamoeba histolytica* ('amoeba').

Dysentery usually begins with flu-like symptoms, which can be quite severe, and include headache, high fever and muscle aches and pains. The diarrhoea may start watery and in large quantities (often explosively), but it usually gets less in quantity and you start to notice blood and mucus (slime) in it, mixed in with the faeces. Painful stomach cramps are often a feature, which usually herald a dash to the little room.

As for any diarrhoeal illness, fluid and salt replacement is important. Because it's usually more severe and complications can occur, specific antibiotic treatment is usually indicated, especially for shigella and amoeba infections, so you should find a doctor and get a laboratory test done. Follow the doctor's advice, but it's usually worth starting a course of norfloxacin 400mg twice daily for three days or ciprofloxacin 500mg twice daily for five days.

! Avoid antidiarrhoeal medications like loperamide or diphenoxylate in dysentery because there is a risk of serious complications, including dilation and bursting of the colon.

DEALING WITH DIARRHOEA

If diarrhoea strikes, here's what to do:

▶ rest – this gives your body the best chance to fight whatever is making you ill, and being on the move with diarrhoea presents a few logistical problems
▶ drink plenty of fluids – see What to Drink later in this section for more guidance on what and how much
▶ take your temperature and note what it is; repeat this to see how the illness is progressing
▶ examine what's coming out of your guts to check for blood or mucus (slime)
▶ check you're not getting dehydrated – be aware of how often you're passing urine and what colour it is
▶ note any other symptoms – diarrhoea can occur in many other illnesses, including malaria (p118) and hepatitis (p158)
▶ remember that diarrhoea is contagious so be scrupulous about washing your hands after you use the toilet

When to see a Doctor

Avoid using antidiarrhoeal remedies (apart from oral rehydration salts) and get medical help in the following situations:

▶ you can't keep any fluids down because of vomiting for more than 24 hours (or less if severe or in a child eg a couple of hours if they really can't take any fluids)
▶ the diarrhoea is coming out of you in a watery torrent
▶ your temperature is 38°C or over

IF YOU GET DIARRHOEA

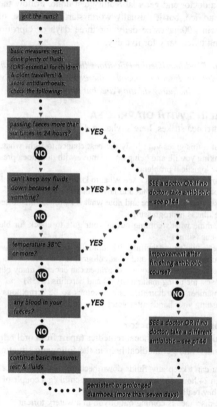

got the runs?

basic measures: rest, drink plenty of fluids (ORS essential for children & older travellers) & avoid antidiarrhoeals; check the following:

passing faeces more than six times in 24 hours?

► YES

NO

can't keep any fluids down because of vomiting?

► YES ►

NO

temperature 38°C or more?

YES

NO

any blood in your faeces?

YES

NO

SEE a doctor OR if no doctor, take antibiotic – see p144

Improvement after finishing antibiotic course?

NO

SEE a doctor OR if no doctor, take a different antibiotic – see p144

continue basic measures: rest & fluids

persistent or prolonged diarrhoea (more than seven days)

▶ there's blood or mucus (slime) in your faeces
▶ the diarrhoea doesn't clear up after four or five days; or more than a day in a child with moderate to severe diarrhoea
▶ you think you may have malaria (see p120)
▶ if you're jaundiced (your skin and the whites of your eyes are yellow) – see p158

Remember that children very quickly become dehydrated with diarrhoea or vomiting, so you need to seek help more readily for them. See the section on diarrhoea (p278) in the Babies & Children chapter for more details.

What to Drink
You need to replace what's being lost in your faeces and through vomiting: mainly salts (sodium, potassium and chloride) and water.

! You can either replace lost fluids and salts by drinking a solution made up from prepackaged oral rehydration salts (essential in children and older travellers with diarrhoea) or you can just drink large quantities of ordinary fluids (usually OK for adults with mild or moderate diarrhoea).

Sachets of oral rehydration salts (ORS) are readily available throughout Asia and contain optimum amounts of glucose (sugar) and salts. Glucose is necessary because it encourages the absorption of sodium and water, and it makes you feel better by boosting your energy levels. Read the instructions and make up the ORS in the specified quantity of purified or bottled water. There's no magic ingredient in these, but the relative quantities of salt and sugar are important.

! Make up your own rehydration solution if necessary by adding six teaspoons of sugar (or honey) and half a teaspoon of table salt to one litre of boiled water. To make it more palatable you can add any flavour you like: lemon, ginger or orange.

Fluid Balance

If you're vomiting or feeling sick, try taking small sips of fluid regularly rather than forcing yourself to down a whole glass in one go. You need to drink the equivalent of two average-sized glasses of fluid every time you have to pass faeces. You should aim for a total fluid replacement of at least 3L over 24 hours, more if you're not eating anything at all.

Use how much urine you're passing as a rough guide to whether you're getting dehydrated. Small amounts of dark urine suggest you need to increase your fluid intake. Passing reasonable quantities of light yellow urine indicates that you've got the balance about right. As a rough guide, drink enough so you produce a reasonable quantity of light-coloured urine every three to four hours while you're awake.

Although ORS is essential in children and older travellers, if you're a normally fit and healthy adult, and the diarrhoea is mild to moderate (up to six bursts a day), you can make do without ORS. Instead, make sure you drink plenty of fluids, including soup (contains salt) and fruit juices (contain glucose and potassium). See the following section for more on eating in diarrhoea, but you should also try to eat small regular amounts of starchy foods like bread, rice, potato, plain noodles or salty crackers (or local variations on these). Starchy foods are recommended in addition to fluids because they encourage more absorption of sodium and glucose.

Other liquids you can drink include weak black tea with a small amount of sugar added (but it's best to avoid Indian-style milky sweet tea), purified water or, if nothing else is available, soft drinks allowed to go flat and diluted with purified water (but avoid colas if possible).

Alcohol, strong tea, coffee and other caffeine-containing drinks (such as colas) are all best avoided because they can irritate the gut and they also promote fluid loss through a diuretic action.

It's best to steer clear of dairy products while you have diarrhoea as you can get an intolerance to the sugar in milk when you have diarrhoea, which then exacerbates the problem.

What to Eat

It's easy to get hung up about what, if anything, to eat when you have diarrhoea. But relax, use your common sense and try to tune in to what your body is telling you – if you feel like eating, go ahead, especially starchy foods which are known to promote salt and water absorption (such as bread, rice, potatoes, noodles or crackers).

Although eating may increase the bulk of the diarrhoea you pass, it won't generally prolong or worsen the illness, so there's no need to starve yourself deliberately. But if you don't feel like eating, don't force yourself to. Unless you've been travelling hard for some time, you're going to be basically well nourished and well able to withstand a couple of days with little or no food. It may make you feel a bit wobbly,

Fit to Eat

When you have diarrhoea, it's good to eat:

- boiled potatoes
- plain rice
- plain bread (chapattis, rotis and naan are all OK if they're not too oily)
- plain noodles
- dry biscuits, salty or not too sweet
- bananas

If possible, it's best to avoid:

- fruit and vegetables, except bananas
- dairy products, including yoghurt
- spicy foods
- greasy foods

so make sure you add a bit of sugar or honey to your drinks to keep your energy levels up.

Your overworked guts will appreciate small amounts of food at regular intervals rather than great big meals, and this may help make you feel less nauseated too. You may find that eating brings on cramps and you have to dash to the toilet. We all have a natural reflex whereby eating increases the activity of the gut, but this can get exaggerated in a diarrhoeal illness. It doesn't make you a great dinner companion, but you'll probably find that once you've answered the call of nature you can return to finish your meal! (But remember to wash your hands very thoroughly ...)

It goes without saying that it's best to stick to a bland diet while you have diarrhoea and as you recover, and to go easy on fibre providers like fruit, vegetables and nuts. Bananas are good as they tend to stop you up, and are a source of potassium and glucose. As the diarrhoea clears up and you start to get your appetite back, add in more foods gradually until you're back to normal – this can take some time, up to a week, but if you feel otherwise well, there's no need to worry.

Antidiarrhoeal Remedies

There are remedies you can take to stop you up if you get diarrhoea, but it's generally agreed that you're better off allowing the illness to run its course.

Antimotility drugs ('stoppers') like loperamide and codeine phosphate slow your guts down, reducing the number of times you have to visit the little room. These are sold under a wide variety of brand names. They can be useful if you have to travel on a toilet-less mode of transport or attend an important meeting, but you should treat them with a bit of respect. If you do need to take them, be careful not to take more than the recommended dose. It's usually best not to take stoppers for more than 24 hours because of the risk of side effects

A Word of Warning

You'll probably find many antidiarrhoeal remedies on sale in pharmacies throughout Asia. In general (apart from rehydration salts), it's best to avoid them. They are unlikely to be helpful and may actually be harmful.

In particular, try to avoid any remedies containing the following substances:

- tincture of opium or morphine
- clioquinol (may be sold as Enterovioform)– this is associated with severe side effects and should be avoided
- combinations of remedies (eg an antimotility medication with an antibiotic)

Two remedies that are not thought to have any effect in the treatment of acute diarrhoea are kaopectate and acidophilus (also known as lactobacillus, found in yoghurt), although studies have indicated that acidophilus may have a limited role in preventing diarrhoea in the first place.

(bursting of the gut and constipation). Another reason not to take them for longer is that diarrhoea is nature's way of flushing out bugs and their poisons, and stopping this may prevent the illness from settling.

Note that these drugs should always be avoided in children because of the risk of side effects and you shouldn't take them if you have a high fever or are passing blood or mucus (slime) in your faeces.

Bismuth subsalicylate (Pepto-Bismol) has been shown to be effective at treating diarrhoea, although it is less effective than the antimotility drugs and is probably better used as a preventive. Bismuth shouldn't be taken if you have asthma or if you are taking aspirin, sensitive to aspirin or have been told to avoid aspirin for any reason. It can cause ringing in the ears and blackening of the tongue. Although it is relatively safe, it's recommended not to take large amounts over a prolonged period of time (no more than three weeks).

Alternatively, peppermint oil is an antispasmodic that may be helpful if you're experiencing abdominal cramps. It has no serious side effects. Homoeopathic remedies for treating diarrhoea include carbo vegetalis and nux vomic (see p62), although these are unlikely to be available locally.

Antibiotics

If you are seriously ill or the diarrhoea just won't go away (see When to see a Doctor earlier in this chapter), you'll probably need antibiotic treatment. In this situation, you should seek medical care for advice on the most appropriate treatment and (usually) a laboratory test to determine the cause of your diarrhoea.

Remember that most cases of travellers diarrhoea do not need treatment with antibiotics, as it will clear up within a few days on its own.

Whether to treat simple watery diarrhoea with antibiotics is much less clearcut, and it's an issue the experts can't agree on. There's plenty of evidence to show that taking a dose of an antibiotic (eg ciprofloxacin 500mg) with loperamide (a 'stopper') can reduce the length of a diarrhoeal illness quite dramatically. Because of this, some doctors may advise you to carry a treatment dose of an antibiotic to take as soon as you develop diarrhoea. Others, however, argue that the benefits are not offset by the risks (which include possible side effects of the antibiotic and the emergence of bacterial resistance) and that in any case travellers diarrhoea is usually a mild illness that will clear up quickly enough on its own.

It's best to discuss this issue with your doctor before you go, as it depends on how long you're going for, how disruptive an episode of diarrhoea would be, and your normal state of health. On balance, it's probably worth having a course of antibiotics with you, but keeping it for a bad attack of watery diarrhoea (eg dashing to the toilet more than about six times a day).

Self-Treatment

! *If you're travelling in remote areas without access to medical care, you may need to self-treat.*

Bear in mind that it is notoriously difficult to make an accurate diagnosis of the cause of your diarrhoea on the basis of symptoms alone, but if you think you have bacterial dysentery, it would be appropriate to take a course of ciprofloxacin (500mg twice daily for five days) or norfloxacin (400mg twice daily for three days). For children, a suitable antibiotic would be co-trimoxazole, with dose based on weight (see also p278). If you think your diarrhoea is caused by a parasite like amoeba or *Giardia*, you could take metronidazole (250mg three times daily for five to 10 days) or tinidazole (2g single dose).

PROLONGED DIARRHOEA

You may find that, perhaps after an acute attack, you just can't seem to get rid of the diarrhoea. Persistent diarrhoea can be a nuisance when you're travelling. You need to get it checked out by a doctor because you'll need a laboratory test to find out what's causing it so that if it's an infection (most likely), a course of appropriate treatment can be prescribed. Use your common sense, but as a rough guide, 'prolonged' diarrhoea is anything lasting longer than about a week with no sign of improvement.Some of the many causes of causes of prolonged diarrhoea in travellers include the following:

- *Giardia* (most common cause in travellers)
- amoeba
- *Cyclospora* (a recently identified algal-like parasite)
- tropical sprue

- intestinal worms
- TB (unlikely)

Noninfectious causes include:

- postinfectious irritable bowel syndrome
- temporary intolerance to lactose (the sugar in milk and milk products)
- inflammatory bowel disease

Tropical sprue is a condition that used to be relatively common in travellers to South-East Asia and the subcontinent, but is now much less common, perhaps because diarrhoea is treated with antibiotics more often than it used to be. This condition is thought to be due to persisting infection, agent unknown, of your small intestine (the top part), causing you to be unable to absorb nutrients properly. It can be very debilitating, with persistent diarrhoea and weight loss. It can be diagnosed by a laboratory test on a sample of your gut, and is effectively treated with an antibiotic such as tetracycline and folic acid.

Giardiasis

This travellers favourite is caused by a parasite, *Giardia lamblia*, and you get it through food or water contaminated by the hardy cysts of the parasite. *Giardia* can infect animals too, and may be found in streams and other water sources in rural areas, especially on trekking routes.

The illness usually appears about a week after you have been exposed to the parasite, but it can take up to several weeks. It may cause a short-lived episode of typical 'travellers diarrhoea', but it can cause persistent diarrhoea. Weight loss is often a feature, as it can prevent food from being absorbed properly in the upper part of your gut.

Giardiasis can start quite suddenly, with explosive, watery diarrhoea, without blood. More often you get loose, bulky, foul-smelling faeces that are hard to flush away (assuming you have the luxury of flushing of course), with

Irritable Bowel Syndrome

This is a very common condition resulting from bowel dysfunction. You probably won't get it for the first time while you are travelling, but a change in diet and increased stress may make symptoms more likely. There is also some evidence to suggest you're more likely to get it following an episode of food poisoning or travellers diarrhoea. Although the symptoms can be troublesome, they aren't life-threatening. Symptoms are very variable in nature and severity but may commonly include:

- abdominal pain and spasm (often in the left lower abdomen), relieved by passing wind or faeces
- abdominal bloating (due to trapped wind)
- diarrhoea or constipation
- passing ribbon-like or pellet-like faeces

Symptoms may last only a few days or can persist for weeks; they often recur. Different people respond differently to treatment. If constipation is the major factor, an increase in dietary fibre will help. If bowel spasm and pain is the main problem, an antispasmodic such as mebeverine 135mg three times daily or peppermint oil capsules may help. Use your common sense and avoid any foods that make the symptoms worse.

If you are not sure of the diagnosis, the symptoms don't fit the pattern described, you have pain that is new or severe or you are unwell in any other way, you should seek medical advice.

Corinne Else

lots of gas, bloating, stomach gurgling and cramps. You can sometimes get a mild fever with it, and you often feel nauseated, with little or no appetite, 'indigestion' (heartburn) and rotten egg burps. Although all these symptoms commonly occur in giardiasis, note that they are nonspecific symptoms and can occur in other types of diarrhoea too. You can't assume you've got giardiasis just because you've got rotten egg burps, for example.

You should ideally get medical advice before starting a course of antibiotics, but if you are in a remote area away from medical help, you could take either metronidazole 250mg three times daily for five to 10 days OR tinidazole 2g single dose (tinidazole is not currently available in the USA).

Amoebic Dysentery

This is worth knowing about because it can cause problems outside the gut (including amoebic liver abscess) and it won't clear up without antibiotic treatment. It's caused by a parasite called *Entamoeba histolytica*, and you get it by eating food and water contaminated by the parasite cysts.

It causes dysentery (ie you get blood and mucus in the diarrhoea), which can be relatively mild and tends to come on gradually. Associated symptoms like fever, vomiting and stomach cramps are much less likely than with giardiasis or bacterial causes, although they can occur.

Complications can occur if the amoeba migrate to your liver or brain, where they can form abscesses, sometimes without diarrhoea beforehand. Signs of an amoebic liver abscess are fever and pain in the right upper abdomen. Treatment is the same as for giardiasis (see that section earlier).

CHOLERA

This diarrhoeal disease can cause rapid dehydration and death. As a traveller you're thought to be at very low risk of getting cholera, unless you are staying in an area which is experiencing an epidemic. Epidemics tend to be widely reported in the media, so you shouldn't have trouble avoiding them.

Cholera is caused by a bacteria, *Vibrio cholerae*. It's transmitted from person to person by direct contact (often via healthy carriers of the disease) or via contaminated food and water. It can be transmitted through seafood, including crustaceans and shellfish, which get infected via sewage.

Cholera exists where standards of environmental and personal hygiene are low, and for that reason tends to affect the poorest of the poor in developing countries. Every so often there are massive epidemics, usually due to contaminated water in conditions where there is a breakdown of the normal infrastructure, such as in a natural disaster like the annual flooding of the Ganges delta in Bangladesh.

The time between becoming infected and symptoms appearing is usually short, between one and five days. The diarrhoea (described as 'ricewater' because it's watery and flecked with white mucus) starts suddenly, and pours out of you. Vomiting and muscle cramps are usual, but fever is rare. In its most serious form, it causes a massive outpouring of fluid (up to 20L a day). This is the worst case scenario – only about one in 10 sufferers get this severe form. It's a self-limiting illness, meaning that if you don't succumb to dehydration, it will end in about a week without any treatment.

You should seek medical help urgently; in the meantime, start rehydration therapy with oral rehydration salts. You may need antibiotic treatment with tetracycline, but fluid replacement is the single most important treatment strategy in cholera.

Prevention is by taking basic food and water precautions, avoiding seafood and having scrupulous personal hygiene. The currently available vaccine is not thought worthwhile as it provides only limited protection for a short time.

OTHER GUT PROBLEMS

INTESTINAL PARASITES

Although high in yuk value, these infections are rarely life-threatening and often cause remarkably few symptoms. It can be some months or even years before symptoms appear, so if you've been on a long trip, especially if you've been roughing it or spending long periods of time in rural areas in tropical

Succulent Seafood?

One of the highlights of a trip to Asia is the wide variety of seafood on offer. However, you might not be quite so tempted to try it when you realise the ways fish and shellfish try to poison us. Shellfish and crustaceans are filter feeders so they concentrate any disease-causing microbes (eg cholera and hepatitis) that might be in the water – they thrive near sewage outflows. Fish and shellfish can also cause disease via toxins they contain. You've probably heard of the poisonous puffer fish (fugu) delicacy in Japan, but it's not the only poisoner.

If tuna and related species are not kept properly refrigerated, they can cause **scombroid poisoning**, a histamine-like (allergic-type) reaction. Often the fish will taste peppery or sharp, then within half an hour of eating it, you get headache, flushing, nausea, vomiting, diarrhoea, dry mouth and sometimes an allergic rash and wheezing. The syndrome doesn't last long (eight to 12 hours) and it's rarely dangerous. However, if your symptoms are severe, especially if you experience difficulty breathing, you must seek medical advice urgently as you may need adrenaline (epinephrine) treatment.

Ciguatera poisoning occurs when you eat normally edible reef fish that contain ciguatoxin. The toxin is not affected by cooking, freezing or drying, and the fish tastes no different from normal. Just about any reef fish can be affected, but commonly affected varieties include barracuda, red snapper, grouper, sea bass and surgeonfish, often on the Indian Ocean coast.

Symptoms usually come on two to six hours after eating the fish, and include some bizarre sensory alterations involving hot/cold sensations, as well as gastro symptoms. Rashes are common, and you can get quite severe symptoms, including

Asia, it's a good idea to get a stool test done to check for these when you get back. Throughout Asia, mind-boggling numbers of people are infected with intestinal worms, and it's quite possible that you could pick up a light infection along the way.

paralysis and transient blindness and, rarely, death. Symptoms usually last about a week but can last several months or years. There's no specific treatment apart from supportive measures. Seek medical help urgently if you think you may be affected.

And then there's **fugu**. The ovaries, liver and intestines of the puffer fish contain a toxin called tetrodotoxin which causes gastro and neurological symptoms, with a mortality rate of 60% (high). There's no known antidote so you'll want to be sure you haven't offended the chef. Various measures have been put in place to prevent fugu aficionados poisoning themselves, so the risk is pretty small.

Shellfish also do their bit to encourage us to leave them alone. In the presence of **red tides** (caused by a type of plankton at certain times of the year) eating shellfish such as clams, mussels and oysters can cause numbness and paralysis within half an hour of eating them. Other types of shellfish poisoning include an illness caused by eating contaminated mussels, giving you nausea, vomiting, diarrhoea and abdominal cramps.

All in all, you'd be wise to give seafood a wide berth, but if you can't resist the temptation:

- seek local advice on the risks of eating seafood (for example, ask about any red tides in the last year or so)
- avoid raw seafood (but remember that steaming doesn't necessarily make it safe)
- remember that you can't tell if seafood is toxic by looking or smelling
- get medical help urgently if you experience pins and needles, numbness or paralysis after eating seafood.

Worms
Different worms are spread in different ways, but the common factor is faeces. Intestinal worms are more common where sewage disposal systems are inadequate or simply

nonexistent and water supplies are likely to be unsafe. Flies contribute to their spread by carrying infective eggs or larvae on their feet.

The larvae of **hookworms** and **strongyloides** can penetrate the skin of bare feet. Both types of worm find their way to the gut, sometimes causing a cough as they pass through the lungs. Untreated, they can live in your gut for years. Hookworms suck blood so if the infection is heavy (unlikely in travellers), it can cause anaemia – a major public health problem but very unlikely to affect travellers.

Roundworms are acquired by ingesting the eggs, often on vegetables. A light infection rarely causes any symptoms, but should be treated because the worms can sometimes get caught in narrow openings (eg into the gall bladder) and cause blockages. **Threadworm** are readily passed from person to person via contaminated hands or food, and they cause intense anal itching, especially at night. They are very small and white, and you may notice them wriggling in your faeces.

Treatment Treatment of intestinal worms is with an anti-worm medicine such as mebendazole, albendazole or piperazine. Mebendazole is not suitable in pregnancy or in children under two.

Tapeworms

Tapeworms have a very high yuk value, and they can make you seriously ill. They are acquired by eating raw or lightly cooked infected meat (eg pork) or fish (eg in raw salmon sushi), or directly swallowing the eggs in the case of the pork tapeworm. Larvae of the pork tapeworm hatch out from the eggs and migrate through the body, forming cysts in the muscles and brain. This condition is called cysticercosis and in Asia, it's common in India, China and Indonesia. Symptoms are variable, depending on what part of your body is affected – if your brain is affected you can get seizures. This can be a serious condition so seek medical advice urgently if you think you may be affected. Treatment is with a drug called niclosamide or praziquantel.

Hydatid disease is caused by the larvae of an animal tapeworm, and you get it by stroking dogs which are infected with the adult tapeworms. Eggs may be present in a dog's fur, and can stick to your fingers. The eggs hatch into larvae which form cysts in different parts of your body, including the liver, lungs, brain and bones. Treatment can be difficult (it usually involves surgery) so prevention is particularly important.

If you're into eating snails and slugs, you need to be aware of a worm that is spread via undercooked snails and slugs in South-East Asia. It can cause blindness and paralysis.

Prevention

With all intestinal parasites, prevention is the main aim:

▶ don't walk barefoot in tropical areas
▶ take care with your food and water and basic personal hygiene
▶ avoid undercooked meat, snails and raw fish
▶ steer clear of dogs

LIVER & LUNG FLUKES

Eating raw freshwater fish or crustaceans is a surprisingly risky activity in Asia – try to avoid it if possible. A tiny worm-like creature called a fluke can be transmitted in this way and, once eaten, can affect the liver, lungs or intestine.

There are a few different varieties of liver flukes, but the distinction is academic as they all cause the same symptoms. Liver flukes are widespread in China, Japan, Korea, Taiwan, Thailand and Vietnam. In northern Thailand up to 50% of people are infected. Lung flukes are widespread in South-East Asia and the Far East.

You can get infected if you eat raw or lightly pickled fish or crustaceans. You can also pick up the infection from serving dishes which are contaminated with affected water. The symptoms you get depend on how heavy the infection is – the more parasites you have, the more likely they are to cause problems. Symptoms of infection with liver flukes include a feeling of something moving about in the liver, fever with tenderness over the liver, and jaundice (yellowing of the skin and eyes). Although as a traveller you're very unlikely to get a prolonged infection, it can lead to long-term liver problems, including cancer.

Lung flukes can cause chest symptoms, including a cough with or without rusty sputum, fever and chest pain. Other problems are caused if the flukes settle outside the lungs – they can cause blindness if they lodge in the eye – and in Korea they are known to commonly cause effects on the brain which mimic a brain tumour.

Infection is diagnosed by a laboratory test on a sample of your faeces. Treatment is simple and effective, and the same for both types of flukes: praziquantel 20 to 30mg per kg twice daily for three days. If you think you may be at risk of these, get a check up done when you get home if you're on a short trip, or you may want to arrange for a test while you are away if you're on a longer trip.

Prevention is obviously the best strategy for these infections, but it can be surprisingly difficult to resist the lure and incipient danger of eating raw fish ...

CONSTIPATION

Far less has been written in the literature about travellers constipation, but all the evidence is that this is a least as common as travellers diarrhoea. Plenty of factors conspire to stop you up while you're travelling, including immobility if you're stuck on a bus, plane or train for hours on end; not drinking enough fluids; disruption to your normal routine; jet lag; and a change of diet. Lack of privacy and time to relax can be enough to bring on constipation if you have a shy bowel or you may find it difficult to get used to squatting (although this is supposed to be a more natural way of defecating). Drugs you have been taking, for example antidiarrhoeals, may cause relatively intractable constipation. The end result is not being able to perform as often as normal, which can make you feel bloated and uncomfortable, with no appetite and no energy.

Dealing with Constipation

If you know you are prone to constipation, consider bringing your own supply of bran with you or a remedy that you know has worked for you in the past. Otherwise, try a few simple measures first before diving into the nearest pharmacy or your medical kit. Make sure you're drinking plenty of fluids, especially if it's hotter than you're used to. Try to increase the fibre in your diet by eating more fruit (peeled) and vegetables (cooked and peeled), but avoid bananas which can stop you up. Porridge, pulses, nuts and dried fruit are also good fibre providers. Prune juice is an old favourite, if you can find it.

A cup of hot, strong coffee can get things moving, especially first thing in the morning, and a large meal can have the same effect (remember that if you're not eating much for any reason, there's not going to be much coming out either). Alcohol has a laxative effect, but don't overdo it.

Finding a decent toilet may help – perhaps consider moving hotel. Exercise is beneficial in many ways, including stimulating your guts. Finally, if you feel like going, don't be tempted to hang on or the moment will pass.

If simple measures fail, you could consider taking something fairly gentle like lactulose syrup (15mL twice daily; takes about 48 hours to work) or senna, a gut stimulant (two to four tablets at night; works in eight to 12 hours).

PILES (HAEMORRHOIDS) & OTHER ANAL PROBLEMS

Piles are swollen veins around the anus, either on the outside (external) or inside (internal), occasionally popping out when you strain. Both are more common in constipation (because of straining), diarrhoea, or when carrying heavy packs, especially up mountains. External piles can be excruciatingly painful.

The pain can be relieved by cutting them open (still with us?), but this needs to be done by a medic ideally under sterile conditions. Otherwise, you may need to take painkillers and hotfoot it down the mountain.

Internal piles can be uncomfortable, with a feeling of something popping out when you strain, and may cause itchiness around the anus. Local anaesthetic creams can be helpful.

If you get excruciating pain when you pass faeces, especially if you've been constipated, often with bright red blood on the toilet paper, you probably have an anal fissure, a small split in the anus. It can be very painful, but there's no specific treatment, apart from taking care to keep the area clean and dealing with any constipation you may have.

Anal itching may be caused by threadworms, chafing and poor hygiene. Check your faeces carefully for worms or, if you really have to know, you can put a piece of tape across your anus at night and examine it for worms in the morning. Treatment of threadworm is with an anti-worm medicine, as described in Intestinal Parasites earlier.

INDIGESTION

A change in diet, stress, anxiety and spicy foods can all make 'indigestion' (burning pains in your upper abdomen) and heartburn (burning in your gullet, often with an acid taste in your mouth) more likely when you're travelling. The discomfort is often worse when you're hungry or just after meals. Smoking and alcohol exacerbate it.

Simple measures you could try are to eat small, regular meals – don't eat a huge meal just before you go to bed, for example. Consider stopping smoking and cutting back on alcohol or at least giving yourself a break for a few days. It can be difficult, but try to avoid spicy hot foods. Milk and yoghurt can be soothing, as can eating plain, starchy foods like bread, chapattis or noodles. You could consider trying antacids (there are many products available without prescription; take them

Kidney Stone

Dehydration (and other conditions) can cause chemicals in the urine to harden and form small stones in the kidney. A stone can become stuck in the tube leading from the kidney to the bladder, and if it does, you experience excruciating pain. The pain usually starts suddenly on one side, in the back just below the ribcage, spreading round to the groin in the front. Typically, the pain is gripey (comes in waves) and you can't stay still with it. It can be so severe that it makes you vomit.

Most (95%) kidney stones eventually work their way down to the bladder and get passed out within about a day or so. However, you should seek medical help if possible as you will probably need a strong painkilling injection.

! if you have a fever, this indicates that the kidney is infected, which is a medical emergency.

If the pain subsides and has not returned by 12 hours or so, this means that you've probably passed the stone, but it's a good idea to get this checked out as soon as possible (or when you get back if you're on a short trip). Make sure you drink plenty of fluids to prevent further problems.

between meals and at night), although stomach acid has a protective effect against infective agents, so this taking antacids may make you more vulnerable to gut infections.

! You need to seek medical help urgently if the pain is severe and not relieved by any of these measures; if it wakes you at night, if it seems to go through to your back; if you have had a stomach or duodenal ulcer in the past; or if you vomit blood.

If you have a gastric or duodenal ulcer, or are taking treatment for one, this may make you more susceptible to gut infections, so it's best to discuss this with your doctor before you go, as you may be able to change to a different anti-ulcer medicine.

APPENDICITIS

If you've still got your appendix, acute appendicitis is a possible cause of severe abdominal pain. It's reasonably common in both adults and children, and you should consider it if you've got abdominal pain that increases in severity over a short period of time (12 to 24 hours). Symptoms can vary, but typically they're as follows:

- central abdominal pain that may be colicky (comes and goes) or constant, and which moves to the right lower abdomen after a few hours, becoming constant
- nausea, loss of appetite and sometimes vomiting
- mild fever (but not usually very high)
- diarrhoea, though this is less common and not usually very severe
- tenderness in your right lower abdomen when you press on it

Seek medical help urgently if you think appendicitis may be a possibility, as you'll need surgery if the diagnosis is confirmed. It's potentially extremely dangerous if it's not treated quickly.

VIRAL HEPATITIS (JAUNDICE)

This infection of the liver can be caused by at least five different viruses: hepatitis A, B, C, D and E. All five viruses cause a similar short-term disease, but three (B, C and D) can cause persistent infection in a proportion of sufferers, resulting in long-term liver problems. The different viruses are transmitted in different ways: A and E are spread by faecal contamination of food and water and B, C and D are spread via blood or sexual contact. A blood test can diagnose which type you have, but you'll probably have a good idea anyway.

SYMPTOMS

You may not realise you've got hepatitis at first as the illness starts with vague flu-like symptoms, including fever, chills, headache and joint aches and pains. You feel listless and washed out, with no appetite. Smokers often report being turned off cigarettes. The flu-like symptoms can go on for two to three days before you get gut symptoms. These include nausea, vomiting, diarrhoea (possibly) and pain in the upper right-hand side of your abdomen. A day or so later you may notice you're passing dark urine and your faeces are a lighter colour than normal. The whites of your eyes turn yellow, and later your skin starts to look yellow. This yellowing is called jaundice and is because your liver isn't able to work properly.

Although these are the classic symptoms, hepatitis can be a mild illness without jaundice in many people, especially children; older people tend to get more severe jaundice.

! *Note that hepatitis is a much more serious disease in pregnancy, so it's important to seek medical help urgently in this situation.*

You usually find that you start to feel better as the jaundice appears. It can leave you feeling very washed out and weak for some time after – about six weeks on average, but sometimes up to three months. It might be one reason to come home early if you're on a long trip.

Rarely, instead of getting better as the jaundice appears, the illness can progress to overwhelming liver failure, which is a very serious condition. Seek medical help urgently if you get suddenly worse or if you have any of the following:

- severe vomiting and dehydration
- bruising for no reason
- bleeding from your gums or nosebleeds
- blood in your urine or faeces
- confusion and drowsiness

TREATMENT

There's no specific treatment apart from rest and tender loving care (although a drug called interferon may be helpful if you've got hepatitis C infection, and a new treatment has recently become available for hepatitis B). You probably won't feel like doing much for a while, so make sure you've got somewhere comfortable to stay. There's no particular need to stay in bed; just do as much or as little as you feel up to doing.

! If you think you have hepatitis, seek medical advice as soon as possible to have the diagnosis confirmed so that people you have been in contact with while you have been infectious can be protected (by having the vaccination)

Drink plenty of fluids, especially if you don't feel like eating because of nausea. Once you do feel like eating again, try to stick to a low-fat (the liver has to work harder to deal with fatty foods), high carbohydrate diet – eat lots of starchy foods like bread, potatoes, rice and noodles. Avoid things that might damage your liver further, like alcohol and medications, including aspirin and paracetamol (acetaminophen). In fact, it's a good idea to avoid any medications if possible while you are ill, because drugs won't be disposed of as efficiently as normal and can have unpredictable effects. If you're using the oral contraceptive pill, you'll need to stop taking it until the illness settles.

If you've got hepatitis, you need to take care not to spread it around. With hepatitis A and E, you're most infectious for about two weeks or so before symptoms appear until a few days after the jaundice develops.

! Anybody you have been in close contact with needs to receive hepatitis A vaccine (or immunoglobulin) if they haven't been vaccinated, unless they have already developed symptoms.

Pay particular attention to your personal hygiene, don't pre-pare food for other people, don't share chopsticks, and avoid sharing drinks or cigarettes. Once you've had hepatitis A or E, you're immune for life.

With hepatitis B you're infectious for the course of the illness, usually about three to six months, and for about a month before symptoms appear. Take care not to spread the disease – practise safer sex by using condoms, let doctors and dentists know of your infection before they carry out any treatment, don't donate blood, and don't share needles.

PREVENTION
Hepatitis A & E

Hepatitis A is common worldwide, but especially where standards of environmental hygiene are low (most of Asia except Japan and Singapore). Hepatitis E also occurs worldwide, but especially in India, Pakistan, Nepal and South-East Asia, and is particularly likely to affect pregnant women. Hepatitis A is common in travellers so it's worth taking steps to avoid it.

The hepatitis A vaccine is very effective, but there's no vaccine against hepatitis E. Prevention of hepatitis A and E is by taking basic precautions with food and water, and making sure your personal hygiene standards are high. Note that shellfish are a source of hepatitis A and E if they have been obtained from sewage-contaminated water, so as a rule it's best to avoid these, especially when they are served raw or you can't be sure they are well cooked (steaming for example won't make them safe). It's also possible to get hepatitis A or E by swimming in water contaminated by faeces – one traveller wrote to tell us that she contracted hepatitis A after swimming in the lake at Pokhara in Nepal.

Hepatitis B

Unlike hepatitis A and E, infection with hepatitis B can persist in about 5% to 10% of people, and these carriers are important sources of infection. Hepatitis B occurs worldwide and is less common than hepatitis A. In Asia it's particularly common in China and South-East Asia. Hepatitis C is a major cause of blood transfusion-related hepatitis in the west and appears to be a growing problem worldwide, but is not going to be a major worry for you as a traveller. Hepatitis D only occurs in conjunction with hepatitis B infection.

You're at risk of hepatitis B if you have sexual contact (especially between men) with a carrier, so take good care to practise safer sex by using condoms. Other risk situations to look out for and avoid are blood transfusions or inadequately sterilised medical (or dental) equipment, including acupuncture needles. Other obvious hazards are needle sharing, getting your ears or other body parts pierced with inadequately sterilised equipment, having a tattoo or being shaved with a reused cut-throat razor.

! *In children, hepatitis B can be transmitted by prolonged contact with a carrier, for example if they play with other children who are carriers.*

Infection with hepatitis B causes a similar illness to type A, but the symptoms can be more severe, and there's a higher risk of liver failure. Note that hepatitis B can take up to six months to appear after infection. Persistent infection carries the risk of long-term liver damage and liver cancer in a minority of cases.

! *If you think you may have been exposed to hepatitis B, a shot of antibody can help protect against it (although this may be hard to find), or you can start a course of the usual hepatitis B vaccination – discuss this with your doctor.*

Prevention involves avoiding risk situations and getting a hepatitis B vaccination (if you have not already been immunised) if you think you might be at high risk of hepatitis B through sexual contact or needle sharing, or if you're planning on living in a highly endemic area or working as a medic.

RESPIRATORY SYSTEM

Coughs and colds can be troublesome when you're travelling and can sometimes lead to worse problems, so make sure you recognise the symptoms early and don't let complications get a hold.

COLDS

It's not just the culture that's different and exciting, the viruses are too. The common cold is common the world over, and because colds are spread by droplets (for example sneezing) and close personal contact, you're more likely to get them in crowded urban environments, by travelling on crowded public transport or by eating in crowded restaurants. Air pollution and the ubiquitous hawking and spitting compounds the problem in Asia.

As for symptoms, you know the score – normal or slightly raised temperature, runny nose, sore throat and perhaps a cough. Colds usually go away in a few days without any special treatment, but when you're travelling you're more vulnerable to complications like sinusitis, bronchitis and ear infection. Recognise the symptoms of a cold as a sign to take it easy for a day or two.

Unless you get complications, antibiotics are no use because colds are caused by viruses not bacteria. Drink plenty of fluids, treat yourself to some good meals and take simple painkillers if necessary for any aches or pains. Make your own cold remedy by adding honey or sugar to lemon or lime juice and top up with boiled water.

If you've got homoeopathic remedies with you, try taking gelsemium or allium cepa. Helpful naturopathic remedies include Combi Q tissue salts, thyme and sage tea or, perhaps most popular of all, echinacea tincture or tablets with or without zinc.

Smog Alert

Pollution is a worldwide issue, but it's something you'll become very aware of in Asia if you're travelling in urban environments, especially in India, Bangladesh, China or the Philippines. Dhaka in Bangladesh is said to have some of the worst pollution of any city in the world, and it has become such a problem that the Bangladesh government has taken steps to ban two-stroke engines from the city. But it's not just auto-rickshaws – industrial pollution is a massive problem, and in 1997 unusual weather conditions meant that parts of Malaysia, Singapore and Indonesia disappeared in a cloud of smog caused by forest fires.

Air pollution can be a health hazard, particularly if you suffer from any lung disease such as asthma. It can also aggravate coughs, colds and sinus problems and cause eye irritation. Consider avoiding badly polluted areas, especially if you have asthma, or you could follow local custom and invest in a surgical mask.

SINUSITIS

This usually follows a cold, and can be a pain – literally. The sinuses are air-filled cavities in the skull above the eyes and on either side of the nose, designed to make our heads lighter so they don't drag on the ground. If the lining of the cavities becomes infected and the normally empty spaces fill with mucus or pus, it causes you pain.

Symptoms are headache (usually over your forehead) or face pain, which is worse when you strain or bend over. Your forehead or cheeks may feel tender when you press them, and you may feel mucus dripping down the back of your throat. Typically the pain isn't there when you first get up in the morning, but comes on during the morning, reaching a crescendo about lunch time before gradually receding. It's possible to be quite ill with it, with a fever and aches and pains.

Try steam inhalations with menthol, eucalyptus, tea-tree oil or tiger balm as a first measure, together with simple painkillers. If this doesn't help, you could try taking a nasal decongestant like pseudoephedrine hydrochloride 60mg four times daily (though not if you have high blood pressure). Antihistamines may also help.

If you have a fever and you feel rough, you'll probably need a course of antibiotics – see a doctor if possible. If not, suitable antibiotics are co-amoxiclav 250mg three times daily (p380) OR cefaclor 250mg three times daily.

Flying can make the pain worse, so start taking a nasal decongestant the day before you fly or use a nasal decongestant spray. Underwater diving also makes it worse, so avoid diving until you feel better.

HAY FEVER (ALLERGIC RHINITIS)

This common condition is usually due to an allergy to something in the air, such as pollen. It can often be difficult to decide whether your symptoms are because of a cold or an allergy, although if they persist and you otherwise feel reasonably well, it's probably hay fever.

Steam Inhalation
In case you don't know, here's how:

▶ get hold of a basin, bucket or bowl, or use a washbasin (you'll need that universal plug)
▶ fill it with boiling water
▶ optional: add a few drops of menthol (which should be widely available), tiger balm, eucalyptus or tea-tree oil
▶ once the heat is bearable, put your face in the steam rising from the bowl and drape a towel over your head
▶ stay like this for as long as you can bear it or until it has stopped steaming

Hay fever involves lots of nose blowing. Other symptoms include sneezing, and itchy eyes, roof of the mouth and sometimes ears too. Your chest may feel tight as you can get asthma with it (see the section on Cough later in this chapter).

If you know you're susceptible to hay fever, it's a good idea to bring all your usual remedies with you. If it's being a real nuisance, try antihistamine tablets to start with (see the Buying & Using Medicines appendix for more details), but if this doesn't control it, you could try a nasal spray containing steroids (the amount used won't cause any general problems) such as beclomethasone dipropionate spray. It needs to be taken regularly to have the best chance of working.

INFLUENZA

Flu and other similar viral illnesses are spread in the same way as colds and are more likely when you're travelling for the same reasons. Although we tend to think of colds and flu as the same thing, they actually have very different symptoms. Flu tends to start quite suddenly, often with a high temperature, and it can make you feel pretty dreadful, with headache and generalised aches and pains. You may have a runny nose and sore throat with it, and often a dry cough that can last for several weeks. Although the illness usually lasts a few days, it can leave you feeling tired and out of energy for some time. There's a vaccine against flu which is recommended for older people.

There's no specific treatment for flu but, as for colds, complications such as a chest infection may be more likely when travelling, so it's worth taking care of yourself. Rest up – you probably won't feel like doing much for a day or two anyway. Simple painkillers can help lower the fever and relieve aches and pains, and any of the remedies discussed under colds may help your symptoms. Drink plenty of fluids because it's easy to get dehydrated with a fever, and once the fever is down, step up the food as you start to feel better.

Bird flu

The term 'influenza' is an Italian word meaning 'influence', possibly because influenza was once ascribed to divine influence. There are three main types of influenza virus, but influenza A is the real villain. It's responsible for regular large outbreaks of flu worldwide, often associated with alarming rates of illness and death. Perhaps the most famous outbreak of all was in 1918-19, when it is estimated that flu killed more people than both world wars combined.

The reason why this little bit of protein regularly outwits the greatest scientific minds is that it is able to continually change its form, often by combining with viruses that affect animals or birds primarily. People can build up immunity to usual strains, but won't have any immunity to markedly different strains, so an epidemic of flu then sweeps across the world. Vaccines are available, but new vaccines have to be manufactured all the time to protect against new strains.

You'll probably remember the last, much publicised appearance of a new strain: the 'bird flu' crisis in Hong Kong in 1997. This strain infected birds primarily and the outbreak was swiftly controlled by killing most of the chicken population of Hong Kong. What next?

As flu is a viral illness, antibiotics won't do you any good unless you get complications.

The trouble with flu is that the symptoms are so nonspecific that lots of diseases can mimic it, and it can be hard to tell if it's flu or something more serious like malaria. To give you some guidelines, you need to see a doctor if:

- your temperature is over 39°C (102°F) and it can't be lowered by any of the measures suggested on p111
- you try all of these measures, but you don't feel better after two days – it may not be flu after all
- you feel breathless, start to cough up green spit or have chest pain – this may indicate a chest infection

- you think it could be malaria or dengue fever – the symptoms can be identical
- you have a severe headache, neck stiffness and hypersensitivity to light – you may have meningitis

SORE THROAT

You can get an uncomfortable throat if you're travelling in dry and dusty situations, if you're mouth-breathing because your nose is blocked or if you're doing strenuous exercise. Drink plenty of fluids, eat moist foods like fruit and vegetables, and consider chewing sugar-free gum if you can get hold of it. Your lips can get very dry under these conditions and cracked lips are uncomfortable, as well as an infection risk. The tender skin of your lips is also very sensitive to the sun, so use a lip salve with sunblock, and reapply it regularly throughout the day. Keep 'em luscious by using a lip balm or plain paraffin jelly at night.

Sore throat can also be caused by infection, usually viral, often with a viral eye infection (conjunctivitis – see p314). Sore throat can occur alone or as part of other illnesses like colds, flu and glandular fever. It usually clears up on its own after a few days without any special treatment. Simple measures for treating a sore throat are to gargle regularly with salty water (buy some table salt and put a few spoonfuls into a glass of purified water) or a solution of soluble aspirin or paracetamol. Having lots of warm drinks will also help: add some grated ginger, lime juice and sugar (honey is better if you can get it) to a cup of hot water.

About a third of sore throats are caused by a bacterial infection. The reason this matters is that some bacterial throat infections can occasionally lead to serious complications, especially in children. Unfortunately, the only sure way to tell bacterial and viral sore throats apart is by a laboratory test, but as a rule of thumb, you need to seek medical advice for severe (if you can't swallow solids for example) or persistent (more

Causes of Sore Throat

- heat and dust
- viral infections, colds and flu
- bacterial infections ('strep' sore throat)
- glandular fever
- toxoplasmosis (p256)
- sexually transmitted infections (eg gonorrhoea)
- diphtheria (rare; p220)

than five days without any improvement) sore throats, as they will need to be treated with antibiotics. Suitable antibiotics are co-amoxiclav 250mg three times a day (see p380) OR cefaclor 250mg three times a day.

! Note that if you've been having oral sex, especially with a new partner, gonorrhoea can cause a sore throat. If you think this is a possibility you should seek medical advice to get it checked out, as you'll need a course of antibiotics.

GLANDULAR FEVER

Glandular fever, also known as the 'kissing disease' because it's passed by saliva, causes a severe sore throat. Suspect this viral disease if you have a severe sore throat that doesn't settle with antibiotics.

Symptoms include a sore throat, swollen glands (lumps in your neck, armpits and groins) and fever. You may also notice that you're jaundiced (yellow skin and whites of the eyes). Very occasionally, it can lead to a serious complication – bursting of the spleen (one of your internal abdominal organs). If you have glandular fever and you develop abdominal pain, particularly in the left upper part of the abdomen, you need to seek medical advice urgently.

Glandular fever can only be confirmed by a blood test; there's no specific treatment. It can leave you feeling weak and washed out weeks, sometimes months, afterwards. Other viral infections can cause similar symptoms.

COLD SORES

Cold sores are caused by a herpes virus infection which recurs periodically. If you've had these before, the stresses of travel are quite likely to make them recur. Other factors that make recurrences more likely include sunlight, fever and menstruation. You usually know when one is coming on because you'll feel a burning sensation on the edge of your lip followed by a blister, usually the next day. They take about a week to clear up. Acyclovir cream (5%) can be effective if you apply it as soon as you feel the burning starting, but it may be difficult to get hold of locally, so take a tube with you. Using a lip salve with sunblock can help prevent recurrence.

Secondary bacterial infection is a risk so try to avoid touching the sore with your fingers. This is good practice anyway, as you can introduce infection in your eye if you then rub your eyes.

MOUTH ULCERS

These are more likely to occur if you're stressed or if you're taking proguanil as an antimalarial, but otherwise they're a bit of a mystery. Regularly swishing your mouth out with salty water or an antiseptic mouthwash (eg chlorhexidine), or even just applying a small amount of toothpaste to the ulcer can help, although all these measures will sting at first.

COUGH

Lots of things can make you cough in Asia, including physical hazards like dust, smoke and air pollution (see the boxed text 'Smog Alert' earlier in this chapter) as well as infections like colds and flu, chest infection (bronchitis), asthma and even malaria. There are some much rarer causes of cough, which you don't need to worry unduly about, including lung flukes (p153), hydatid disease (p153) and various worm infestations (p149).

Many chest infections are caused by viruses, unless you've got a chronic lung condition or it follows another illness like flu. We know you know, but it should be pointed out that all chest infections are more common in cigarette smokers.

Bronchitis usually begins with an irritating, dry cough and a feeling of tightness in the chest. You may have a mild fever. After a day or so, you start coughing up yellow or greenish gunk. It usually clears up on its own in about five to seven days.

Antibiotics aren't usually needed (they don't work against viral infections), but there are some situations when you do need to see a doctor:

▶ you're pretty sick, with a high fever – it may be malaria or a more serious chest infection
▶ you're still coughing a week later
▶ you're feeling increasingly short of breath
▶ you have pain in your chest on coughing or taking a deep breath
▶ you cough up blood

If you do need antibiotics, appropriate treatment would be amoxycillin 250mg three times a day OR, if you're allergic to penicillin, erythromycin 250mg four times a day (see p380).

If you're asthmatic, you'll probably know about it before you go travelling, and you should take a plentiful supply of your usual medicines with you. Symptoms include a cough, wheeze, chest tightness and shortness of breath, which may be worse at night or brought on by exercise.

It is possible that asthma may start for the first time while you are travelling, especially if you are travelling in some of Asia's notoriously polluted cities. It's very common in children and young adults, and appears to be a disease of 'westernisation'. Some drugs can make it worse and should be avoided, the most common one being aspirin.

If you're worried, seek medical advice so that appropriate medication can be prescribed if necessary. If you are very short of breath or wheezy, you should seek help urgently.

EARS, EYES & TEETH

Grouped here are three parts of the body you probably would not give much thought to normally. However, they can be troublesome if they go wrong, and some aspects of travelling can make this more likely.

EARS

FLYING

Cabin pressure is normally kept at levels equivalent to those at altitudes of 6000ft to 8000ft. At these pressures, gas in body cavities (like your ears) expands by about 30%. Normally, this isn't a problem because you can equalise the pressure difference in your ears by swallowing, yawning or sucking on a sweet. However, if your ear is blocked for any reason (for example if you've got a cold or hay fever), you can get a pressure build-up which is very painful, and sometimes your eardrum can burst.

It's best not to fly if you've got a cold or severe hay fever, and you shouldn't fly at all if you've got a middle ear infection (see later in this chapter). If you have to fly with a cold, the following measures should help:

▶ take a decongestant, such as pseudoephedrine hydrochloride 60mg four times daily (but not if you have high blood pressure), starting the day before you fly
▶ take an antihistamine before and during the flight (follow the dose instructions on the packet)
▶ try a nasal decongestant spray – use it an hour before the expected time of arrival, and every 20 minutes after this
▶ during the descent, pinch your nose firmly and blow hard down it – this should force the pressure to equalise, and you should feel your ears pop; do this as often as necessary

Burst Eardrum

If these measures don't work, your eardrum may burst. You'll get a gradual build-up of severe pain, followed by sudden relief. You may notice a bit of bleeding from the ear. If this happens, ideally see a doctor to get it checked out. If it has burst, it'll take about six weeks to heal up. During this time, you should avoid getting water in the ear – use ear plugs or a cottonwool ball covered in petroleum jelly when you shower or wash your hair. It's best to avoid swimming altogether until it's healed, and you should definitely avoid swimming underwater. If you do swim, protect your ear with earplugs. If possible, you should get your ear looked at again in about six weeks. If you have any persistent symptoms (eg discharge from the ear) you should seek medical advice before this.

EARACHE

The most common cause of earache is fluid build-up behind the eardrum during or just after a cold. This will respond to simple painkillers and doesn't need antibiotic treatment.

Sometimes earache is due to infection, either in the outer ear (the bit you can stick your finger into) or in the middle ear (the bit behind the eardrum). The causes and treatment differ depending on where the infection is. You can tell them apart by pulling on your ear lobe – if the pain increases, it's a problem in the outer ear; if there is no difference, it's a middle ear problem.

Outer Ear Infection

This is very common in swimmers, and is sometimes called 'swimmer's ear' or 'tropical ear'. It's caused by swimming in dirty water, especially in hot, humid conditions. Microbes thrive in these conditions, and you can get an infection even if the water was clean.

'Tropical ear' is very itchy, and you may notice a discharge, as well as earache. If it's very painful, it may indicate that you have a boil in the ear canal.

Simple painkillers will help relieve the discomfort. Warmth also helps – you could try putting a water bottle filled with warm water and wrapped in a towel against your ear. If you can get hold of some eardrops, appropriate treatment is either aluminium acetate drops (this helps to toughen the skin) OR antibiotic drops, usually combined with a steroid and ideally with an antifungal too (eg neomycin with hydrocortisone and polymyxin B sulphate).

Note that antibiotic eardrops shouldn't be used for longer than a week because long-term use can lead to secondary fungal infection. If your symptoms haven't settled in a week, seek medical advice as you may need a change of antibiotic or treatment to clean out your ear canal.

! To give the infection a chance to get better, make sure you don't get water in your ear for at least two weeks; use earplugs if you're washing your hair, taking a shower or swimming, and avoid swimming underwater.

Allergic reactions, for example to eardrops or swimming pool water, can also cause itching. If so, try to keep your ears dry and think about stopping the eardrops.

! It's tempting, but avoid cleaning your ears out with the corner of a towel, a cotton bud or anything else as this makes infection much more likely.

Middle Ear Infection

Typically, you get this during or just after a cold. It starts as a blocked feeling in the ear and progresses to pain, often with a fever. Later, you may notice a discharge from the ear (for example on your pillow) if your eardrum bursts, followed by relief from the pain.

If it doesn't start to get better in 48 hours, seek medical advice as you'll probably need a course of antibiotics (usually amoxycillin). In the meantime, simple painkillers will help the discomfort and to bring any fever down. Warmth against your ear may help. You should avoid using eardrops or getting water in your ear in case your eardrum has burst. See the section under Flying earlier for guidance on this.

Note that earache in both ears is unlikely to be due to infection. It's more likely to be due to blockage by mucus, and it may respond to decongestants (eg pseudoephedrine) or antihistamines.

Earache sometimes isn't to do with your ears. Problems outside the ear – such as in the jaw, throat or teeth – can sometimes cause earache and may be the reason why the treatments described earlier don't work.

Diving into the water when you've got a cold may push germs into your ears and make infection more likely, so it's best avoided.

DEAFNESS WITHOUT PAIN

This is usually due to wax. Don't attempt to poke anything in your ear as this makes infection more likely. Try wax-dissolving eardrops (eg Cerumol) or warm almond or olive oil. If this doesn't work, your ears may need to be syringed out, but you might want to wait until you get home before getting this done. It's annoying, but not dangerous/harmful.

EYES

This section was compiled by Graeme Johnson, an ophthalmic surgeon based in Sydney, Australia.

If you use regular medications for a preexisting eye condition like glaucoma or diabetes, remember to take plenty of supplies with you, as well as a letter from your doctor saying why you need to carry them, to avoid any problems at customs.

If you have had recent eye surgery, get advice on from your eye doctor on what you can and cannot do (eg diving into swimming pools is not advisable for some time after surgery).

When you're travelling it can be hard to keep your hands clean, and general environmental cleanliness can be far from ideal in many countries, so try to touch your eyes as little as possible, especially when you're out and about. Don't wipe your eyes with cloths or towels that could be dirty – if necessary, use a clean tissue.

SPECTACLES

If you wear glasses, remember to take a spare pair with you and consider having a pair tinted as sunglasses. Optical prescriptions are understood in all languages, so if you take a copy you can always have a new pair made. You could carry a miniature screwdriver to tighten the screws in glasses frames; these always work loose at the most inopportune times.

CONTACT LENSES

If you wear contact lenses, you will know what to take – remember that the various solutions and cleaners can take up a fair bit of luggage space. It's a good idea to take back-up glasses. Maintaining your usual hygiene standards could be difficult, especially if you're roughing it or the local water supply is suspect. If necessary, you can use boiled and cooled water in place of your usual cleansers. Take extra care to wash your hands with soap and water before handling the lenses.

If your eye becomes red or irritated, remove the lens, clean and sterilise it and leave it out until your eye is better. Bathing your eye in clean salty water may help. If your eye hasn't improved after 48 hours, you should seek medical advice as it may indicate an infection that needs to be treated promptly.

MALARIA PILLS

If you're taking chloroquine, you may notice some blurring of vision – this doesn't indicate any permanent damage. A more serious, but rare, complication is permanent damage to the retina (the back of the eye), but this is only likely to occur if you take chloroquine in high doses for a long time (usually for more than three years).

SUN

Sunlight can damage your eyes; take good (not necessarily expensive) sunglasses, and wear them. Sunglasses that block out light from the sides (ie wraparound ones, or ones with side pieces) are best. Sunlight is reflected off water and snow. If you're going to be trekking in snowy conditions, ski goggles may be better. Snow blindness, or sunburn of the surface of the eyes, can be excruciatingly painful and may take a couple of days to resolve. It doesn't have any lasting effects.

DRY OR ITCHY EYES

Air conditioning, especially in aircraft, can exacerbate dry eyes and allergic eye conditions. Take lubricant drops with you (available without prescription from pharmacies) and use them frequently.

Note that anti-allergy drops containing a decongestant ingredient shouldn't be used more than every few days – these are eyedrops that usually claim to make red, tired eyes look white.

SOMETHING IN YOUR EYE

Dust, particles of sand and travel companion to wash the particle out with copious amounts of water – see the boxed

Bathing your Eyes

If you've got an eye bath, this is obviously designed for the purpose, but good substitutes include any small container or glass, or an egg cup. If you have a ready-made saline (salt) solution, you can use that; alternatively, you can make up your own by dissolving a level teaspoon of salt in about 600ml (a pint) of boiled and cooled water or add a pinch of salt to a cup of water.

Fill the eye bath or container, bend your head over it with your eye open and blink rapidly in the water. You could get someone to pour the water into your eye if you prefer, but you'll get pretty wet. Alternatively, get someone to soak a tissue or a clean cloth in the water and squeeze it into your eye from a height of a few inches while you are lying down.

text for guidance on how to do this. Salty water is better in theory, but clean water is fine if nothing else is available.

If a particle can be seen on the white of the eye or under the upper eyelid (turn the eyelid over a match or a small key), it can be gently removed with the corner of a tissue or (even more gently) a cotton bud. The clear central part of the eye is too sensitive for you to be able to do this. If you can't wash the particle away, you'll need to go to a doctor, who may be able to remove it after anaesthetising the eye.

RED EYE

If your eye is red and sticky, with a discharge, you've probably got an infection (conjunctivitis). Another cause of red eye is a haemorrhage on the surface of the eye, on the white of the eye. It can look fairly spectacular, but if your sight is unaffected and you don't have any pain, there's nothing to worry about. You don't need any specific treatment and it will clear up in a week or so.

Conjunctivitis

This eye infection is quite common, especially in children. When you're travelling, it can be difficult to keep your hands clean, which is a source of infection if you then put them up to your eyes. You can also get it by swimming in crowded pools or dirty rivers, or through flies landing on your eyes (although you usually have a reflex blink that prevents flies landing).

Conjunctivitis can be caused by bacteria or viruses. Bacterial conjunctivitis usually quickly affects both eyes, whereas viral conjunctivitis is more likely to affect one eye only, and you don't usually get such a copious discharge. Viral conjunctivitis often comes with flu or a cold.

In addition to looking red, your eye may feel irritated, as though there's something in it. If you have a bad infection, your eye can be quite uncomfortable, and you'll find bright light difficult to tolerate.

Treatment If you've got a red, sticky eye, bathe it frequently in clean (boiled and cooled) plain or salty water. Try not to touch or rub your eye as this makes the infection more likely to spread to your other eye – or to other people.

If the redness doesn't clear up in a couple of days or you've got ready access to medical care, see a doctor as you will probably need a course of antibiotic eyedrops or ointment.

A common and effective antibiotic for eye infections is chloramphenicol (eyedrops or ointment); other commonly used antibiotic eyedrops and ointments that may be available include neomycin, gentamicin or sulphonamides. Start by putting one drop in every two hours, decreasing this as the redness and irritation improve. If you've got an ointment as well, apply the ointment at night before you go to sleep. If you've got ointment alone, apply it three to four times daily.

Ointment should be put directly into the eye, as follows: hold out the lower eyelid and squeeze about 1cm of cream into the pouch made behind the lid, then close the eye on it.

Bacterial conjunctivitis usually improves (ie the redness clears up) in two to three days, but you need to continue using the drops or ointment for three more days to make sure. If you don't notice any improvement within 48 hours of using the antibiotic, it may be that the cause is not bacterial. Viral conjunctivitis won't respond to antibiotics – it will clear up on its own, although it may take a week or two. If you're in doubt, using antibiotic eyedrops won't do any harm.

! As a rule, you should avoid using eyedrops containing a combination of an antibiotic and steroids (the names of these usually end in '-sone' like betamethasone), as this can sometimes cause a serious problem if the infection is not bacterial.

Trachoma

This type of conjunctivitis, spread by flies, is most common in dry, rural areas of Asia and other parts of the world. Untreated and repeated infection results in serious damage to the eyes, and it is a major cause of blindness worldwide. Before you get too alarmed, it's not likely to be a big problem for you as a traveller in the region, as you'll generally wave off any flies that approach your eyes. Treatment is with antibiotic eyedrops (chlortetracycline) or tablets (eg a single dose of azithromycin).

STYE

If you develop a painful red lump on the edge of your eyelid, it's probably a stye. This is a bit like a pimple and it usually clears up in a couple of days without any special treatment. Try putting a clean cloth soaked in clean hot water (not scalding) on your closed eyelid – do this several times a day.

If it doesn't go away, it might be something called a chalazion. This is a blocked and infected gland in the eyelid, and you'll need to see a doctor about it.

BLACK EYE

If you receive a blow to the eye, you may get a black eye. This is due to bruising around and behind the eye, usually with swelling of the eyelids, but your sight is not usually affected (unless your eyelids are so swollen that you can't open them). If your sight is not normal, then you need to get medical advice as soon as possible. Minimise the bruising by putting an ice pack (or anything cold, including snow) onto your closed eye.

OTHER EYE INJURIES

You can get a scratch on the eye if the branch of a bush or tree whips back in your face. You usually get pain straight away, which may become worse after an hour or two. If you put a pad on the eye this makes it more comfortable, although walking on rough ground is not easy with one eye! Keep the pad on for a few hours or even a couple of days if the pain persists, although you might find it's more trouble than it's worth.

If you've got a tube of antibiotic eye ointment (such as

Signs of Serious Eye Problems

If you experience any of the following symptoms, you should seek medical advice urgently:

- any blurred vision or loss of vision that can't be improved by blinking or washing your eye
- sudden loss of vision
- painful eye, especially if it is also unusually sensitive to light
- double vision
- eye injury followed by loss of vision or blood in the eye

chloramphenicol), you could use that. If the abrasion is not too deep, it should heal in one or two days.

A blow to the eye can cause bleeding inside the eye, which your travel companion may see as a fluid level of blood in the iris (the coloured part of the eye). This is a potentially dangerous situation – seek medical help urgently; in the meantime, rest in bed with the eye covered.

LOSS OF VISION

! If you lose your sight, partially or totally in one or both eyes, you need to seek medical help urgently.

If you suddenly lose your sight (blurring or total loss) without any pain, it could be due to a haemorrhage inside the eye or detachment of the retina (the back of the eye). You may notice a curtain obstructing part of the vision in one eye, which may be preceded by seeing lightning flashes on one side of the vision. Retinal detachment can also follow injury.

If you have blurring or loss of vision associated with intolerance of light and severe aching pain in the eye, it could be due to inflammation inside the eye (iritis) or glaucoma (where the pressure inside the eye is abnormally high). Glaucoma is

Migraine
Bear in mind that migraine headaches can be associated with flashing lights and other eye symptoms such as tunnel vision. The visual symptoms usually last about 20 minutes, and may or may not be followed by a headache. If you have had it before, you will know what it is, but if it is the first time, it can be frightening.

All sorts of factors can trigger migraines when you're travelling: tiredness, movement, stress and sunlight. Try taking simple painkillers as early as possible to prevent the attack worsening. Natural remedies like feverfew can be helpful (although you will need to have a supply with you) and many traditional therapies available in Asia like acupuncture and massage are good for migraine sufferers.

more likely to occur in older people. Both these conditions need urgent medical attention.

Partial loss of vision associated with giddiness (especially if you experience weakness in an arm or leg) is likely to be a stroke – a blockage of the blood vessels in the brain. This is also more likely to occur in older people.

TEETH

UK-based dentist Iain Corran gives you the complete low-down on staying out of the dentist's chair while you're away.

There are lots of reasons why dental problems are more likely when you're travelling. You tend to consume sugary drinks (soft drinks or sweet tea or coffee) in much larger quantities than you would at home, while practical difficulties with water supplies – or simply the lack of a washbasin – may mean that you take a break in your usual dental hygiene routine just when it's needed most. You'll probably want to avoid having to get dental treatment while you are away because it may be unreliable, expensive and could carry a risk of hepatitis B or HIV if instruments are not properly sterilised.

BEFORE YOU GO

It's a good idea to have a dental checkup about four to six weeks before you plan to travel, as this allows time for you to have any necessary treatment. Let the dentist know you're going away so you can have a really thorough examination. If you wear a brace, be sure to get it checked before you leave, and let your dentist know how long you are going to be away so any necessary alterations can be made.

DENTAL KIT

Consider taking a dental kit with you, or ask your dentist to provide you with a small tube of temporary filling material (which is a bit like chewing gum) or even a plastic filling tool (a spatula thing to help you put the filling in), but make sure you're clear about when and how to use these. Commercial dental kits are available from many travel health clinics, and usually include a dental mirror and temporary filling material, as well as instructions on how to use them. They tend to be quite expensive, but are probably worth considering if you're planning to be away for a long time or trekking in remote areas. Other useful items for dental emergencies include painkillers (for example co-codamol), a course of antibiotics (discuss this with your doctor) and oil of cloves (for toothache).

If you have been advised to have antibiotic cover for any dental treatment, for example because you have heart valve disease, then remember to carry the necessary medication with you (ie amoxycillin 3g sachet, or erythromycin if allergic to penicillin).

AVOIDING DENTAL PROBLEMS

The two main preventable causes of dental problems are tooth decay and gum disease. Tooth decay arises when refined sugars are turned into acid by bacteria in the mouth. The acid erodes the outer layer of the tooth, called enamel, eventually resulting in a cavity. Gum disease is caused by a build-up of plaque (a layer of bacteria and food gunk) on the tooth surface near the gum margin. This can cause sensitivity, particularly to hot and cold foods, and you may notice bleeding from the gums, especially when you brush your teeth.

As a general rule, try to avoid sugary foods and drinks, especially carbonated soft drinks and local-style tea (which is often very sweet), and rinse your mouth out with clean water after you eat. In hot climates you may find your mouth gets really dry. Keeping your mouth moist, for example by chewing on a sugar-free gum, helps reduce the risk of tooth decay, as the saliva neutralises the acid by bacteria in the mouth.

Avoid plaque build-up by brushing your teeth, ideally with a fluoride toothpaste, at least once a day. Remember to take generous supplies of your favourite toothpaste with you, as it may not be available locally. If you run out of toothpaste, you can use a small amount of salt instead on a moist brush. If you're on a long trip, remember to pack a spare toothbrush; if you can't get a replacement, you can use your finger as a toothbrush, possibly with a small piece of clean cloth around it.

! In some places making a toothbrush from a piece of wood, by splitting the end to make bristles, is quite common, but beware of splinters in the gums.

It's also a good idea to use dental floss or tape to clean the areas between your teeth where the toothbrush doesn't reach. If you run out of floss, toothpicks can do the same job, and are widely available. Dental floss can come in handy for a multitude of minor repairs, so is well worth tucking into your pack.

! Remember that you need to use clean (bottled or purified) water for brushing your teeth or flossing – it's obvious, but surprisingly easy to forget!

If you wear a brace, it's particularly important to avoid sticky or hard foods which may damage it, as specialist treatment may be required to fix it.

DENTAL PROBLEMS
In spite of your best efforts, you may experience some problems with your teeth while you're away.

Broken or Lost Fillings
This can happen if you bite on something hard such as nuts or the ubiquitous crunch in a rice dish. You may feel a sudden pain, a gap where the filling was, and pieces of the filling in your mouth. As an immediate measure, rinse your mouth out with some warm salty water (add a couple of teaspoons of salt to a glass of boiled and cooled water) to clear any debris from your mouth.

If you have some temporary filling material (from your dentist or a commercial kit), you can use it to plug the hole up or you can use a piece of sugar-free chewing gum. It's important to plug it up so that the hole doesn't get filled with food, which can cause more problems. You'll need to get dental treatment for a permanent filling as soon as possible. If you're on a short trip, and it's just a small surface filling, it could wait for a week or so until you get back.

If the filling has cracked rather than fallen out, you may notice that it's sensitive to hot/cold/sugary foods and drinks. A cracked filling can lead to toothache, so try to get a permanent filling placed in the tooth, as soon as is convenient.

As a general rule, avoid sugary, hot and cold foods in all these situations.

Toothache
There are lots of causes of this most unpleasant of symptoms: an injury to a tooth, a filling breaking or falling out, or tooth decay can lead to a tooth abscess.

Unless it settles quickly, you are going to need to find a dentist or doctor. In the meantime, take painkillers (such as co-codamol) regularly. Note that you shouldn't put aspirin directly on a painful tooth, as this can cause a sore patch on the gum. If you have oil of cloves with you, it can help relieve the pain when applied to the offending tooth on a clean cotton bud, although applying it may be uncomfortable.

Wash your mouth out regularly (after meals) with warm salty water. Try to avoid sugary foods, hard foods (such as nuts) and hot and cold foods. It goes without saying that you should avoid biting on the tooth.

If the pain is severe and unrelieved, perhaps with a bad taste in your mouth, you've probably got a tooth abscess, and you may need to have the tooth extracted eventually, although root treatment may save the tooth (but you'll need a good dentist). Seek medical or dental help urgently, but if you're in a remote area away from help, start taking a course of antibiotics, for example amoxycillin OR erythromycin OR metronidazole, or whatever you have with you (so long as you're not allergic to it).

If your face becomes swollen or you develop a fever, you must seek medical help as soon as possible as it means that the infection is spreading. In the meantime, drink plenty of fluids and start a course of antibiotics.

Another cause of pain in the mouth is a gum abscess, which can occur around a partially erupted wisdom tooth or when the gum has receded around a tooth, but hopefully both of these will have been picked up by your dentist before you left. Treatment is the same as for a tooth abscess.

Chipped Teeth

This can be caused by a fall, or a direct blow to the tooth. It can cause toothache immediately or after a delay, and an abscess can develop. You need to seek treatment as soon as possible as you may need root canal treatment or, possibly, extraction of the tooth. In the meantime, take simple pain-killers if necessary.

Crowns & Veneers

If a crown comes out, stick it back in and then find a dentist to glue it back on. If a crown breaks (usually front porcelain ones), it's unlikely that you'll be able to get a new one made, but you should be able to find a dentist to put a temporary crown on, which should last you till you get home.

If a veneer cracks, chips or breaks off, you probably don't need treatment until you get home, as it's unlikely to cause any damage to the tooth if it's not replaced in the short term. A rough edge may initially cause some irritation.

If a Tooth is Knocked Out

If you can find the tooth, wash it in milk (better) or clean water and, if practical, place it back in the socket to reimplant it. Get dental help as soon as possible. If it's in a child, remember that milk teeth won't need to be replaced.

If it is not practical to attempt to reimplant it (for example if it's chipped or broken or you've got other injuries in your mouth), keep the tooth in milk, and try to get a doctor/dentist to attempt to reimplant it.

Reimplantation may not be successful, but it is worth try-ing. If more than two hours have passed between the tooth being knocked out and reimplantation, the chance of success is slim.

If you are left with an open socket, rinse your mouth out with warm salty water. Don't rinse too vigorously as this may dislodge the clot forming in the socket. Avoid strenuous exer-cise for a few hours.

If there is persistent bleeding from the socket, place a clean piece of cloth across the top of the socket and bite onto it for 20 to 30 minutes. If bleeding persists, seek expert advice as soon as possible, as the socket may need stitching. Make sure you know what type of stitches have been put in, and whether or not you need to go back to have them removed.

Sometimes the socket can become infected and very painful. Use warm salty water mouthwashes and take painkillers as an immediate measure. Seek treatment as soon as possible for specialist treatment and possibly a course of antibiotics.

GETTING DENTAL TREATMENT

The same rules apply to finding dental treatment as for medical treatment, and a personal recommendation from a reliable source is probably the best way to go. Five star hotels, the local expatriate community, embassies or your travel insurance hotline may be able to point you in the right direction. If possible, try to find a dental teaching hospital – most capital cities should have one. Charges for treatment vary, but it's probably best to negotiate the price before treatment starts.

A major concern when receiving any dental treatment is the risk of contracting infections like HIV or hepatitis B from the dentist or the instruments being used, but there are some basic precautions you can take. Check that the dentist is wearing a clean pair of dental gloves, and make sure they wash their gloved hands if there's any doubt in your mind. Ideally, they should put on a new pair for each patient, but this may not be possible in some areas. You should consider taking a pair of disposable surgical gloves in your medical kit. If you need an injection, make sure the dentist uses a new, sterile needle.

Always tell anyone who is going to give you dental treatment of any existing medical condition or medication you may be on before they start treatment.

SKIN

○ For guidelines on safe sun exposure see the Staying Healthy chapter.
○ See the First Aid appendix for treatment of cuts, burns and scalds.
○ Something biting you? Turn to the Bites & Stings chapter for more guidance on what to do.

The skin is your body's first line of defence against the outside world. When you're travelling it's subjected to assaults from all directions: there are physical hazards like the sun, wind and cold; insects and parasites of all shapes and forms attack it with glee; and bacterial and fungal infections thrive in hot and humid conditions. Although there's a great line-up of weird and wonderful 'tropical' skin diseases, your skin problems are likely to be much more prosaic: sunburn, skin infections and allergic rashes are the most common afflictions.

Fungal infections of your feet can be a real nuisance when you're travelling, especially in hot, humid conditions. Happy, healthy feet are vital if you're going to enjoy all the tramping around that travelling often seems to involve – this is why we've devoted a special section to them at the end of this chapter.

RASHES

Skin rashes may occur as part of a more generalised disease. It'll be obvious, because you'll usually have a fever and other symptoms, such as sore throat or nausea and vomiting, in addition to the skin rash. Some diseases that are associated with a skin rash include:

- the 'childhood' illnesses (can occur at any age if you haven't had them before): measles, rubella and chicken pox (p220)
- glandular fever and other viral infections (p169)
- food poisoning or allergies
- dengue fever and other viral haemorrhagic fevers (p115)
- meningococcal meningitis (p126)

- tick and mite-transmitted fevers (p338)
- schistosomiasis (bilharzia) (p331)
- worm infestations of the gut (p149)

PRICKLY HEAT

This uncomfortable rash is caused by blockage of the sweat ducts. It's called 'prickly heat' because as sweating tries to occur in the blocked glands, you get an uncomfortable prickling sensation. It's common in hot, humid conditions, and can strike you when you first arrive or further down the track. It's very common in babies and children.

! Nappy rash can be a big problem in hot climates – see the Babies & Children chapter for more guidance on this.

At its mildest, prickly heat consists of a rash of painless clear blisters without any redness. These usually burst quickly and don't cause any other problems. The next step up is prickly heat proper. You get itchy areas of redness, with spots and

Causes of Itchy Skin Rash

dermatitis	(p191)	often on hands or other exposed areas
prickly heat	(p190)	armpits, waist, groin, head (babies and children)
fungal infections	(p193)	sweaty areas: armpits, groin, under breasts, between toes
insect bites	(p334)	any exposed area
scabies	(p196)	intense itchiness, especially at night
reaction to medicines		rash all over
swimmer's itch	(p332)	anywhere that was in contact with water
geography worm	(p198)	moving red tracks, usually on feet and legs

small blisters, usually in covered, sweaty areas like around your waist, chest or back, under your breasts or in the groin. You may get it on the backs of your knees or in the elbow creases. Babies and young children commonly get it on their heads too.

Because the problem is the build-up of sweat in the blocked ducts, treatment is aimed at preventing sweating:

▸ stay cool: rest and use fans, cool showers, damp cloths or an air-con hotel
▸ wear loose cotton clothing
▸ wash with water: overuse of soap may destroy the skin's natural oils and defences and is thought to be a contributory factor
▸ applying calamine, calendula or comfrey cream to the rash can be soothing
▸ taking antihistamine tablets will help stop the itching
▸ watch for signs of bacterial infection (see p400)

Prickly heat usually clears up in a few days. On rare occasions, the rash refuses to go away and becomes widespread. Because your sweat ducts are blocked all over, this affects your heat controlling mechanisms and you can get heatstroke because of it. This is more likely after you've spent several months in a hot climate.

DERMATITIS

Dermatitis is a general term for an itchy skin rash. It's very common worldwide and can be caused by a whole range of factors, from simple chemical irritation to reactions to plants and insects. It may be an in-built tendency in some people, when it can occur without any obvious cause. In this situation it's known as atopic dermatitis or eczema, and may be associated with asthma or hay fever. Most people with eczema will have had it for some time, often since childhood, and it is unlikely to develop for the first time on your travels.

Itching is the main feature of any dermatitis, which appears as thickened, red and often cracked skin. There may be some

Close Encounters

Many plants and creatures can cause an irritant or allergic skin reaction if you come into contact with them. Some plants that have been implicated include the Japanese lacquer tree (and anything that has been lacquered), raw cashew shells, mango rind and the fruit of the gingko. Philodendron is a common plant allergen in India.

Certain species of caterpillars have hairs that can be very irritant, so they are best avoided. Some beetles can cause blisters or other reactions if their body fluids come into contact with you, for example, if you squash one on your skin.

blistering, particularly if it has been caused by contact with a plant. Where you get it depends on what's causing it: eczema usually affects your hands, inside of the wrists and backs of the knees; while contact dermatitis, caused by something you've touched, will appear wherever contact was made.

If you haven't had dermatitis before and it suddenly appears when you're travelling, it's most likely to be due to contact with something ... the question is what. It may be a chemical irritant, for example soaps or detergents, or something that you are allergic to, for example an ingredient in a new skin lotion or a plant you've touched or brushed past.

Some unlucky people can get a dermatitis, often with blistering, as a result of mild to moderate sun exposure – consider this possibility if it only occurs on parts of your body that have been exposed to the sun. Or it could be a reaction to the suncream you're using. Or it could just be sunburn.

It's not always easy to work these things out, but a bit of common sense and a certain amount of trial and error can help. For example in this case, you could see if covering up or changing suncream helps. Don't forget that you can develop a sensitivity or allergy to something you have used without problems in the past.

Treatment

Most contact dermatitis will gradually settle once the irritant or allergy-causing substance is removed. If you can work out what the culprit is, avoid it! Otherwise, finding the cause only really matters if it doesn't go away.

If the rash is mild, try liberally covering it with a simple moisturiser (like aqueous cream or white soft paraffin). The trouble with 'cosmetic' moisturisers is that they can contain ingredients that may exacerbate the rash, but if you've got nothing else it may be worth giving them a try.

 Calendula or comfrey cream may help to soothe an itchy rash.

If this doesn't work, a weak steroid cream can help, such as hydrocortisone 1% cream or ointment, and is quite safe to use for a short period of time. You may find that if the skin is thick, for example on the palm of your hand, a stronger steroid cream is needed, such as betamethasone 0.025% or 0.1% cream.

If the skin is cracked and weeping, it's likely to be infected and an antibiotic cream will be helpful.

Note that all steroid creams should be used as sparingly as possible, twice a day. Don't use anything stronger than hydro-cortisone 1% on the face or genital area. If you're using these creams for the first time, discuss it first with a doctor or phar-macist if possible.

If a steroid cream makes a rash worse, stop using it – you've probably got the diagnosis wrong! Steroid cream on its own will make fungal and bacterial infections much worse.

FUNGAL INFECTIONS

These are common diseases worldwide, but are even more common in hot, humid conditions. (A piece of bread in a plas-tic bag quickly goes mouldy in the heat, and it's the same principle with your skin and fungal infections.) If you've already got a fungal infection before you leave, you'll probably find it gets worse when you're travelling.

Fungal infections can affect different parts of your body, but the basic principles for preventing them are the same:

▶ wear loose fitting, cotton clothing
▶ wash regularly and dry yourself carefully, especially between the toes, the groin area and under the breasts

You can get fungal infections from other people, animals or the soil, and they can affect different parts of your body.

Treatment of these rashes is generally with an antifungal cream – there are many different creams available (eg clotrimazole, ketoconazole, miconazole, nystatin, terbinafine and amorolfine), but all need to be applied daily or twice daily and used for at least a couple of weeks.

Scalp

Ringworm of the scalp (tinea capitis) gives you flaky, round lesions and is more common in children. Treatment is with antifungal tablets, such as fluconazole 50mg daily for two to four weeks OR griseofulvin 500mg (10mg/kg/day in children) daily for six to 12 weeks (avoid in pregnancy).

Body

Ringworm on the body appears as flaky, red areas which spread outwards, leaving a clear patch in the middle. Treatment is with antifungal cream.

Another fungal infection that is common in the tropics is tinea (also called pityriasis) versicolor. It often affects young adults and can be difficult to get rid of. You get round slightly scaly, itchy patches which may be lighter or darker than the surrounding skin, usually over your shoulders, chest and back.

Seek medical advice, but treatment options include selenium sulphide shampoo OR an anti-fungal cream OR itraconazole

200mg daily for seven days OR fluconazole 50mg daily for two to four weeks for persistent problems.

Crotch

Tinea cruris or jock itch appears as a red, flaky rash in the groin crease, especially in men; there's often a fungal infection of the feet too. Treatment is with antifungal cream.

Feet

Athlete's foot is extremely common in hot, humid climates. You get a flaky rash between the toes, which can progress to splitting of the skin. Dry carefully between your toes and use an antifungal cream or powder, or calendula tincture.

BACTERIAL INFECTIONS

○ For more guidelines on preventing and treating bacterial skin infections, see the First Aid appendix.

Warmth, humidity, dirt and dust make bacterial infections of the skin very common when you're travelling. They're extremely common in local populations too, occurring in one-tenth of adults and up to one-third of children in the tropics.

Sores

A sore, or ulcer, is any breach of the skin, usually taking a long time to heal up. These are common in hot, humid climates. The commonest cause is scratching a mosquito bite open, but other causes include:

- insect bite
- tropical ulcer
- leishmaniasis (p216)
- Buruli ulcer (p215)
- guinea worm ulcer (p215)
- cutaneous diphtheria (p220)

Bacterial infections usually have pus as their main feature. Any break in the skin, however small and insignificant it may seem, can get infected if you don't take steps to prevent it. If the infection spreads, it can make you seriously ill with blood poisoning. Boils and abscesses are also more common in hot climates. Folliculitis, a rash of pimples caused by infection of the hair follicles, is more common in hot, humid conditions, especially if you swim in dirty water.

Impetigo is an extremely common skin infection, especially in hot, humid climates. It typically affects children but is common in adults too. It usually starts on the face, often around the mouth or from a mosquito bite. The first sign of this infection is the appearance of blisters on the face, often looking a bit like a cold sore. These then burst, forming golden crusty sores, which can spread quickly to other areas of the skin. Impetigo is very infectious, and can easily be spread by fingers and towels or face cloths. Treat impetigo as follows:

- wash the crusty sores regularly (eg twice a day) with soap and water or an antiseptic solution like povidone-iodine
- apply an antibiotic cream (such as fusidic acid) three times daily for five to seven days on the sores after washing the crusts off
- seek medical advice or if it's not available take a course of antibiotics (eg flucloxacillin OR erythromycin if penicillin-allergic – see p380) if it's severe or doesn't respond to treatment

SCABIES

You're not likely to get this infestation unless you're planning on intimate contact with a sufferer. The villain is the scabies mite, which burrows into your skin(usually between the fingers or on the wrists and genital areas) where it lays its eggs.

It causes intense itching, which is much worse at night, and there's a high risk of secondary bacterial infection. The itching isn't actually due to the mites themselves, but it's a sensitivity reaction they produce in you, six to eight weeks after you've been infected. It can persist even when the mites themselves have gone. You may see typical burrows between your fingers. It's not a tropical disease as such, but it's encouraged by poor personal hygiene, especially when water isn't readily available for washing. You get it from intimate, prolonged contact with an infected person.

Treatment is with malathion or permethrin lotion (preferably); benzyl benzoate lotion may still be available locally, but should be avoided in children. You need to cover your whole body apart from your head (except in young children) and leave it ideally for 24 hours, but overnight treatment (10 to 12 hours) is probably adequate.

Itchiness may persist for 10 to 12 days even after successful treatment of the mite. It can be treated with calamine cream or antihistamine tablets. You need to wash all your clothes and anything you've been sleeping in (eg your sleeping bag and liner) to prevent reinfection. Anybody who has shared a bed with you will also need to be treated. Scabies mites are not known to transmit any diseases.

LICE

These are a definite possibility in many Asian countries, especially if you're roughing it. There are three types of lice which infest different areas: head, body and pubic (crab louse). They all cause itching due to bites. You may not see the lice themselves as they're transparent, but they lay eggs that look like white grains attached to hairs. Lice are passed by close contact between people (sexual intercourse for pubic lice) and via infected bedding or clothing for body lice.

Head lice can be treated with carbaryl, malathion, permethrin or phenothrin lotions – apply the lotion to your head and leave for it for 12 hours before washing off. Alternatively, use any hair conditioner and get a (good) friend to comb through your hair – the lice just slip off. You'll need to repeat this every three days or so for two weeks after you spot the last louse. Treat anyone you share a bed with as well. The empty egg cases can stick around after the lice themselves have gone.

Treat body lice by getting rid of them: wash all bedding and clothing in hot water (kills the lice). Body (clothing) lice can, rarely, transmit typhus via their faeces.

Pubic lice should be treated by applying malathion OR carbaryl lotion all over your body (not just the pubic area) and leaving it overnight. You'll need a second treatment after seven days to zap any lice appearing from surviving eggs.

BEDBUGS

You're very likely to get acquainted with these, especially if you're on a shoestring budget. Bedbugs are 3mm by 4mm oval insects that live in mattresses, cracks in the walls etc, but not on you. They merely visit you for a meal when it's dark. Bites, which can be itchy, are usually in a line of two or three on your face, arms, buttocks, ankles or anywhere else accessible. If bites are itchy, try some calamine cream or Tiger Balm.

The best way to get rid of them is to spray furniture and wall cracks with an insecticide, or to use a permethrin-impregnated mosquito net. Better still, find another hotel.

There's been much debate about whether bedbugs can transmit HIV, as in theory at least it's a possibility, but there is no evidence to suggest they do.

GEOGRAPHY WORM

This migrating rash (also known as cutaneous larva migrans) is caused by the larvae of various worms, usually the dog or cat hookworm, which are passed in their faeces. It occurs worldwide, but it's more common in hot, humid environments. You're at risk anywhere contaminated with dog and cat faeces, usually by walking barefoot or sitting on sandy beaches.

You can get mild itching and a rash when the larvae first enter your skin, but the real fun begins when they start to migrate a few days later. They produce intensely itchy red tracks that advance slowly day by day. They're desperately hoping you're a cat or dog, as they can't live in humans and will die after a few weeks.

You could just wait for them to die naturally, but you're probably not going to want to leave it that long. Treatment is by freezing the head of the track with ethyl chloride spray or applying an anti-worm medicine like thiabendazole (made up into a 10% solution) directly to the track. Alternatively, albendazole 400mg twice a day for five days is very effective. As for any skin condition in the tropics, look out for secondary infection.

A similar rash can be caused by intestinal worms (see the Digestive System chapter), but they tend to be much speedier.

JIGGER FLEA (TUNGIASIS)

These fleas live in sandy soil and infest pigs, humans and other mammals. You're most likely to pick them up by going barefoot or wearing open sandals in risk areas (in Asia, the west coast of India).

The flea burrows into your skin, commonly the soles of your feet or on your toes, under the toenails. It forms a swelling the size of a pea with a central black spot (the back end of the flea).

Treatment is aimed at getting rid of the flea and preventing any secondary bacterial infection. Textbooks talk of microsurgery, but it is possible to dig it out relatively painlessly using a sterilised needle and plenty of antiseptic solution. You should make sure you remove it whole, and take care to keep the open wound very clean afterwards.

FEET

Chris Wheeler, Melbourne-based podiatrist (when he's not off road-testing his own advice), has the following to say about that most vital piece of travel equipment – your feet.

To paraphrase the sage: 'while travel makes the heart grow fonder, it is true that the smile comes from the feet'. Your feet come in for a lot of wear and tear when you're travelling, and even minor afflictions can make your life a misery. The good news is that with a bit of care you can avoid most problems.

FOOTWEAR

If you're not going too far off the beaten track, your best bet is likely to be light-weight walking shoes (the next step up from running shoes). These are supportive where they need to be (around the heel), cushioned where they should be (under the base of the heel and under the ball of the foot) and allow the foot to bend where it's happiest to. Most importantly, you have a wide range of brands to choose from so you can find one that suits the shape of your foot best. Unless you're planning on trekking, it's probably best to avoid serious hiking boots because they're heavy and stiff. Open footwear such as sandals or thongs are tempting in a hot climate, but they leave your feet open to injury (and subsequent infection), and over a long period of time they can cause your skin to dry out, giving you cracked and painful heels.

FOOT HYGIENE

Try to make sure you wash your feet once a day, and dry them carefully, especially between the toes. If you're a sweaty foot person, consider wiping between the toes with methylated spirits (pre-injection swabs are available from pharmacists and won't take up much space in your medical kit).

If you wear open footwear, you can help prevent cracked heels by using a skin-softening agent (any simple moisturiser will do) and a pumice stone to remove dry skin.

Deliciously soothing foot sprays, moisturisers and balms are available for tired feet – well worth the extra weight in your pack.

BLISTERS

The scourge of hikers, blisters occur when there is repeated friction to the skin. Prevention is all-important. Make sure your footwear is well worn in before you set off sightseeing or on a hike. At the very least, wear them on a few short walks before you leave – don't plan to wear them in for the first time while you are away. Your boots should fit comfortably with enough room for you to move your toes, and make sure your socks fit properly. If you're going to be doing lots of walking, it's worth investing in socks specifically made for walkers. Socks made from a synthetic fibre called orlon have been shown to decrease the size and frequency of blisters. Wet and muddy socks can also cause blisters, so slip a spare pair of socks in your daypack and change your socks when necessary. Keep your toenails clipped, but not too short.

If you do feel a blister coming on, take immediate action. Apply a simple sticking plaster or preferably one of the special blister plasters which act as a second skin, and follow the instructions on the packaging for replacement. 'Second skin' products reduce the shearing forces that cause blisters. You could try stretching the offending part of the shoes or wearing a different pair of socks.

If you're planning on going on a hike and you haven't time to toughen the skin of your feet up by graduated walking, you could consider soaking your feet in a weak solution of potassium permanganate for 20 minutes daily (add a teaspoon of crystals to 4L of warm water) to toughen the skin. In the army, new recruits were once told to urinate on their feet to toughen the skin, but this probably won't endear you to your travelling companions.

A blister won't get infected as long as it is intact. If the blister looks as if it is about to burst or is already broken, apply an antiseptic ointment such as chlorhexidine to reduce the risk of infection and cover it with a thick pad of sterile gauze (preferably over a nonadherent dressing like melolin). If you have a hydrodermic dressing such as Duoderm with you, apply it and leave it in place for seven days or so.

HIV/AIDS & SEXUAL HEALTH

For a general discussion about sex and travel, including how to avoid sexually related health problems, see the section Sex & Travel in the Staying Healthy chapter earlier in this book.

HIV/AIDS

AIDS stands for acquired immunodeficiency syndrome, and it describes the collection of diseases that result from suppression of the body's immune system by infection with the human immunodeficiency virus (HIV). HIV targets cells in the blood that are an important part of your immune system, which protects you from infections. At present, although there are effective (but toxic) treatments that can keep AIDS at bay for a period of time, there is no known cure.

TRANSMISSION

In Asia, heterosexual sex is the most common way in which HIV is passed from person to person. HIV can be transmitted through vaginal, anal or oral sexual intercourse between men and women or between men.

In Asia, the other most important ways in which HIV is transmitted are from mother to unborn child and via infected blood transfusions. In many western nations, the risk of HIV infection from blood transfusions is practically zero because of stringent screening procedures, but in many developing countries, including most parts of Asia, blood is not screened or is inadequately screened – see the section on Blood Transfusions in the Staying Healthy chapter for further discussion of this issue.

Other ways in which HIV is transmitted are through needle sharing among intravenous drug users and inadequate sterilisation or reusing of needles, syringes and other equipment in medical and dental procedures, as well as acupuncture, tattooing, ear and body piercing, and using cut-throat razors.

FACT OR FICTION?

It may be all old hat to you, but it can be confusing trying to separate fact from fiction with HIV; here's the current wisdom on it:

- a vaccine against HIV is looking promising, but there's a long way to go so don't throw away those condoms just yet
- worldwide, most HIV infections are acquired through heterosexual sex
- the more sexual partners you have, the more at risk you are for HIV/AIDS
- you can be perfectly healthy for 10 years or more after infection before any signs of the disease show up
- you can't tell by looking at a person if they are infected or not
- HIV can be transmitted through infected blood transfusions
- HIV is not thought to be transmitted by saliva
- acupuncture, tattooing, ear and body piercing, injections and other medical and dental procedures with unsterilised equipment can all transmit HIV infection
- HIV is a sensitive little virus and needs pretty intimate contact to be transmitted – it's not transmitted by hugging, social kissing, using the same toilet seat or sharing a cup
- it's not passed in swimming pools
- insects like bedbugs and mosquitoes do not transmit HIV

RISKS

The risk of acquiring HIV per exposure varies enormously, from one in 20 to one in 1000 for different types of sexual intercourse, one in 20 for needle sharing, to near certainty for a contaminated blood transfusion. In general, it's twice as easy to transmit HIV from men to women than the other way around, and receptive anal intercourse is especially risky. Many other factors can affect the risk, including the stage of infection (early and late are the most risky), the strain of HIV and whether you have another STI. Having another STI increases your risk of getting HIV; if you are already HIV-infected, having an STI increases the chance of you passing HIV on.

HIV INFECTION & AIDS

There aren't any immediate signs of infection, although you may get a glandular-fever-like illness a few weeks after infection, with fever, aches and pains, a skin rash and swollen glands. After this you may have no more symptoms for 10 years or more, although this time is very variable. This is when you're HIV-positive, and is the danger period in terms of passing the infection to others. Because you're healthy with it, you may not realise that you've got HIV. Eventually, your immune system starts to show signs of strain, and the syndrome of AIDS starts.

A blood test can show if you're infected or not, but it won't show positive for about three months after you may have been exposed to HIV.

HIV & YOU

While you are away, you could put yourself at risk of HIV infection if you

- have sexual intercourse with an infected person
- receive an infected blood transfusion or injection
- share needles with HIV-infected injecting drug users

You're obviously going to want to take steps to avoid these risk situations, wherever you go: always practise safer sex; avoid getting into situations where you might need a blood transfusion; and never share needles with injecting drug users.

If you're worried you may have put yourself at risk of HIV infection:

▶ don't sit and brood on it, but phone an AIDS helpline as soon as possible to talk about your concerns; either wait until you get back home if you're on a short trip or check your guidebook or a phone book for the local number

▶ play fair with partners and always practise safer sex

▶ make an appointment with your doctor or at a sexual health clinic when you return to your home country to discuss what your best course of action is

Remember that an HIV test won't be able to tell you either way for about three months after the risk situation; in the meantime you will need to practise safer sex.

You may have heard about a 'morning after' treatment for HIV, called post-exposure prophylaxis. It's a cocktail of antiviral drugs that, in theory, stops HIV infection getting a hold after you've been exposed to it. Although it may be of value for health workers who accidentally get jabbed by contaminated needles, its use after sexual exposure is very controversial. It's not guaranteed to work, and there are enormous practical problems associated with its use – it's extremely expensive, several different drugs have to be taken every day for at least six weeks and it can cause unpleasant side effects. And it's not guaranteed to work. For most travellers, this isn't an option and you shouldn't rely on it.

AIDS IN ASIA

Because the HIV/AIDS epidemic is relatively recent in Asia, HIV/AIDS statistics are only beginning to emerge, and the picture here could change dramatically over the next few years. Currently, about one-fifth of all people living with HIV/AIDS (30 million worldwide) are in this region. There's much concern that the recent economic and political upheavals in South-East Asia may impact significantly on the problem. Only time will tell. One of the main barriers to forecasting the future is the variable quality of the AIDS surveillance systems in the region.

There are many different behavioural, cultural and economic factors affecting the spread of HIV in this region, making it difficult to generalise. Thailand, for example, had all the prerequisites for a rapid spread of infection: a large number of heroin addicts, a large commercial sex industry, and many seasonal migrating workers. This resulted in a rapid spread of infection during the late 1980s and early 1990s among injecting drug users and female sex workers, followed by rebound

What Is Safer Sex?

Using a latex (rather than natural membrane) condom is extremely effective at preventing transmission of HIV and other STIs. Use only water-based lubricants, as petroleum or oil-based lubricants can damage rubber.

You may feel awkward about discussing condoms because of cultural differences or a worry that you might be seen as 'forward' or as having planned it, but it's a small price to pay for peace of mind and your good health.

Your local health centre, any travel health clinic and any sexual health clinic will be able to provide you with more information on safer sex or you could check out the UCSF safer sex web site at www.safersex.org. The Terrence Higgins Trust web site (www.tht.org.uk) also has loads of information on all aspects of preventing and living with HIV/AIDS.

waves in male clients of sex workers, then their wives, and finally in their children.

In Cambodia and parts of Myanmar and India, heterosexual transmission via the large-scale sex industries has also been the most important form of transmission, and it's now spreading into the community through infected regular partners. This rapid spread makes for a large infected population, which can go largely unnoticed because they are not actively sick.

Epidemics in injecting drug users are recognised in several areas, thought to be associated with a change in habit from smoking (traditional) to injecting purer forms of drugs like heroin. These include the Golden Triangle area (encompassing northern Thailand, eastern Myanmar, also Manipur in India, Yunnan in China and probably Bangladesh too) and the Mekong Delta area (Cambodia and southern Vietnam).

In some countries, like Indonesia and the Philippines, there may be smaller numbers of people living with HIV/AIDS and, so far, a slower rate of spread among the general population (but not among certain groups, including sex workers). Other countries like Nepal, Malaysia and Vietnam have the same prerequisites as Thailand but in varying proportions and appear to be on the verge of large-scale epidemics,.

It's easy to get the impression that India is in the grip of a major epidemic, especially as the absolute numbers of people living with HIV/AIDS in India is the highest in the world. However, when you take into account the fact that India's population is currently about a billion, this translates as quite a low rate of transmission (0.3% compared with 3% in badly hit Cambodia). The potential for an epidemic on a truly alarming scale is certainly there, given that about half of India's vast population is in the sexually active age group, but currently much of India is relatively unaffected by HIV/AIDS. Some areas are very severely affected, including Maharashtra, Tamil Nadu and Manipur, as well as large metropolitan areas like Mumbai (currently the hardest hit area in India), Chennai and the India/Nepal border area.

Countries in Asia have varied in their response to the problem of HIV/AIDS transmission, and there are many cultural factors that impact on this, including, for example, India's total denial of sex, the persecution of sex workers in China and the refusal of the Philippines to condone condom use (because of Catholic religious beliefs).

In contrast, Thailand is a much-lauded example of a country which had a rapid and effective response to the problem, with extensive public education campaigns on the risks of unsafe sex and the need to use condoms, as well as genuine attempts to change Thai male sexual behaviour, and some coercive elements (such as the 100% condom program in brothels). There have been some remarkable results in a relatively short time, with new infections with HIV and other STIs slowing significantly.

Other countries have effectively turned a blind eye to the problem which they have neither the will nor the resources to combat.

OTHER STIs

Although some of the 'traditional' STIs like syphilis and gonorrhoea have faded from the picture somewhat in most developed countries, they're alive and kicking in most other parts of the world, including Asia.

Why do you care? Because travellers regularly roll up at STI clinics back home with infections they've acquired on their travels. There's a long history of an association between itinerant populations (sailors, soldiers and long-distance truck drivers) and the spread of STIs. Most famously, Christopher Columbus and his crew have been accused of initiating a syphilis epidemic that spread through Europe in the 16th century. The two world wars were associated with epidemics of STIs, while more recently, the spread of HIV through Africa can be directly related to long-distance truck routes.

Many STIs (including gonorrhoea and syphilis) can be simply and effectively treated with antibiotics if they're caught early. However, others can make you seriously ill and may have long-term effects, especially if they are not treated early, including infertility (eg *Chlamydia*, gonorrhoea), liver disease (eg hepatitis) and an increased risk of cervical cancer (genital warts).

Hepatitis B is the only sexually transmitted infection for which there is an effective vaccine. See the Immunisations section in the Before You Go chapter for more details.

AIDS Amma

AIDS is making an impact in India: a new goddess has been added to the list of Hindu divinities. A group of students, inspired by the AIDS-related death of a local couple, have built a temple dedicated to the goddess of AIDS in Karnataka in South India. Worshippers pray here for a cure for the disease, and the temple is decorated with awareness-raising messages.

Some STIs cause no symptoms or only mild symptoms that may go unnoticed. Sometimes fertility problems are the first sign that you have had an infection. If STIs do cause symptoms, these are usually an abnormal vaginal or penile discharge, pain or irritation during intercourse or when you urinate, and any blisters, lumps, itches, rashes or other irritation on or around your genitals or anus.

! Because STIs can go unnoticed, it's best to get a checkup when you get home if you have had unprotected intercourse with a new partner while you were away.

If you notice any symptoms, it's best to get expert help as soon as possible. You can't tell accurately from your symptoms what infection you're likely to have, and it's common to have more than one STI at the same time. Taking the wrong treatment or inadequate treatment leaves you at risk of complications like infertility later, or you may think you're cured when you're not. Try to find a reputable doctor or STI clinic for a thorough examination and laboratory tests, and see your doctor when you get back so they can confirm that the infection is gone and there are no other problems. If you think you may have an STI:

▶ seek medical advice for investigation and treatment
▶ self-medication is best avoided as it can be disastrous

What's in a Name?
Bear in mind that clinics dealing with sexual health go by many different names in different countries in Asia. These include VD or dermato-venereology (everywhere), 'social hygiene' (Hong Kong) and the National Skin Centre (Singapore). You'll probably find that local people may be reluctant to go to clinics (or they can't affford to) and that they often self-treat with medicines from the drug store, often with disastrous results.

▸ your partner will need treatment too
▸ avoid intercourse (assuming you still feel like having sex) until you have finished the course of treatment
▸ play fair and don't spread it around

SOME DETAILS

In this section we've summarised a few details about some of the STIs you may be at risk of acquiring. We haven't included specific antibiotic treatments because the sensitivity of infections to antibiotics varies from region to region and with time, and it's near impossible to diagnose STIs without a laboratory test. In any event, you always have time to find medical help.

Trichomoniasis is another STI women may be at risk for – we've covered this in the Women Travellers chapter (p244).

Gonorrhoea

Caused by a bacteria, this STI occurs worldwide, affecting hundreds of millions of people. It usually causes a penile or vaginal discharge and burning on urination. You can also be infected in the throat or rectum. It can lead to serious complications like pelvic inflammatory disease and infertility if it's not treated promptly. Gonorrhoea used to be effectively treated with high-dose penicillin, but multiple antibiotic resistance is a major problem worldwide, and treatment is now usually with one of the newer antibiotics. You'll need a couple of check ups to make sure it has gone completely.

Syphilis

This ancient disease occurs in three stages, and can cause serious complications in a proportion of sufferers if it's not treated early. Initially it causes a painless ulcer (on your genitals, rectum or throat) and a rash. Later you may get a feverish illness with painful ulcers and rashes, and later still (up to 50 years) you can get problems involving major blood vessels or the brain. Diagnosis is by a blood test. Treatment needs to be administered and monitored by an expert, and usually involves multiple injections of penicillin.

Chlamydia

Known as the silent STI because it often causes mild or no symptoms, this STI is extremely common worldwide. It's also known as NSU (nonspecific urethritis) and if symptoms are present they're similar to gonorrhoea but milder. It's a major cause of pelvic inflammatory disease and infertility in women. Antibiotic treatment is effective at treating this condition.

Genital Herpes

This is a very common cause of genital ulceration. Ulcers can be very painful, occur in clusters, and may recur. It's caused by a virus similar to the one that causes cold sores on your lips, and if your partner has a cold sore it can be transmitted to your genitals by oral sex.

The initial infection is usually the worst, and can last about three weeks. You can feel quite miserable with it, with a fever, aches and pains and swollen glands. Herpes is not curable, but subsequent attacks are usually less severe, and you may recognise and be able to avoid triggers like stress or being

Condoms

What condoms won't protect you against:

- genital herpes
- genital warts
- pubic lice
- scabies

Condoms do help protect against STIs transmitted through the exchange of body fluids. These infections include:

- HIV
- hepatitis B, C
- gonorrhoea
- chlamydia
- syphilis

run-down. Note that any genital ulcers make transmission of HIV more likely.

Treatment is with simple painkillers and bathing the ulcers in salty water or a mild antiseptic solution; a local anaesthetic jelly applied to the ulcers may help. Antiviral drugs (eg acyclovir 200mg five times daily for seven days) can help shorten the length of an attack and reduce the severity, but they are expensive and only moderately effective.

Genital Warts

These are usually painless, and can appear on the vagina, vulva, penis or anus. Warts can be painted with an acid solution that makes them dry up and fall off, or you sometimes need to have them removed in hospital or can be frozen or burnt off. Occasionally they may need to be surgically removed. They can recur, and although stress and smoking may be associated, it's often for no reason. Fortunately, they usually disappear completely, but in women they are associated with cancerous changes in the cervix, so it's important to have regular cervical smear tests if you have been infected.

Chancroid

This highly infectious STI occurs in tropical and subtropical areas, where it is the most common cause of genital ulcers. It is endemic in South-East Asia. The ulcers are painful (and can get secondarily infected) and you often get swelling of the glands in the groin. It is much more common in men than women, and it often occurs together with syphilis. Antibiotics are effective against chancroid.

Lymphogranuloma Venerum

This is caused by types of chlamydia (see earlier in this section) and occurs worldwide. Hot spots in Asia include India and parts of South-East Asia. Symptoms are variable, but you may notice a blister or small painless ulcer or, more commonly, tender swelling of the lymph glands with fever and

Genital Ulcers

Causes of these lesions include:

- chancroid (common in tropical regions)
- genital herpes
- syphilis
- lymphogranuloma venerum
- granuloma inguinale (donovanosis)

Genital ulcers make transmission of HIV infection more likely.

general aches and pains. Late problems, if it's not treated, include bladder and rectal problems and swelling of the genitals (genital elephantiasis). Antibiotic treatment is effective in the early stages.

Donovanosis (Granuloma Inguinale)

You probably don't need to worry about this one as it's pretty rare, but hot spots in Asia are southern India and Vietnam. It causes a persistent genital ulcer. Antibiotic treatment is effective, but may need to be prolonged over several weeks.

Other infections

Just be aware of some other infections that can be transmitted through sexual intercourse:

- viral hepatitis (p158)
- pubic lice (p197)
- scabies (p196)
- intestinal infections (p132)

RARITIES

Grouped here are some infections you're generally going to be at very low risk of getting, except under special circumstances or, in the case of the 'childhood' infections, if you are not up to date with your immunisations. We've listed these infections in alphabetical order.

EXOTIC INFECTIONS

If you get one of these, you're either exceptionally unlucky, or you were just in the wrong place at the wrong time.

BURULI ULCER

Named after the place in Uganda where it was first diagnosed, this condition is rare and extremely unlikely to affect travellers in Asia. It is caused by a relative of the tuberculosis bacteria.

A firm, painless lump appears, usually on the limbs. This then breaks down and spreads rapidly, causing huge damage to the skin. The ulcer tends to heal spontaneously after some months or years, but it leaves extensive scarring and deformity. Treatment is with antiseptic solutions and skin grafting, and some antituberculosis drugs have also been found to be useful.

GUINEA WORM

This ancient scourge, described in the Bible and by Hippocrates, is the target of a World Health Organization eradication program, and you'll be relieved to know that much progress has been made towards this end, especially in India. It presents a very small risk indeed to travellers in Asia.

Larvae of the guinea worm live in small fresh water crustaceans called *Cyclops*, which you swallow by drinking contaminated water (which gets contaminated when ulcers are bathed in it). The step wells in India are notorious for being part of this cycle. Once in your gut, the larvae are released from the *Cyclops* and develop deep in your body tissues. The female worms are the ones that cause the problems, and they can grow up to 1m in length.

When the female is mature, she migrates towards the skin in order to release the larvae from her uterus. Most (90%) worms emerge from the legs but they can emerge from anywhere (yes, anywhere). Symptoms occur as the worm matures, and include pain at the site of emergence, swelling, itching and fever. A blister appears over the end of the worm which then bursts leaving a small ulcer. You can usually see the swollen uterus of the worm in the centre of the ulcer.

The aim of treatment is to remove the worm and to prevent secondary infection, although worms that are left just die and the wound usually heals up without any other problems. Surgical removal is effective, but the traditional method is more fun to describe – and may be the only option available.

▸ Empty the uterus of the worm by repeatedly washing the ulcer in clean (boiled) water (this makes the worm easier to extract).
▸ Pull the worm out a little way, taking care not to pull too hard.
▸ Attach the worm to a preferably sterile piece of wood with thread.
▸ Gently draw the worm out until you feel resistance by rolling it round the stick. It's important to remove the worm intact because it can cause a severe reaction if it breaks.
▸ Roll the worm up a little bit day by day – it can take up to two weeks to remove it this way.
▸ Cover the wound with a sterile dressing to prevent it from getting secondarily infected.

LEISHMANIASIS

This parasitic disease is rare in travellers, but is an important cause of illness and disfigurement worldwide. It occurs in some parts of Asia, mainly the Indian subcontinent and China. Leishmaniasis is caused by parasites of the *Leishmania* family, and is spread through the bite of infected sandflies (see the Bites & Stings chapter for more on these bloodsuckers). There are three main forms of the disease: skin (cutaneous or CL);

visceral (VL, affecting the internal organs); and mucocutaneous, which occurs in Latin America only.

Development of a vaccine seems likely in the near future, although one isn't available commercially yet. Recovery from an attack gives lifelong immunity to both forms of the disease. The best prevention is to avoid sandfly bites. Animals like dogs can act as reservoirs of infection in certain areas, especially in central Asia.

CL is the most common form of the disease worldwide, although it is relatively uncommon in Asia, mainly occurring in northern India and Pakistan and a few parts of China. This form of the disease causes a skin lesion or sometimes several lesions that usually heal spontaneously, often with scarring.

VL (also called kala-azar) is a more serious form of the disease which can be fatal. Large outbreaks of kala-azar occur periodically in Bangladesh and India, and China has been experiencing something of a resurgence in VL recently. More than 90% of VL cases in the world are from Bangladesh, Brazil, India and Sudan. The increase in VL in some areas of the world, including parts of India, has been linked to levels of HIV infection as HIV makes the disease reappear in people who have been exposed to the infection in the past.

Symptoms
VL develops anything from three to 18 months after you get bitten by an infected sandfly, and sometimes the parasites can persist in a dormant state for many years. Initially a nodule called a leishmanioma may appear. Later you get a fever, usually irregular and intermittent, and massive enlargement of internal organs, usually the spleen and liver.

Diagnosis & Treatment
Leishmaniasis isn't something you are going to be diagnosing in yourself. VL can be diagnosed by laboratory examination of a sample of tissue. Seek medical advice if you think you may have it, and remember it can have a long incubation period.

Diagnosis of CL is by laboratory examination of a small piece of tissue from the ulcer. Treatment of simple, single ulcers is nonspecific – just the usual measures to prevent secondary bacterial infection.

Drug treatment is available with antimony drugs, and is used for multiple ulcers and for kala-azar.

LEPROSY

Although you're extremely unlikely to get this disease yourself, you'll probably see sufferers on your travels through India and Asia. This disease was well known to the ancient world, and used to be widespread in Europe in the Middle Ages. Crusaders are known to have returned with it from the Middle East. It's now estimated to affect 15 million people worldwide, over half of whom live in Africa and India, and with substantial numbers in South-East Asia.

The disease is caused by a bacteria which attacks the nerves. This deadens feeling in the extremities, and sufferers damage themselves without realising it. Secondary infection of wounds due to poor hygiene completes the picture. Although the stereotyped image of a leprosy sufferer is of someone with deformities and weeping sores, there is a wide spectrum of disease, from simple depigmented, pale patches of skin to characteristic deformities like claw hand.

You won't catch leprosy by touching a sufferer. Prolonged contact with a sufferer (eg living in the same house) is needed for spread of the disease, possibly through nasal secretions. Socioeconomic conditions are thought to play a big part in determining spread – malnutrition, for example, is known to increase susceptibility to the disease. An animal reservoir may be important – the nine-banded armadillo is the only animal known to be affected by leprosy, and it may act as a reservoir of the disease in some areas.

Specific treatments are available and, if started early, the disease can be halted before deformities occur. The problem is that diagnosis is often delayed because of fear of the disease and the social stigma attached to it. Leprosy is unique for the place it has had in society – sufferers have been stigmatised to an extraordinary degree, shunned by society and banished into ghettos. Because it's such an emotive term, leprosy is now officially known as Hansen's disease, after the person who first identified the causative organism in 1873.

LYMPHATIC FILARIASIS

This disease is caused by blockage of the lymph channels by long thread-like worms (filaria) which are transmitted by the bite of several varieties of mosquito.

You've probably heard of the most severe form of this disease, elephantiasis, when male sufferers have to carry their enormously enlarged genitals in wheelbarrows – an image that is bound to stick in your mind.

The risk to you as a traveller is minute, however, as it takes prolonged (three to six months at least) and intense exposure to infected mosquito bites for infection to become established, and elephantiasis also only occurs in a small proportion of heavily infected people living in high risk areas. However, it's still sensible to avoid insect bites in these areas. There's no vaccine available against lymphatic filariasis.

With light infections, you may get no symptoms at all. If you do get symptoms, these include fever, painful swellings of the lymph glands (eg in your armpits, groin, elbows) and, in men, swelling of the testes with scrotal pain and tenderness. Note that symptoms usually develop about six months or so after infection. If the infection is not treated, you can get permanent damage to the lymph system, leading to swelling of the arms, legs, breasts or scrotum, with associated thickening and wrinkling of the skin that's supposed to resemble elephant skin, hence the name 'elephantiasis'.

If you think you may have filariasis, seek medical advice as soon as possible for appropriate treatment. Infection can, in some cases, be diagnosed with a blood test. An effective treatment is available with diethylcarbamazine or ivermectin.

INFECTIONS COVERED BY ROUTINE IMMUNISATIONS

In most western nations, national immunisation programs ensure that you are usually protected against the infections listed here. See the Immunisations section of the Before You Go chapter for details about travel-related immunisations.

DIPHTHERIA

Vaccination against this serious bacterial disease is very effective, so you don't need to worry if you've been properly immunised against it.

This disease occurs worldwide, but has been controlled by vaccination in most developed countries. It mainly affects children and causes a cold-like illness which is associated with a severe sore throat. A thick white membrane forms at the back of the throat which can suffocate you, but what makes this a really nasty disease is that the diphtheria bacteria produces a very powerful poison which can cause paralysis and affect the heart. Otherwise healthy people can carry the bacteria in their throats, and it's transmitted by sneezing and coughing.

It can also cause a skin ulcer known as a veldt sore. Vaccination protects against this form too. Treatment is with penicillin and a diphtheria antitoxin, if necessary.

MEASLES, MUMPS & RUBELLA

These diseases are now much less common in most western nations because of widespread immunisation programs, but they are still prevalent in many parts of Asia, especially in countries with limited resources for adequate immunisation programs. You are generally at low risk of these diseases, especially if you have been fully immunised. Although they are thought of as 'childhood' illnesses, all these diseases can occur in adults and tend to be much more serious when they do.

Measles starts a bit like a cold, then appears to get worse, and a fever develops. At about the third or fourth day, a rash appears on the skin, starting on the face and moving down. The rash is red, raised and tends to conglomerate together. It starts to fade after about five days. You can get ear and chest infections with measles, and also diarrhoea. Occasionally, severe complications (affecting the brain) can occur, which is why you should seek medical advice if you think you may have measles.

Mumps is a viral infection of the salivary glands. It makes you feel generally unwell; you get swelling around the jaw, extending towards the ear, which is painful, especially when you eat. It usually resolves after about a week without any special treatment. It's not generally a serious illness, although there is a risk of infection affecting the testicles in adult men who get measles, but not in children.

Rubella (German measles) is generally a very mild illness, a bit like a mild cold, associated with a pink, non-raised rash that starts on the face and spreads downwards. It can, however, cause severe problems in unborn children, so it is extremely important that you are immunised if you are a woman of child-bearing age.

POLIO

The World Health Organization aims to eliminate polio worldwide by the year 2000, and immunisation programs have made this seem like a real possibility in Asia. Polio has been eliminated from Japan, but still occurs in other parts of Asia, especially where resources for health care are limited. It's an important cause of disability worldwide.

The polio virus is spread from person to person by coughing and sneezing or by contamination of food and drink with faeces from an infected person. Polio attacks the nerves, causing paralysis of muscles, and commonly affects young children. At first, infection causes a flu-like illness with fever, headache, muscle aches and pains, nausea, vomiting and sometimes diarrhoea, then it appears to settle for a few days before you get more muscle pains and paralysis of a limb or more generalised paralysis. Paralysis occurs in less than one in 100 infected people. It can be dangerous if the muscles controlling breathing are affected – you may have seen old photos of polio sufferers in 'iron lungs'; the technology is a bit more sophisticated these days, but the principle is the same. The paralysis does improve with time but a proportion of people are left with some disability, often a wasted, paralysed limb. Polio can be diagnosed by a blood test.

If you are up to date with your immunisation, it's very unlikely that you will get infected. Prevention is through immunisation and taking care to avoid contaminated food and water.

TETANUS

You probably know that you have to be up to date with this vaccination, but do you know what you're being protected against? Spores of the tetanus bacterium are widespread in soil and some animal faeces and occur worldwide. They can be introduced into your body through injury – for example through a puncture wound (even a very trivial one), a burn or an animal bite. The tetanus bacteria produce a toxin in your body that causes severe, painful muscular contractions and spasm leading to death through spasm of the respiratory muscles. It's old name is 'lockjaw' because of the spasms of the jaw muscles.

If you have tetanus, you need specialist treatment in hospital, but you shouldn't get it if you make sure you are up to date with your vaccination.

You may still need a booster dose even if you are up to date with your vaccination. Clean any wound immediately and thoroughly with soap and water or antiseptic and, if you have not been vaccinated against tetanus within the last 10 years or the wound is particularly dirty, get medical advice on having a booster dose of the tetanus vaccination as soon as possible.

MENTAL WELLBEING ————————

The author of the Sanskrit texts on which traditional Indian (Ayurvedic) medicine is based outlined three prerequisites for health: 'a balanced diet, proper sleep and a healthy sex life, and mental hygiene'. We've given you some guidance on the first earlier in this book (see the section Eating for Health at the end of the Staying Healthy chapter), we'll leave the second up to you, and in this chapter we discuss the third, keeping your mind healthy.

STRESS, PHYSICAL & MENTAL WELLBEING

You'll probably find that sooner or later you get stressed out by the travel experience. Stress is the traveller's diarrhoea of mental health on the road.

Everything that makes travelling good is also a potential source of stress. There's a different physical environment to cope with, your lifestyle is completely different and you've lost all your usual points of reference; in addition, you're cut off from your usual support network of family and friends. Language difficulties combined with unfamiliar social and cultural cues can make communication problematic, even on a basic level.

Often the lead-up to the trip has been less than relaxing, as you rush around trying to get things done before you leave, and you may be jet lagged for the first week. And then you're expected to enjoy yourself ...

Unless you're on a short trip, you may find it helpful to factor in some time and emotional space for adjusting to your new situation. You may want to bear in mind some of the following points:

- high levels of stress can make you less able to cope; even minor difficulties and setbacks can seem like insurmountable hurdles
- you may feel frustrated and angry, taking your frustrations out on your travelling companions and other people you have to deal with – not good for personal or international relations

- stress can make you feel anxious or depressed, irritable, tired, unable to relax, and you may have difficulty sleeping (although this is often due to external causes)
- because you don't feel 100%, you may think you are physically ill, especially as the physical manifestations of anxiety can easily be mistaken for illness – see Anxiety later in this chapter
- stress affects your immune system, making you more liable to infections. Conversely, being physically ill affects you emotionally, often making you feel low and less able to cope
- if you know you're sensitive to stress, or you've had emotional problems before (you may even have come away to escape them), you may find that, in the short term anyway, travelling exacerbates your problems

Half the battle is recognising that the way you're feeling is because of stress rather than some worrisome physical disease you've acquired. An acute stress reaction is to be expected to some degree at the start of your travels and will probably ease by itself over the course of a few days, but you might want to activate some damage-control measures:

▶ take some time off to unwind: quit the tourist trail for a few days and do something completely different
▶ rest and try to catch up on any sleep you've missed because of jet lag, overnight bus journeys or noisy hotel rooms
▶ exercise is a great de-stresser, and worth a try if you've been stuck in trains or buses, or you're on an overland tour
▶ catch up on missed meals – stress is very energy-consuming
▶ try a de-stressing routine like aromatherapy, massage, yoga, tai chi or meditation – see the chapter on Traditional Asian Medicine later in this book for more details on therapies that may be available locally
▶ talk with fellow travellers – they may be experiencing similar emotions

CULTURE SHOCK & TRAVEL FATIGUE

You experience a well-recognised set of emotional reactions following any major life event; when this occurs as a result of living (or travelling) for an extended period of time in a culture markedly different from your own, it's called culture shock. The culture shock syndrome is a well known hazard of living overseas for any length of time. It's unlikely to strike hard on a short trip, but you may notice it if you're on a long trip, especially if it is compounded by travel fatigue.

Culture shock is a sort of psychological disorientation which results from a conflict between your deeply ingrained cultural values and the different cultural cues and behaviours of the society you have relocated into. It seems that however broad-minded you may hope you are, deep down we all have a fundamental assumption that our own culture is right.

Four basic stages in adjustment can be recognised. Culture shock doesn't happen all of a sudden, it progresses slowly, affecting some personalities more markedly than others. Sometimes it doesn't progress, and you may get stuck at one of the early stages. If you've been travelling a while, you'll probably recognise some of the stages and symptoms, as identified by Myron Loss in *Culture Shock – Dealing with Stress in Cross-Cultural Living*:

- euphoria, when everything is new and exciting
- hostility as the novelty wears off and the differences start to irritate: you feel critical of your host country, stereotyping local people; you may feel weepy, defensive, homesick, lonely and isolated, and perhaps you are worried about your physical health
- adjustment is when you start to feel more comfortable in your new lifestyle and with the new culture
- adaptation occurs when you lose that 'us and them' feeling

Travel fatigue is bound to affect you after you've been on the road for many months. It's a combination of culture shock, homesickness and generally feeling fed up with the hassles and inconveniences of life on the road.

Some strategies for minimising the impact of culture shock on you, and people in contact with you, include the following:

▶ accept that everyone experiences some degree of culture shock, and be prepared to recognise the symptoms as such

▶ find out about the country, people and culture before you go and when you're away – surprisingly, it doesn't have a huge effect but there are other good reasons for doing it

▶ look after your physical health – it's easier to feel positive if you feel well

▶ friendships and keeping in touch with home can help you feel less isolated

▶ you don't achieve anything by succumbing to the temptation of disparaging everything local

▶ having a sense of humour can help you keep your head above water – just think what good stories you'll be able to tell later

ANXIETY

A certain degree of anxiety is a natural reaction to a change in lifestyle and environment, and you'll probably accept it as such. But there are situations when anxiety is a worry, either because it's over the top or because you misread the symptoms as something else.

Anxiety can take a number of forms, any of which can strike you for the first time when you're away, especially if you're a worrier by nature. If you have any preexisting anxiety-related problems, travel may exacerbate them.

For the forms of anxiety described in this section, we've suggested some short-term strategies for coping; you'll probably want to discuss longer term methods of anxiety reduction with your doctor when you get home, especially if the problem is new or persistent. This is important because some physical diseases like thyroid and diabetic problems can cause anxiety symptoms, and your doctor may want to test for these.

Generalised anxiety often affects worriers; you feel restless, irritable and tired, stretched to the limit, with tension headaches and sleep problems.

Any of the strategies listed earlier for stress reduction may help; also try cutting out coffee and strong tea, both of which make tension symptoms worse. Drug treatment is only indicated if your symptoms are very severe and disabling.

Feeling Anxious?

Anxiety is the body's way of preparing for an emergency: the so-called fight or flight reaction. Symptoms are a result of physiological changes that take place, and include:

- palpitations, missed heartbeat or discomfort in chest
- overbreathing, shortness of breath
- dry mouth and difficulty swallowing
- stomach ache, bloating and wind, diarrhoea
- needing to pass urine frequently
- periods stop
- premenstrual tension
- tremor and aching muscles
- pricking sensations
- headache
- dizziness and ringing in the ears

! Remember that alcohol withdrawal, perhaps after a binge or if you're a habitually heavy drinker, can be a cause of acute anxiety; it's best to avoid binges in the first place, and if you are a heavy drinker it's best to cut down gradually.

Panic attacks can occur without warning and can be terrifying. They're marked by frightening physical symptoms as well as thoughts, and there's rarely a recognisable trigger. You feel like you're suffocating, you can't get enough air, and have palpitations, light-headedness, faintness and pins and needles. Often you have a feeling of being outside yourself, and everything seems unreal.

You'll probably recognise the symptoms if you've had an attack before, but if it's the first time you may think you're dying. Sounds silly, but breathing in a controlled way in and out of a paper bag for a short time can help the symptoms of a panic attack. This is because when you panic, you start to overbreathe and this causes you to feel light-headed and gives you pins and needles.

The main thing is to recognise what's happening, and to be reassured that you're not having a heart attack, and that it will pass eventually. Some general stress reduction as described earlier is probably a good idea in the short term.

DEPRESSION

The blues can strike any time, even when you're on holiday. Stress, anxiety, disappointment, isolation and poor physical health can all make an attack of the blues likely. You know you've got it bad when you feel teary, listless, tired; you can't be bothered to do anything and nothing is enjoyable any more. You lose interest in sex and food (although sometimes you over-eat instead), you may have trouble sleeping and you just want to withdraw from the world.

Any physical illness can make you feel low, but some diseases are known for causing depression and fatigue, often for prolonged periods of time. Some notable culprits are viral diseases like flu, glandular fever and hepatitis; dengue fever is also notorious for this, and malaria. Other causes are anaemia and low thyroid function.

If it's just a simple case of the blues, you'll probably find you bounce back in a few days, especially if you can identify and deal with the cause.

▸ Try any or all of the de-stress strategies mentioned earlier and reassure yourself that it will pass.
▸ If you know you suffer from depression, try anything that has worked in the past.
▸ Exercise is known to stimulate the production of endorphins which are natural feel-good factors.
▸ Maybe it's time to stop and re-think what you're doing, and perhaps to head home.

If your depression is a follow-on from a physical illness, it may be reassuring to recognise this. It's also worth seeking medical advice as antidepressant drug treatments may be helpful in this situation.

Strange Experiences
Some serious illnesses like schizophrenia could theoretically be kick-started by the stress of travelling. If someone you are with starts experiencing unusual things like visual or auditory hallucinations, and delusions, they may need urgent medical help. They may not recognise that they are ill, which can make it frightening and confusing.

If you think you may be depressed and things haven't improved over a couple of weeks, you should think about getting medical help. Depression is an illness and it can be treated, with medication ('conventional' antidepressants or herbal remedies such as St John's wort) or counselling. Severe depression can be very frightening and if it's not treated, you're at risk of suicide.

PHYSICAL DISEASES & MIND PROBLEMS

Depression and tiredness can follow several diseases, as discussed earlier under Depression. Delirium can be caused by any serious physical illness, but especially infections. This shows itself as confusion, restlessness, disorientation, sometimes hallucinations, and it can be difficult to persuade someone who is delirious to stay in bed or to take treatment. Treatment of the underlying illness will settle it. If you or someone you are with is this ill, you need to seek medical attention urgently; in the meantime take steps to bring down a fever and make sure the person doesn't hurt themselves.

Alcohol withdrawal is a specific form of delirium, and strikes people who are habitually heavy drinkers who suddenly stop (for example if they're ill and miss their usual alcohol intake). It's a serious, life-threatening condition, and you must seek medical advice urgently

Some therapeutic drugs can cause mind problems. You may be aware that the antimalarial mefloquine can cause a variety of symptoms, from abnormal dreams to panic attacks, depression and hallucinations. They're all more likely if you've had emotional problems in the past, and your doctor will usually have recommended an alternative drug in this case. If you're taking mefloquine, it will probably have been prescribed well before you leave, and you'll have had a chance to deal with any potential problems before you go. However, if you do experience problems while you're away, stop taking it and seek medical advice about alternative protection. Since mefloquine is only taken once weekly, you should be able to organise an alternative antimalarial without any break in protection. For more details on antimalarial medication see the Malaria Pills section of the Before You Go chapter.

Some diseases affect the brain and can cause changes in behaviour or level of consciousness, such as concussion following a head injury (p407), meningitis (p126) and Japanese B encephalitis (p125).

ALCOHOL & RECREATIONAL DRUGS

It's not just a question of what these substances can do to you, it's also what they make you do to yourself. Before you begin a session, assess your situation for potential risks. You're much more likely to have an accident while under the influence of alcohol or other drugs, and you're more likely to take unnecessary risks that you might regret later, like having unprotected sex with a new partner.

You might want to be a bit wary of some local brews, especially distilled spirits, as they can contain additives you probably don't want to treat your system to. They can also contain methanol, a highly toxic form of alcohol which has the potential to cause permanent blindness among other things.

Other mind-altering substances are readily available throughout much of Asia. In most tourist haunts you'll be offered drugs at every opportunity. It's not surprising when you consider that most of the west's heroin comes from countries in or just outside Asia: Afghanistan, Pakistan and the Golden Triangle countries of Laos, Myanmar and Thailand.

It's a personal decision whether or not you take these substances, but be aware that there are legal and health consequences if you do. By definition, these substances affect your mental state – this is the reason you take them – but they can have effects that are unwanted or unexpected, especially if you're taking them for the first time. There's no quality control on the drugs you get, and locally available substances can be unexpectedly strong or may be mixed with other harmful substances. You are at the mercy of sellers when it comes to quality of ingredients, and their main concern is unlikely to be your good health.

Some unwanted effects you could experience include:

- acute anxiety or panic attacks – cannabis, LSD or mescaline; common, and more likely if you're taking them in a stressful situation
- acute paranoia – cocaine, amphetamines, ecstasy; can be very frightening
- an overdose – can be fatal anywhere, but especially where you can't rely on the emergency services

Because unexpected reactions can occur, including accidental overdose, you should never take drugs when you are alone. Anxiety attacks or acute paranoia are likely to resolve themselves without any specific treatment, although they may be pretty unpleasant at the time.

WOMEN TRAVELLERS

Travelling in Asia isn't particularly hazardous to your health but women's health issues are relevant wherever you go, and can be a bit more tricky to cope with when you are on the road.

PRACTICALITIES

It's a good idea to take with you all the sanitary towels/pads/napkins or tampons you think you'll need. Women all over the world menstruate, but they often have very different ways of dealing with it. In many countries, including Japan, Singapore and Thailand, tampons and sanitary towels are of good quality and relatively easy to find. However, in other countries in the region, especially in rural areas, tampons can be difficult or impossible to find and may be expensive or of poor quality. Sanitary towels are generally easier to obtain, but again you may not be able to find the quality or variety you're used to.

Disposal of used tampons and sanitary towels is a major concern, especially if you are travelling in remote or environmentally sensitive areas. It's an issue that doesn't only affect travellers, but you become more acutely aware of it when waste disposal systems are inefficient or nonexistent, as goes for much of Asia and India. There's no easy answer to this problem, although from an environmental point of view the best – but not necessarily the most practical – option is to burn them. If you're in a rural area, other options are to bury them carefully (dig a deep enough hole and cover it over with a decent layer of soil) or to carry them out with you and dispose of them carefully later.

Alternatively you could consider reusable items, such as washable sanitary towels, available from specialist shops selling environmentally friendly products, or tampons made from sea sponges, which can be washed out in cold water and replaced. Again, there are practical problems, as both these options rely on you having access to adequate water and washing facilities – often in short supply when you're on the road.

Another option you could investigate is a rubber cap device which is worn in the vagina, similar to an upside down diaphragm. You need to remove it every six to 12 hours, give it a rinse and replace it. Between periods you carry it in a cotton bag in your luggage. It can last up to 10 years. The Keeper is one brand, and they've got a web site (wouldn't you know it) at www.keeper.com where you can find out more.

You'll appreciate that cleanliness is even more important when you're travelling, and you're going to want to wash your hands carefully before and after changing tampons. Remember that most infective agents in the vagina come from your own bowel. Toxic shock syndrome is a rare but serious disease that can be associated with the use of tampons and, theoretically anyway, may be more likely in travellers. It's thought to be caused by bacteria entering the bloodstream from the vagina. The risks are very low, however, if tampons are used hygienically (ie if you take care to wash your hands carefully, change the tampons regularly and don't use them continuously).

MENSTRUAL-FREE TRAVEL

If all this sounds too daunting for words (for example, if you're going on a trek in a remote area) it is possible to take measures to temporarily prevent menstruation. If you think you will need or want to stop your periods for any reason while you are away, it's a good idea to discuss this with your doctor before you go.

If you're taking the combined oral contraceptive pill, you could carry on taking the pill without the usual break (or skip the seven days of inactive pills), although it's not advisable for more than three cycles at a time and, if you're unlucky, you may have some breakthrough bleeding.

Menstrual Myths

Heard the one about menstruating women being attacked by wild animals? The accepted wisdom is that many animals can detect menstruation in humans. Some monkeys, for example, are thought to be able to detect hormone cycles in humans and can react accordingly, although it's not to menstruation as such. In Asia, monkeys are probably the most likely hazard to you, as you may find yourself in close contact with them at temples and in urban areas. Monkeys can transmit rabies, so take care around them – never be tempted to feed them or walk around eating food when they are in the vicinity.

Be reassured that predators like lions are not thought to be attracted to menstruating women in any situation travellers would be likely to get themselves in to.

As for sharks, you'd probably want to avoid swimming in shark-infested waters anyway!

For a short trip, norethisterone (a progesterone) can be used to postpone a period. You need to start taking it three days or so before menstruation is due to begin and continue until the end of the holiday (for up to two to three weeks); menstruation occurs again two to three days after stopping. The dose is 5mg three times daily and side effects are rare, but it's not suitable for long term use. It's not a contraceptive.

Alternatively, an injected progesterone contraceptive produces light, infrequent periods or none at all in most women – great for when you're travelling, but you need to have injections every eight to 12 weeks and the effect on periods is initially unpredictable.

PERIOD PROBLEMS

If you normally get period pains and premenstrual bloating, you may find these are worse while you are travelling, for a variety of reasons, including physical and psychological stresses, unaccustomed heat and prolonged immobility (on long bus or plane journeys). If you know that you are prone to these problems, take a good supply of a painkiller or any other remedies that you know work for you, or you could consider starting the oral contraceptive pill before you leave (you'll need to sort this out well in advance of your planned departure date).

Alternative or complementary remedies include evening primrose oil, which can be taken in capsule form or as the oil, and vitamin B6, magnesium or calcium supplements. Herbal treatments that have been found to be helpful include the delightfully named Chaste tree (Vitex agnus castus) or dong quai (toki in Japanese), known as the Chinese women's herb. Ginger and cinnamon tea is used in Chinese medicine for menstrual problems. Acupuncture has been shown to be effective in the treatment of menstrual cramps, and Ayurvedic medicine (herbs, diet and massage), shiatsu and reiki can all be helpful and should be readily available depending where you are.

You often find that your periods disappear or become irregular periods when you're on the road, probably because of the mental and physical stresses of travel and the change to your usual routine. Other causes are pregnancy, drastic weight loss and hormonal contraceptive problems. Obviously the most important cause to exclude is pregnancy – see the section 'Am I Pregnant?' for more guidelines.

New, severe period pains can be a result of infection (eg sexually transmitted) or a tubal pregnancy (if there's a chance you may be pregnant), so seek urgent medical advice in this case.

If there's no chance you are pregnant, there is usually nothing to worry about, although if you don't have a period at all for more than about three or four months it's a good idea to get a check up. Periods usually get back to normal once you have finished your travels.

Light or absent periods are great, but you can find that your periods become heavier or more frequent while travelling, so to cope with this possibility take more supplies of towels or tampons than you think you'll need.

! If you are having heavier periods than usual, you may develop a mild anaemia – if possible, boost your diet with fresh fruit and green vegetables, or consider taking a multivitamin and iron supplement.

Heavy bleeding is often due to hormonal problems. If you suffer heavy persistent bleeding for more than seven days which shows no sign of lessening and you are in a remote area and unable to get medical advice, you could try the following treatment. This is only for emergencies, and you should not take it if there is any chance you may be pregnant or if you have a history of gynaecological problems or are otherwise unwell – you must seek medical advice in all these cases.

If you can find it, take norethisterone (a progesterone tablet) 5mg three times daily for 10 days. If you're prone to unpredictable bleeding, you might want to discuss taking a supply of norethisterone with you. Bleeding should stop by the end of the course and you should expect to have a period after about seven days of finishing the course. If the bleeding does not stop, you will need to seek medical advice urgently.

! Abnormally heavy or long periods can be an indication of problems with the cervix or womb (eg pelvic inflammatory disease, fibroids, miscarriage), so you should try to find a doctor to get it checked out as soon as possible.

MENOPAUSAL & POSTMENOPAUSAL TRAVELLERS

Hot flushes can be worse while you are travelling, as hot weather, spicy meals and any sort of emotional upset can trigger them. It's probably worth discussing this with your doctor before you go so you can work out ways of dealing with it; for example if you're not taking hormonal replacement therapy, this may be an option to consider.

Asian Menopause – Soy Good
Fed up with hot flushes? A trip to Asia may be just what the doctor ordered. Rates of menopausal symptoms vary in women throughout the world, and the good news is that the lowest rates occur in women in Asian countries. For example, about 80% of menopausal women in Europe suffer hot flushes compared with 18% in China, and there is a similar difference in the occurrence of bone thinning in postmenopausal women.

The reason? The humble soy bean. There are probably many other contributory factors, including genes, lifestyle and culture, but a diet high in soy products has been shown to be linked to low rates of menopausal symptoms.

When you are away, you could try simple measures to keep cool, such as wearing loose cotton clothing, not overexerting yourself, resting during the heat of the day and, if evening flushes are a problem, it may be worth making sure you have a room with a fan or air-conditioning. Cool drinks and eating small, frequent meals may also help.

Dry, itchy skin can be a problem at and after menopause. The physical hazards of travelling can exacerbate this, so it's worth taking particular care to protect your skin from the sun and wind by using sunscreen and moisturisers.

Cystitis can occur at any age but is very common after the menopause, and travelling can make an attack more likely. You'll probably already know if this is a problem for you – see the section on cystitis for more details on preventive measures and treatment.

!*If you're postmenopausal, and you're not on HRT, you need to seek medical advice for any vaginal spotting or bleeding that occurs, although if you're on a short trip, this can probably wait until you get back.*

Many alternative or complementary remedies can be helpful for menopausal symptoms, including the herb dong quai (for flushes), St John's wort (Hypericum perforatum; for depression), ginseng (to reduce sweating) and Bach flower remedies, so check these out with your practitioner before you go, and take a good supply with you. You might like to try traditional Chinese medicine, Ayurvedic medicine, shiatsu or tai chi for menopausal symptoms while you are away.

TRAVELLING ON HRT

As for any medication, it's best to take all you'll think you'll need with you; if you have an implant, will it be due for renewal while you are away? If you're swimming, or you're going to be travelling in the heat, sweating may mean your patches stick less well, so you could consider changing to a tablet or gel preparation before you go.

If you're taking a preparation that induces bleeding, it may be possible to change to a different one that induces periods every three months instead of every month if a period is going to be inconvenient while you're travelling. Periods can be postponed by manipulating your progestogen dose, but this can sometimes lead to heavy bleeding, so it's best to discuss this with your doctor before leaving.

HRT makes you slightly more prone to thrombosis (blood clots) in your leg veins or lungs, especially if you're immobile for long periods of time, for example on a long flight or bus journey – take regular walks and, when you're sitting, wriggle your toes and flex your calf muscles; alternatively you could wear support stockings or tights. Drink plenty as dehydration makes clotting more likely. If you're going to be at high altitude for any length of time, it's a good idea to discuss this with your doctor before you leave because this may make blood clots more likely

If you have been on HRT for some time and you develop heavy or irregular bleeding while you are away, it could indicate a problem with the lining of your womb (eg thickenings called polyps or even early cancer) and you should seek medical advice as soon as possible.

BREAST LUMPS

If you notice an irregularity or lump in your breast while you're on the road, see if it disappears after your period. If it's still there, and you're going to be away for some time, seek medical advice so that it can be checked out. If you're post-menopausal, it's a good idea to have it checked out as soon as possible.

CYSTITIS

This is an infection in the bladder, often caused by bacteria that normally live in the bowel. It's a very common condition in women, probably because the urethra, the tube leading to the bladder, is short in women (compared with men, who relatively rarely get cystitis), making it easy for bacteria to enter the bladder. This is also why bladder infections often occur after sexual intercourse, and are more common in women who use the diaphragm for contraception.

You're more likely to get cystitis when you're on the road because you often have to hang on for longer, and you may drink less. The answer is to drink plenty of fluids and empty your bladder at regular intervals.

Symptoms of cystitis include needing to empty your bladder more frequently but passing small quantities of urine, pain or discomfort on emptying your bladder and lower abdominal discomfort. If you think you have cystitis:

▶ drink plenty of fluids to help flush the infection out; citrus fruit juice or cranberry juice (unlikely to be available, but you can try!) can help relieve symptoms

▶ if available, an alkalinising agent like potassium citrate, sodium bicarbonate or sodium citrate can help relieve discomfort – preparations with various brand names are available over the counter in many western countries, or add a teaspoon of bicarbonate of soda to a glass of water

▸ if symptoms persist without improvement for more 24 hours despite these measures, you may need a course of antibiotics

If you have the symptoms described earlier, you almost certainly have cystitis, and it will almost certainly respond to one of the antibiotics listed as follows. If it does not, or if the symptoms recur quickly, you should seek medical advice so that a urine test can be done to clarify what's causing your symptoms.

Although traditionally longer courses are used, there is good evidence that single dose treatment is just as effective; it's also more convenient when you're travelling. Single dose treatment options (avoid all three in pregnancy) include trimethoprim 600mg OR norfloxacin 800mg OR ciprofloxacin 500mg. Other antibiotics (suitable in pregnancy) include amoxycillin 3g take two doses 12 hours apart (not if allergic to penicillin) OR nalidixic acid 1g four times daily for seven days.

If cystitis is left untreated, there's a risk of the infection travelling up to the kidneys, which causes a much more serious illness. Symptoms of a kidney infection include a high temperature, vomiting (sometimes) and pain in the lower back – you should seek medical attention in this case.

About a third of women with symptoms of cystitis don't have an infection (it may be a sort of 'irritable bladder' syndrome), so it's definitely worth trying some simple nonantibiotic measures first.

Also remember that 'cystitis' can be caused by a sexually transmitted infection, so you should get this checked out if you are concerned, especially if you have any other symptoms like an abnormal vaginal discharge.

If you know that you are prone to cystitis, arrange to take a couple of courses of treatment with you in your medical kit.

THRUST (VAGINAL CANDIDIASIS)

This common condition is due to an overgrowth of vaginal yeasts, usually the species called *Candida albicans,* which is present normally in the vagina and on the skin. Symptoms include itching and discomfort in the genital area and, often, a thick white vaginal discharge (said to resemble cottage cheese, but it can be variable).

A variety of factors, including diet, pregnancy and medications, can trigger the infection, which is normally kept at bay by the acid conditions in the vagina and the normal balance of organisms. Heat, the oral contraceptive pill, antibiotics and wearing tight trousers or nylon underwear can all make an attack more likely, so it's no surprise that it's even more common while travelling.

There's no evidence that it's a sexually transmitted infection, although it does make sense to treat your regular partner with an antifungal cream on the genital area for five days.

To help prevent thrush, wear cotton underwear and loose-fitting trousers or a skirt, and maintain a reasonable cleanliness regime (but note that some soap and bath salts can cause vaginal irritation and upset the normal acid environment of the genital area, so are best avoided).

If you do get thrush, the most effective and convenient treatment is a single dose of an antifungal pessary (vaginal tablet) eg clotrimazole 500mg. Short courses of three to 14 days are also available (eg econazole nitrate 150mg for three nights), but are less convenient. Alternatively you can use an antifungal cream (eg clotrimazole 1% OR econazole nitrate 1%) inserted high in the vagina (eg on a tampon) instead of a pessary. You should use this treatment even during menstruation. Antifungal cream can be used in addition to a pessary to relieve vulval itching. A vaginal acidifying gel may help prevent recurrences.

! If you know you are prone to thrush, take a supply of pessaries or cream with you in your medical kit.

Lesbian Health

Lesbians around the world have created some of the many resources that are now available to make your trip easier – it's worth the effort to do some research before leaving home. Make sure you are as healthy as possible before leaving home. You could check out a lesbian health guide like *Caring for Ourselves, The Lesbian Health Book* (Jocelyn C White & Marissa C Martinez eds, Seal Press) or any general women's health guides.

One of the many issues you might want to consider is the safe expression of your sexuality during your travel. Although many cultures allow a greater display of tenderness between women than the western world, this does not necessarily extend to overt displays of desire. Be sensitive and if you are not certain you can safely let your feelings be known, we suggest you wait. Web sites such as the following may help give you more of an idea of what you might encounter before you set off:

- www.utopia-asia.com/womens.html – a list of Asian lesbian resources
- www.qrd.org (Queer Resources Directory) – has a list of of organisations and publications worldwide including Asia

Other options, if you're in a remote area and can't obtain medication, include using natural yoghurt to soothe and help restore the normal balance of organisms in the vagina. You can use plain yoghurt directly on the vulva or dip a tampon in it and insert it in the vagina. Sitting in or washing with a weak solution of vinegar or sodium bicarbonate may also help.

If thrush is really being a nuisance, you might want to try some nonspecific strategies such as cutting down the amount of sugar and alcohol in your diet, and eating more plain live yoghurt.

Enjoy your travel experience, but remember that simple safe sex precautions are even more vital when you don't know your partner's medical history. Lesbian sex is low risk, but this doesn't mean that it's no risk.

Avoid touching or tasting blood or body fluids. Use gloves and dental dams or another latex barrier with plenty of wet stuff and your favourite water-based lubricant. Note that extremes of heat can melt dental dams in their packaging.

Depending on where you are travelling you may need to be creative, but never be careless. Do not share sex toys without washing them between each use; alternatively, cover them with condoms. Travelling into some countries with your toys on board can be a bit embarrassing, but let's face it, if tampons are in short supply then other womanly essentials will be totally out of stock. So plan ahead if you intend to play around.

If you need further guidance on what women safely do together, then check out www.safersex.org/lesbianss.html, call your gay and lesbian switchboard for a local clinic or visit any good gay and lesbian bookstore before you leave.

And a final warning ... beware the dreaded love bug. The authors of this section, one European and one Australian, met in North America fell in love and have never recovered ...

Leonie Englefield & Caz Price

OTHER VAGINAL INFECTIONS

Although thrush ('yeast' infection) is probably the best known cause of vaginal problems, and the one women are most likely to self-diagnose, it's worth remembering that it probably accounts for only 20 to 30% of all vaginal infections, which a relatively small proportion. If you think you've got thrush, but it's not getting better with treatment, it may be another infection.

If you've got a vaginal discharge that is not normal for you (eg more copious, abnormal colour, smelly) with or without any other symptoms:

▶ seek medical advice: you need a laboratory test to see what is causing it so that the most appropriate treatment can be prescribed

▶ remember that sexually transmitted infections (for example gonorrhoea) are an important cause of vaginal discharge – if you think you may be at risk, read the following section on Sexually Transmitted Infections

▶ if you've had thrush before and you think you may have it again, it's worth self-treating for this (see previous section)

▶ it's best not to self-medicate with antibiotics because there are many causes of vaginal discharge which can only be differentiated with a laboratory test – the treatment details given here are for guidance only, after the diagnosis has been made

Two important causes of vaginal discharge are trichomoniasis and bacterial vaginosis (you may recognise its old names: non-specific vaginitis or *Gardnerella* vaginitis).

Bacterial vaginosis is the most common cause of abnormal vaginal discharge. Although it is more likely if you are sexually active, there's no evidence that it is transmitted by intercourse. It's not caused by any one organism – instead there's a general change in the whole vaginal environment, with the good guys, the lactobacilli that normally keep the vagina healthy, being replaced by a variety of other bad guy species. It can cause a wide range of symptoms, but the most common are odour (fishy) and discharge (white-grey). Treatment is with an antibiotic, metronidazole 500mg twice a day for seven days.

Trichomoniasis is a sexually transmitted infection of the vagina caused by the organism *Trichomonas vaginalis*. It often occurs together with other sexually transmitted infections. Symptoms include discharge (thick yellow), itchiness and sometimes discomfort on passing urine. Just to confuse things, about 50% of women with the infection don't have any symptoms. Men rarely have any symptoms, but partners must be treated to prevent reinfection.

Treatment is with an antibiotic, metronidazole EITHER in a single dose of 2g OR 250mg three times daily for seven days.

SEXUALLY TRANSMITTED INFECTIONS IN WOMEN

Prevention is the name of the game here. Symptoms include sores in the genital area, any abnormal vaginal discharge and sometimes symptoms of cystitis. For a more detailed discussion, see the HIV/AIDS & Sexual Health chapter earlier in this book.

- Signs of a sexually transmitted infection (STI) are usually an abnormal vaginal discharge or sores in the genital area; sometimes it can cause symptoms of cystitis (see earlier).
- Casual intercourse is risky anywhere in the world; asking your partner to use a latex condom helps prevent transmission of STIs, but is not 100% effective.
- Having an STI can make you more vulnerable to HIV infection.
- STIs need to be diagnosed and treated properly as they can cause chronic pelvic inflammatory disease (in women) or infertility (women or men) later, so it's worth finding a doctor or clinic to get it checked out.
- It's important that your partner is treated for the STI as well.
- You may have an STI even if you have no symptoms – if you think you may have put yourself at risk, get a full checkup when you get home.

CONTRACEPTION

It makes sense to discuss your contraceptive needs with your doctor or a specialist family planning clinic well in advance of travelling. Even if you're planning on celibacy, it's always worth being prepared for the unexpected ...

There's a whole range of options available to you, so if one method doesn't suit, there's plenty more to choose from. Seek professional advice, but the table over the page summarises the major players, with some of the pros and cons for travellers.

!New sexual partner? Go 'double Dutch' – use a barrier method in addition to a non-barrier method to protect yourself against HIV and STIs.

AVAILABILITY OF CONTRACEPTIVES

Contraceptives are generally widely available in Asia and India, but it's best to take your own supplies as you may not be able to find exactly what you want when you want it. (Interestingly, until recently Japan was the only industrialised country not to sanction the use of the pill for contraceptive purposes – thought to be one reason for the prevalence of abortion here.)

If you need advice while you're away, you could try a local doctor, hospital or family planning clinic. If you do have to see a doctor, use common sense and choose someone you trust. If you can't find a reputable female doctor, insist on having a chaperone present if you need to be examined.

CONTRACEPTION & TRAVELLING

Travelling can present challenges for any method you use, so it's a good idea to discuss potential problems with your doctor before you leave.

IPPF

You can't visit Asia without being aware of the importance of reproductive health issues in many countries here, from China's controversial one-child policy to India's alarming population explosion. If you're looking for information on these issues, a good place to start is the International Planned Parenthood Federation (IPPF), a voluntary organisation concerned with all aspects of sexual and reproductive health.

IPPF can provide you with information on the availability of contraceptive methods in Asian countries, as well as local attitudes to contraception and abortion. They also have heaps of good information on contraception, sexual health (including HIV/AIDS prevention) and lots of useful resources and links.

Check out their web site (www.ippf.org) or contact them in the UK on ☎ 020-7487 7913 or by mail at Regent's College, Inner Circle, Regent's Park, London NW1 4NS.

method	advantages on the road	disadvantages on the road	protects against STIs?
combined oral contraceptive pill	effective and reliable; periods may be lighter and PMS less	only effective as long as you remember to take it! diarrhoea and vomiting, and some antibiotics, can reduce effectiveness; fluid retention may be worse in hot climates	No
progestogen-only pill	useful for a selected group of women (eg older women heavy smokers, migraine sufferers); not affected by antibiotics	effectiveness reduced by diarrhoea and vomiting; small margin for error if you forget to take it	No
hormonal implants	effective and reliable; nothing to remember or lose; not affected by diarrhoea and vomiting or antibiotics; periods usually lighter and may disappear; injection lasts eight or 12 weeks	irregular bleeding can be a problem, especially at first; if you're going to be away on a long trip you will need to arrange when and where to have the next injection	No
intrauterine copper devices ('the coil')	convenient – nothing to remember or lose; reliable	STIs more likely to cause long term problems, so this method is not advisable if casual sex is likely; tubal pregnancy may be more likely	No
intrauterine progestogen	convenient and reliable; period pains are improved and periods are usually lighter and may disappear; STIs less likely to cause problems than with the coil and less risk of tubal pregnancy	periods may be unpredictable at first	No
diaphragm or cap	no hormonal side effects	hygiene may be a problem when travelling; difficult to replace if lost; you need a refit (diaphragm) if you lose a lot of weight (4kg)	some STIs, but not HIV
female condom	available over the counter; less likely to rupture than male condoms	useability could be improved, but sense of humour may help	Yes
male condom	readily available; no mess – important if washing facilities are in limited supply; can be carried just in case	can split or leak – needs to be used correctly to be effective	Yes

Oral Contraceptive Pill

As for any medication, take enough (and some more) to last the entire trip, as your brand may not be available locally. If you are crossing time zones, or travelling at night, it can be easy to forget to take a pill:

- combined oral contraceptive (COCP) – make sure that you do not leave more than 24 hours before taking the next pill; take it earlier rather than later
- progesterone-only pill (POP) – the timing needs to be much more precise with this; if you're more than three hours late, you'll need to take additional contraceptive precautions for the next seven days

Vomiting or diarrhoea can mean the hormones are not absorbed properly and therefore that you are not protected. For either the COCP or POP:

▶ if you vomit or have severe diarrhoea less than three hours after taking the pill, take another pill
▶ if more than three hours, or if vomiting and diarrhoea persists,

---

Missed a pill?

If you miss a pill (either the combined oral contraceptive or progestogen-only pill), take the missed pill straight away, and take the next pill on time, even if it is the same day.

You'll need to use a different form of contraception for the next seven days in the following situations:

- progestogen-only pill: if you took it more than three hours late
- combined pill: if you took it 12 or more hours late

In addition, for the combined pill, if the seven days extend into the pill-free gap (or into the inactive pill interval), you should start the next course straight away without the usual break.

---

take the pill as normal, but take additional contraceptive precautions for the rest of the cycle

You should stop taking either the COCP or POP and use an alternative method of contraception if you get hepatitis (jaundice) as the jaundice can interfere with the usual way in which the body deals with the pill.

Be aware that some common broad-spectrum antibiotics (eg ampicillin) can reduce the effectiveness of the COCP (but not POP); the UK Family Planning Association advises that you should use additional contraceptive methods during a short course of these antibiotics and for seven days afterwards (the leaflet accompanying the packet will give you more guidance on which drugs to be careful with, but if in doubt, take additional precautions anyway). If you get to the end of the pill packet during the week after finishing the antibiotics, you should start the next packet straight away and take additional precautions.

Because one way your body adapts to high altitude is with an increase in circulating red blood cells, there's a theoretical risk that side effects of the COCP like blood clots in the leg veins or lungs may be more likely at altitude. If necessary, discuss the issue with your doctor before you go.

Intrauterine Copper Devices ('the Coil')
Remember that if you can't feel the strings, assume that you are not protected and use an alternative contraceptive method until you can get it checked out by a doctor.

!You should seek medical advice urgently if you develop low abdominal pain, especially with a fever and vaginal discharge; if you miss a period; or if you develop unusually heavy or painful bleeding.

Barrier Methods
See also Contraception in the Men Travellers chapter for more details on condoms. A couple of points to bear in mind:

- heat can cause rubber to perish so check your diaphragm for holes periodically, and try to keep it in a cool place
- consider taking a second diaphragm with you, especially if you are going to be away for a prolonged period of time

EMERGENCY CONTRACEPTION

In an emergency, you can try to prevent pregnancy following unprotected intercourse by taking a couple of high doses of oestrogen, which helps prevent the fertilised egg from settling in the lining of the womb.

Ideally, you should see a doctor who can prescribe the so-called 'morning-after' pill. You need to take two doses 12 hours apart, and you need to take the first dose as soon as possible within 72 hours of unprotected intercourse. The high dose of oestrogen may cause nausea and vomiting. If you vomit within two hours of either dose, the dose should be repeated. You should not take the morning-after pill if you are suffering from a severe migraine at the same time. Your next period may be either early or late. If you are taking the oral contraceptive pill, continue taking it as normal.

The morning-after pill is not 100% foolproof. It's for emergencies only and should not be used as a regular method of contraception.

The morning-after pill usually prescribed contains ethinyl-oestradiol 50µg and levonorgestrol 250µg, and the dose is two tablets followed by another two 12 hours later. The important ingredient is oestrogen, which is usually in the form of ethinyl-oestradiol.

If it's not practical to seek medical advice, then see if you can buy a pill containing the same dose of oestrogen (check the packet to see what dose of oestrogen it contains or ask the pharmacist to tell you), and treat yourself as indicated in the previous paragraph.

If you can't find a high strength pill, you could use a 'normal' contraceptive pill, as follows:

▶ if the pill contains 20µg of oestrogen, take five pills and then another five 12 hours later

▶ if the pill contains 30µg of oestrogen, take three pills and then another three 12 hours later

Another method of preventing pregnancy is to have an intrauterine contraceptive device inserted within five days, but you'd want a reliable doctor for this.

AM I PREGNANT?

If you have reason to be concerned about pregnancy, be suspicious if you miss a period (or have an unusually light one); other signs are enlarged, tender breasts and, although this is usually a later sign, nausea ('morning sickness').

So what do you do if you think you may be pregnant? It's probably best to continue (or start) using a reliable contraceptive method (there is no evidence that the contraceptive pill harms the fetus, for example, so it's probably best to continue taking it until you know for certain you are pregnant, especially if you are still sexually active).

Get a pregnancy test as soon as possible so that you have got plenty of time to make any necessary arrangements – you may be able to buy a kit from a pharmacist in some big cities, otherwise go to a doctor, clinic or hospital and ask for a pregnancy test to be done (note that a pregnancy test won't show positive before the first missed period). If it's negative, but you still think pregnancy is a possibility, wait two weeks and then repeat it.

If you're happy to be pregnant, you should see a doctor as soon as possible for blood tests and advice on optimising the outcome for you and the fetus. Some medications you may be taking (eg antimalarials) are known to be harmful to the fetus, also some diseases (eg malaria and hepatitis A and E) may be more serious in pregnancy. For more details on travelling while pregnant, see that section later in this chapter.

If you decide you want to terminate the pregnancy, timing

could be important: abortions are best done before the 12th week of pregnancy (counting day one of pregnancy as the first day of your last menstrual period). In many developed countries, abortion is effectively available 'on demand' but this is not the case in many parts of the world, including Asia and India. In addition to social and ethical constraints, it may also actually be against the law of the country, so you should check this as soon as possible.

In addition, consider carefully where you would want to have the procedure done – it may be worth changing your travel plans to accommodate this. Remember that any surgical procedure carries a risk of HIV or hepatitis B transmission in a country with less developed medical services. In addition, in less competent hands, abortion carries significant risks of infection, blood loss and permanent infertility. You should avoid a 'back street' abortion at all costs – these are notorious for resulting in death and illness.

PREGNANT TRAVELLERS

The days of seeing pregnancy as an 'indisposition' are long gone, and many women either choose or end up having to travel while they are pregnant, without any adverse effects on mother or fetus. However, there are some important considerations to bear in mind if you are planning to travel while you're pregnant, which we have summarised in this section. We should stress that this is to give you an idea of the issues that may be involved – you should seek expert medical advice well before you plan to go on any trip.

If you've had complicated pregnancies before or you're expecting twins, it would be best to postpone your trip.

WHEN?

Most doctors would suggest that the best time to travel in pregnancy is during the middle 12 weeks, when the risk of complications is less, the pregnancy is relatively well established and your energy levels are getting back to normal.

Before the 12th week, there is a relatively high chance of miscarriage (which could require treatment with a surgical procedure like a scrape of the womb lining and possibly a blood transfusion), or a tubal pregnancy, which occurs in about one in 200 pregnancies and nearly always requires surgical treatment – it's an emergency situation. In addition, many women experience morning sickness in the first three months (sometimes for longer), which could make travelling less than enjoyable. Occasionally, it can be severe enough to require treatment in hospital. More mundane, but just as incapacitating for travelling, is needing to empty your bladder more frequently as the enlarging womb takes up more room in the pelvis and presses on the bladder.

In the last three months, major complications such as premature labour, blood pressure problems and problems with the placenta can all occur, so you would probably not want to risk a trip of any length during this time.

!Note that most airlines prohibit flying after the 36th week of pregnancy (sometimes this can be waived if you have a doctor's certificate to say that there are no complications) – this is because they don't want to risk a woman going into premature labour on a flight, not because there's thought to be any intrinsic danger to the pregnancy.

WHERE?

When deciding where to go, you should take into account the standard of medical facilities for dealing with any complications that may occur, including the safety of blood for transfusion. For the same reason it's probably not a good idea to plan a trip to remote areas while pregnant, in case complications occur that need to be treated urgently.

It's sensible to avoid travelling to a high-risk area for malaria (like rural areas of Thailand near the border with

Cambodia, although the coastal resort areas are fine) because malaria is very much more serious in pregnant women, and can have disastrous effects on the fetus. Some of the more effective antimalarial drugs are not suitable to take in pregnancy, which makes it even riskier.

High altitude trekking or scuba diving, assuming you'd want to do either of these activities in mid-pregnancy, are not advisable either.

Some vaccinations are best not given in pregnancy, so this is something else to bear in mind before deciding where to go.

IMMUNISATIONS & MALARIA PREVENTION

Your best bet is to make sure you're up to date with all your vaccinations before you get pregnant! Generally, it's best to avoid all vaccinations in the first 12 weeks of pregnancy, as there's a theoretical risk of harm to the fetus they might increase the chance of miscarriage;. In addition, so-called live vaccines should be avoided at any time during pregnancy, although sometimes the risk of the illness outweighs the harm the vaccine may cause. Live vaccines include yellow fever and oral typhoid.

Note that an inactivated polio vaccine can be used instead of the usual oral live vaccine in pregnant women if necessary. A tetanus booster can be given safely in pregnancy, and tetanus protection is conferred to the newborn.

Hepatitis A is a common illness in travellers that can be prevented by vaccination. In pregnancy it can be a much more serious illness, so vaccination with immunoglobulin (the new, more effective, vaccine is live and therefore not advised) is an important preventive step, as is taking sensible precautions with food and water.

Taking antimalarials is considered safer than risking the disease in pregnancy. However, it's worth stressing that you should seek medical advice well before any trip, as most doctors would advise against going to a malarial area while you're pregnant. If necessary, chloroquine and proguanil are considered safe in pregnancy, although a folic acid supplement may need to be given with proguanil. Mefloquine can be used in the last 24 weeks of pregnancy, if travelling to an area with a known high incidence of chloroquine resistance, although it shouldn't be used for emergency treatment. If prevention fails, quinine is known to be safe in pregnancy for emergency treatment (for more details, see Malaria in the Fever chapter earlier in this book).

SPECIAL CONSIDERATIONS

All the predeparture preparations discussed in that section earlier apply to pregnant women too, but there are some special considerations too.

Be prepared, especially if this is your first pregnancy. It's a good idea to read up on pregnancy before you go so you have an idea of what to expect (eg tiredness, heartburn) and are familiar with any minor problems that may arise. Discuss these with your doctor, and work out strategies for coping in advance.

Discuss with your doctor, but all pregnant women should avoid unnecessary medications. Don't take any medications while you are away unless you know for certain that they are safe in pregnancy (read the information leaflet or packaging, or ask a reliable doctor or pharmacist). It's a good idea to take a well-stocked medical kit with you, having discussed fully with your doctor medications for common problems, so that you are clear on what you should and shouldn't take while you are away.

! Make sure you are clear on what your travel health insurance covers you for during pregnancy.

Long flights or bus rides increase the risk of blood clots in the legs, so if possible try to get up and walk around, drink plenty of water and consider wearing support stockings to reduce this risk on a long flight.

Every traveller should take steps to avoid illness, but this is even more important in pregnancy when illnesses can have more severe effects both on your health and on the fetus: prevent insect bites, take particular care with what you eat and drink, and avoid risk situations for accidents. During pregnancy, immunity is lower; infections, such as cystitis and chest infections, can be more severe and should be treated with antibiotics early. If possible, medical advice should be sought. In the tropics you may be less tolerant of the heat. Rest, drink plenty of fluids and give yourself lots of time to adjust.

Make sure you eat a well-balanced, nutritionally sound diet during the trip, avoiding in particular potential problem foods like raw or partially cooked eggs, peanuts and peanut products, and soft cheeses. You can get toxoplasmosis by eating undercooked meat in many countries in the region. It can cause a mild flu-like syndrome in adults, but can result in congenital deformities in the fetus.

To maximise your baby's health (as well as your own), don't smoke during pregnancy. Alcohol should be avoided in the first three months and, if necessary, taken only in moderation after this.

If you do need to seek medical advice when you are away, choose a reputable doctor and make sure there is a chaperone present if you need an examination.

MEN TRAVELLERS

There are some conditions that only men travellers are in line for … besides, we didn't want you to feel left out.

○ If a sexually transmitted infection is a possibility, turn to the chapter on HIV/AIDS & Sexual Health for more guidance.

JOCK ITCH (CROTCH ROT)

Hot, humid climates, tight underwear and infrequent washing all make this fungal infection more likely while you're travelling. It can occur in women, but it more usually affects men … as you might have guessed from these affectionate terms.

It produces itching and soreness in the groin area and inner thighs. Inspection reveals a red, flaky rash, sometimes with blisters. Keep the area clean and dry, but do not overwash with soap, as this may increase the irritation. Wearing cotton shorts rather than close-fitting underpants can also help. An antifungal powder or cream (such as clotrimazole, econazole or miconazole) should be applied twice a day for at least seven days.

PAINFUL TESTICLE

You should seek medical advice urgently if you develop a sore testicle. If the pain started suddenly, and the testicle is swollen and red, it may be due to torsion. This is when the testicle gets twisted, which cuts off the blood supply to it with the risk of irreversible damage. This is an emergency situation, as you may need surgery to fix the problem.

If the pain has come on more gradually it may be due to an infection, often a sexually transmitted one like chlamydia (common) or gonorrhoea (less common). You may have a fever as well as other symptoms such as a discharge from the penis, and the testicle will feel hot and tender. You will probably need a course of antibiotics to treat the infection, so it's best to seek medical advice. Pain in the testicle can be due to a problem elsewhere, for example stones in the urinary tract (see p157), when the testicle will look and feel normal to the touch.

LUMP ON TESTICLE

Feeling your testicles for lumps is a good habit to get into, although travelling may not provide the ideal environment for doing it in – it's usually best in a hot bath or shower. If you do feel a lump, or you think one of your testicles has changed in shape or feel (eg it feels harder) you should get this checked out as soon as possible. Testicular cancer, although uncommon, tends to strike younger men. If diagnosed and treated early, it often has a very good outlook. Note that it's normal for one testicle to be larger than the other, so you should be looking for any change in either testicle.

CONTRACEPTION FOR MEN

If you're planning on being sexually active with a new partner (or even if you're not), you'll probably want to make some preparations in this department. Your choices are limited, admittedly, and probably boil down to condoms, which are sensible anyway as you will need to protect yourself from STIs and HIV. Condoms are generally widely available throughout the region, although they may be difficult to obtain in rural areas and in places like the Philippines because of cultural and religious reasons.

Some points to bear in mind about condoms:

- rubber condoms can disintegrate in the heat – try to keep them cool if possible and check them carefully before use
- if buying locally, check expiry dates and buy only items that are likely to have been stored properly (out of direct sunlight)
- local brands may be less reliable than international brands, and sizes can vary, so you may want to take a supply with you
- many commonly available lubricants cause rubber to perish, so be careful with what you use

PROSTATE PROBLEMS

While there's no reason why you shouldn't travel if you've got symptoms of prostate enlargement, it's probably a good idea to discuss this with your doctor in advance, especially if you are going to be travelling in remote areas. That way you can work out strategies for dealing with any problems that might arise while you're away. The main concern is if you become unable to pass urine at all; in this scenario you will need to have a tube (catheter) inserted up the penis into the bladder to drain it manually. It's not something that you can accurately predict, so in certain situations it might be appropriate to take a sterile catheter set with you.

!If you are unable to pass any urine at all for more than 24 hours (you'll probably feel very uncomfortable before this) seek medical advice urgently.

TRAVEL HEALTH FOR GAY MEN

Glen Monks, UK-based Health Promotion Specialist for gay men and drugs, has the following tips for gay men.

BEFORE YOU GO

Try to get hold of the telephone number of a gay advice/support agency in the country(ies) you are visiting and also the number of an HIV/AIDS advice/support service or helpline. Try your travel guidebook or *Spartacus*, the international gay guide, which has listings for each country. Your local service at home should also have listings.

If you're HIV-positive, it's a good idea to consult your specialist for advice on possible risks before you travel – for more information on travelling with HIV, see the Travellers with Special Needs section in the Before You Go chapter.

CONDOM CARE

Extra-strong condoms and water-based lubricant form the essential safer sex toolkit for gay men. You need to protect yourself from HIV and other sexually transmitted infections (STIs) even more when travelling than you do at home. For more information about condom availability and care, see the section earlier. Note that in some countries it is impossible to find extra-strong condoms and water-based lube, so it's best to take a plentiful supply with you.

IMMUNISATIONS
See Immunisations in the Before You Go chapter for general recommendations on this, but note that hepatitis A and B can both be transmitted through sex and are fairly common among gay men. Hep A is passed on through human faeces, so sex or even handling used condoms may present a risk.

GAY ABANDON
Everyone, no matter their sexuality, tends to be less inhibited away from home. Letting you hair down and having some fun is fine, so long as you don't put yourself and others at risk.

Personal safety is paramount. If you're the new boy in town and agree to go back to some other guy's place are you getting into a vulnerable position? Is there someone else who knows where you'll be? How will you get home?

Remember that the law on sex between men varies greatly around the world, as does the policing of public sex venues and cruising sites. Public attitudes differ too, so find out about this before you go – try your travel guidebook or gay groups at home for information on this.

Be prepared: some people will be very up-front about safer sex and others very coy. The key thing, whatever your cultural disposition, is to avoid getting or passing on HIV and other STIs. To do this, however awkward it might feel and however many language barriers there seems to be, you will need to raise the subject of condoms and lubricant and make sure that you use them. Remember, you're the one on vacation, not HIV.

AFTER THE FUN
Few of us are saints all the time. If you have any concerns at all, it's a good idea to pay a visit to your sexual health or HIV clinic when you get back home.

BABIES & CHILDREN

The whole of this book applies as much to children as it does to adults, (except where we've indicated otherwise), but in this chapter we've highlighted some of the health issues that are especially relevant when you're travelling with babies or young children. Children can be surprisingly adaptable to climate and time changes, but you need to bear in mind that they are more susceptible to disease and accidents, and to take appropriate precautions to protect them. Children also change very quickly – they can deteriorate or improve within a matter of hours – so it's important to be vigilant, especially with young children.

BEFORE YOU GO

Good preparation is the key to a successful trip with babies or children so it's worth putting a bit of effort into this before you go.

CONSIDERATIONS

You might want to think about and perhaps do a bit of home-work on some of the following issues before you go.

Age

On the plus side, babies are easy to feed if they are exclusively breastfed, they're relatively easy to carry around in a sling and you don't need to worry about them getting bored by sightseeing. But they are a concern if they get sick, they can quickly become dehydrated and are very sensitive to heat and sun. Toddlers are more complicated to feed, transport around and to keep amused and safe, particularly around water! Obviously it's best to avoid travelling during toilet training …

Type of Holiday

Staying in a resort is probably going to be easier than a back-packing-style holiday that involves lots of long journeys, although this may depend on your children's temperament and ages. It's worth researching exactly what is available for the children before you go.

Health Risks

This can depend as much on the type of holiday you're planning as on the location. Backpacking through remote areas exposes you to more risks than staying in an upmarket hotel in a resort area. Don't assume that international-type hotels will necessarily have the standards of water quality and general cleanliness that you are used to. You may be able to get away with taking a few risks with your own health, but you may not want to take the same risks with your children's.

Medical Facilities

This is especially important to find out about if your child has an ongoing condition like asthma, diabetes or epilepsy that may need treatment while you are away.

SOURCES OF INFORMATION

For up-to-date information on current health risks of your destination and advice on immunisations, go to your family doctor or a travel health clinic at least six weeks before you intend to travel. It's best not to rely on your travel agent for health advice. See the earlier Before You Go chapter for contact details of travel health clinics and other information sources.

Some travel health providers and other commercial organisations have good leaflets and information sheets for travelling parents, including Nomad Travellers Store & Medical Centre (listed in Information Sources in the Before You Go chapter earlier in this book) and the UK-based chain of pharmacies, Boots The Chemist.

Many of the travel health web sites listed in the Before You Go chapter have items on travelling with children, some more informative than others. Try the TMVC web site for a good, helpful summary written from personal experience.

If your child has an ongoing condition (such as diabetes or asthma), contact your national organisation or support group as they often have good information for travellers – for more details, see the section on Travellers with Special Needs in the Before You Go chapter.

An excellent, comprehensive guide for parents is *Your Child's Health Abroad* by Dr Jane Wilson-Howarth and Dr Matthew Ellis. For a useful insight into travelling with children of various ages, Lonely Planet's *Travel With Children* has loads of practical suggestions.

DOCTOR & DENTIST

It's a good idea to make sure your child is as healthy as possible before you go. When you see your doctor to discuss any immunisations and malaria preventives your child may need, take the opportunity to discuss basic problem prevention strategies and to work out a plan of action for problems that are likely to occur such as diarrhoea or fever.

If your child has an ongoing condition like eczema, diabetes or asthma, it's best to be clear about what to do if the condition worsens while you are away, and to make sure you have a plentiful supply of any medications they normally take.

It's worth making sure your children have a dental checkup before going away, but remember to leave enough time for any treatment to be carried out if necessary.

IMMUNISATIONS

It's just as important for children to be protected against diseases through immunisation as it is for you. They should be up to date for all routine childhood immunisations and, in addition, they'll need the same travel-related vaccines as you – see the Immunisations section in the Before You Go chapter for more guidance on this. This is especially important if your child is going to be in close contact with local children while you are away. Most fully immunised school-age children won't need further doses of routine immunisations, but babies and younger children who haven't completed their normal childhood immunisations may need to complete the schedules earlier than normal. You should discuss this with your doctor when you start planning your trip.

Note that some vaccines have age limits or are best avoided in childhood. Discuss this with your doctor, but to give you some idea:

- diphtheria and tetanus (usually given with pertussis, as DTP) – the first dose can be given at six weeks of age if necessary
- polio can be given at six weeks if necessary
- measles can be given at six months of age if necessary (it's normally given as part of the MMR vaccine at 15 months of age); measles is common in many Asian countries and can be a serious illness, although mumps and rubella are less of a worry

Travel-related vaccines your child may need include:

- hepatitis A vaccine can be given from the age of one year (or two years in the US); younger children should be given immunoglobulin
- typhoid and meningococcal meningitis vaccinations aren't normally given below two years of age; note that young children may be more susceptible to meningitis
- rabies (preexposure) vaccine isn't normally given before the age of one year; you should be aware that children are more at risk of rabies because they tend to want to pat animals and they may not tell you if they have been bitten; they're also more likely to get bites to the head and neck area which carry a greater risk of rabies
- Japanese B encephalitis can be given at any age (although half the dose is used in children under three years of age); side effects tend to be more likely in children
- yellow fever can be given from nine months
- BCG (rarely used in the US) and hepatitis B vaccines have no lower age limit

If your child is going to have a reaction to an immunisation, this usually occurs about 48 hours after the injection and it generally settles with a dose or two of paracetamol (acetaminophen) syrup or suppositories. Note that children can have further reactions and sometimes develop rashes 10 days after the immunisation, so the earlier you get this organised, the better.

MALARIA PILLS

For more general information on malaria risk and prevention, see the Malaria Pills section of the main Before You Go chapter earlier in this book.

Note that it's generally not recommended to take babies or young children into malarial zones because they can rapidly become ill and die from malaria, so you should think very carefully carefully about putting your children at risk of this disease. Discuss this with your doctor or travel health clinic, but if you do take children into a malarial area, it's particularly important to protect them by using antimalarial medications and taking steps to avoid mosquito bites.

Chloroquine, proguanil and quinine are known to be safe in children of all ages, and mefloquine can be given to babies over three months. Mefloquine should be avoided if your child has any history of seizures. Doxycycline should not be given to children under 12 years because of potential side effects (may stain teeth and retard growth). Note that if you are taking antimalarials yourself and you are breast feeding your child, you will still need to give your child antimalarials.

! Be careful to keep antimalarials out of reach of children – even a few tablets overdose of chloroquine can be fatal in small children.

Getting your children to take their malaria pills can be a real challenge, as only chloroquine is available in suspension form (in some countries). You may have to resort to crushing the tablets into a powder and disguising them in a small amount of food or drink.

If it's a battle to persuade your child to take the medication, you may be tempted to stop as soon as possible; however, it's very important your child carries on taking antimalarials for four weeks after leaving a malarial area otherwise they are at risk of getting malaria.

EMERGENCY TREATMENT FOR MALARIA

If you are going to a malarial area in Asia (see the cautions in the previous section), it may be necessary to carry a dose of malaria treatment for your child. You need to discuss this fully with your doctor or travel health clinic before you go.

NAPPIES, FORMULA FEED & BABY FOOD

It's worth taking a plentiful supply of nappies with you. Washable nappies and liners tend to take up less luggage space than disposable nappies and are more eco-friendly. Generally, you'll find that the use of disposable nappies correlates with how 'westernised' a country is. You'll find them easily enough in Japan, Hong Kong and Singapore, and in big cities or tourist centres elsewhere, but they may be less easy to find, if at all, in other places, especially in rural areas. It's the same story for tins of baby food, although formula feed is widely available throughout most countries in Asia and India.

Disposing of nappies can be a headache as well as an environmental nightmare, especially in countries where waste disposal systems are less than ideal (most of the developing nations in Asia). Washable nappies (worn with a liner) rely on you having access to water and washing facilities but are a good alternative. You could burn disposable nappies (not a very practical option); otherwise, it's probably best to take a supply of large plastic bags or nappy sacks with you and to dispose of them as thoughtfully as you can.

MEDICAL KIT & MEDICATIONS

It's a good idea to take a child-specific medical kit in addition to your own basic medical kit (for detailed suggestions on what to take for yourself, see the What to Take section in the Before You Go chapter). If your child takes any medications regularly (for example for asthma, eczema or diabetes), remember to take a good supply of these with you.

You'll need to include something for pain and fever, for example paracetamol (acetaminophen) syrup or suppositories for little ones, Junior paracetamol (acetaminophen) for older children or ibuprofen paediatric syrup.

Consider taking a course of antibiotics with you for treating common ailments like ear infections or coughs, especially if you are planning on going off the beaten track, without ready access to medical care. Discuss your individual needs with your doctor but some suitable antibiotics include co-amoxiclav, cephalexin or clarithromycin (if your child is allergic to penicillin). See the section on Antibiotics in the appendix on Buying & Using Medicines for more details.

Take a plentiful supply of oral rehydration salt sachets, barrier cream for nappy rash, calamine cream or aloe vera gel for heat rash and sunburn, motion sickness remedies, sunscreen, antiseptic wipes and antiseptic liquid or spray. Sterilising

Medications to Avoid
Some drugs you might be prescribed if you get ill should be avoided in children under the age of 12 years because of the possibility of side effects. Drugs to avoid in children include:

- for pain and fever: aspirin and aspirin-like drugs
- antibiotics: ciprofloxacin and doxycycline
- antidiarrhoeals: loperamide, diphenoxylate, bismuth
- antimalarials and malaria treatment: mefloquine before the age of three months; Maloprim under one month; doxycycline

If you are uncertain about the dose or whether the medicine is suitable for children, check with a doctor before giving it.

tablets are a good idea for cleaning feeding utensils, or you might want to consider taking a sterilising unit with you.

If you do need to give your child medication, remember that they will generally need a child-sized dose, and that some medications are best avoided in children. Follow the dosing instructions given by your doctor or on the packet. Doses are generally worked out from how much your child weighs, so have a rough idea of this before you go away.

It's a good idea to carry plastic spoons (eg 5mL and 2.5mL capacity) with you for measuring out doses of liquid medications. A plastic syringe (5mL or 10mL) can be handy for giving medicine (and fluids) to a reluctant patient.

ON THE MOVE

Long journeys aren't going to be a bundle of fun with children, so be prepared! Consider arranging your itinerary to minimise the number of long journeys you have to do, or consider alternative means of getting around (such as flying instead of taking a two-day bus journey). For toddlers or older children, travelling at night may be one solution, although it might be exhausting for you. Take plenty of travel games, puzzle books, reading books, colouring books and electronic games. A new toy might just provide enough interest to last a journey.

Trains tend to have more scope for running around than buses. It might be worth checking on the toilet situation for any mode of transport you choose, although most bus drivers are likely to be sympathetic to the vagaries of children's bladders. It's always worth checking the seating arrangements for young children, as you may be expected to keep your child on your knees for the journey.

On flights, air pressure changes can cause ear pain in babies and young children – for more details, see the Ears section of the Ears, Eyes & Teeth chapter earlier. Older children can be encouraged to blow their noses. Younger children and babies can be given decongestant nose drops if necessary (get these from your doctor or pharmacist before you go) as well as paracetamol (acetaminophen) syrup to ease the pain. Give the syrup approximately one and a half hours before landing. If you are bottle feeding during the flight, try to sit the baby or toddler upright as far as possible as feeding can sometimes increase the ear discomfort. If your child has an ear infection or a bad cold, you should postpone flying until it is better.

You might also want to bear in mind that children can get thirsty and hungry on plane journeys very quickly, which is one preventable reason for bad temper.

Motion sickness is extremely common in children – if you know yours is prone to it, consider using an anti-sickness remedy like promethazine (follow the dosing guidelines, and note that it's not recommended for children under two years) or ginger. Promethazine has the added advantage that it often makes your child sleepy – possibly sanity-saving on a long journey – although the effects are very variable. A naturopathic alternative is chamomile, which can be soothing.

Coping with Jetlag

Travelling eastwards is potentially the most difficult for your child to cope with. Allow your child to get plenty of sleep. You could consider using a mild sedative, for example an antihistamine like promethazine. When you arrive, slot your child into their new routine immediately. Serve their meals at the correct time and put them to bed at the local time. Also spend plenty of time outside because light (particularly sunlight) and physical activity in the first half of the day will help the body clock to adjust faster.

Be aware that our body temperature falls during the night and initially this will occur in the middle of your new day. Even though you may have travelled to a warmer climate, your child may require warmer clothes for a few days before their body clock adjusts.

John Mason

You might want to make up some milk beforehand if you're bottle feeding, although it will only keep for a limited amount of time, or you can get bottles with powder and water which you can mix up when you need. It's always a good idea to take a few snacks and cartons of drink for giving out to little ones on the journey. A change of clothing is always good to have on hand in case of the inevitable spills etc.

STAYING HEALTHY

FOOD, WATER & CLEANLINESS

It depends to a certain extent on where you're going, but for most destinations in Asia, you'll need to be particularly careful about food and water, and be meticulous about maintaining good cleanliness habits. If possible, breastfeed babies and young toddlers as this reduces their risks of getting diarrhoea through contaminated food and water. If you give babies and children water, use only boiled water (allowed to cool) or bottled water, and if you are bottle feeding remember to use only boiled or bottled water to make up the formula. You'll probably want to avoid giving children carbonated and other soft drinks, but packet fruit juices and UHT milk are often available and make safe substitutes.

If you can, try to prepare any food for babies yourself, making sure that the utensils you use are sterile (take sterilising tablets with you). For more details on food to avoid, see the Safe Food section in the Staying Healthy chapter earlier.

Children who are crawling or just walking are particularly at risk of diseases spread via dirt, so take care to wash hands and faces frequently throughout the day, especially if you're travelling on public transport, and discourage wandering hands in the mouth, eyes and nose as far as possible. A supply of wet wipes can be invaluable, especially on long journeys.

If you get a bout of diarrhoea yourself, be extremely careful to wash your hands after using the toilet to avoid passing diarrhoea to your child. However, it works both ways: be careful with nappies and other sources of contamination if your child has diarrhoea to prevent it passing to you.

DIET & NUTRITION

Several factors may make your child less inclined to eat while you are away. New foods can induce surprise and a reflex refusal; stress and new surroundings can distract children from eating and the heat can often reduce even the healthiest of appetites. Try to introduce new foods gradually, perhaps starting before you leave, and consider taking a supply of familiar dry foods with you to provide an element of continuity. If the local cuisine is not proving a hit, western-style dishes are often available, especially in touristed areas. Take a spoon with you if you are going to a country where chopsticks are the norm.

If you're on a long trip, try to make sure your child has as balanced a diet as possible, including a source of protein (lentils, pulses, meat or fish), fresh fruit (peeled) and vegetables (peeled and cooked). Even if your child is not inclined to eat, fluids are a must, especially if it's hot.

INSECT BITES

Biting insects carry a number of serious diseases, including malaria and dengue fever, the current scourge of Asia, so it's extremely important to protect your child from this hazard. For more details, see the main section on Insect Bites in the Staying Healthy chapter earlier, but the main messages are to cover up with long-sleeved tops, long trousers and socks and shoes, and to use DEET-containing insect repellents or the new natural repellents containing lemon eucalyptus on exposed areas. Permethrin-soaked mosquito nets are very effective at preventing bites at night and during daytime naps (the mosquito that spreads dengue bites during the daytime).

Try to discourage scratching of bites if they do occur, as this often leads to secondary infection. Keep fingernails cut short and use calamine cream or a sting relief spray to ease irritation.

ACCIDENTS & OTHER HAZARDS

Children tend to be accident-prone at the best of times, but the hazards are even greater when you're travelling, so you need to be even more vigilant than normal. Road traffic is often chaotic and unpredictable, and pavements nonexistent. If you're travelling in a motor vehicle, seat belts and child safety seats are often absent. Most hotel rooms and restaurants are not built with children in mind and may have a nightmare-inducing lack of safety features, particularly where windows and balconies are concerned. Some sensible precautions include:

▶ look out for potential risk situations and unsafe features
▶ keep all medications in child-proof containers and out of reach of prying fingers
▶ try to be aware of what your child is doing at all times, especially if they're playing outside
▶ consider using a harness for toddlers when you're travelling or walking in crowded places
▶ make sure your child has some form of identification on them at all times, including details of where you are staying
▶ never let your child touch any domestic or other animals
▶ if you're planning to travel by car, consider taking a child safety seat with you
▶ drowning is surprisingly common – be particularly vigilant around swimming pools or at the beach, and remember that drowning can occur in shallow water as well as deeper water
▶ check new beaches for debris, discarded hypodermics, glass and tins as well as various offerings left by people and animals

Children's natural curiosity and fascination with all creatures great and small also make them more vulnerable to insect and scorpion stings, snake bites and animal bites. For details on these hazards, see the Bites & Stings chapter later in this book.

CUTS & SCRATCHES

This is something else that's worth being particularly vigilant about, as it can be difficult to keep children clean, especially if they are running or crawling around. Any break in the skin

Poisonous Plants

Small children are attracted like magnets to plants, particularly if the plants are colourful and look appetising. Toddlers will eat almost anything, regardless of taste. Children need to be supervised, especially if they are somewhere outdoors with access to plants and bushes. Contact with some plants and grassess may go unnoticed until a reaction occurs.

Some plants and grasses can cause toxic or allergic reactions when they come into contact with bare skin, so it's best to make sure your child is covered up if they are playing in grassland. This will help protect them from insect bites too.

If you catch your child eating a plant, keep a sample for identification. Watch for any symptoms, and encourage your child to drink plenty of fluids to help dilute any potential toxic effects. If possible, seek expert advice. If this is not available, you can induce vomiting by giving your child ipecacunha syrup (if you can find it) – but be aware that some experts believe children should never be given ipecacunha. This is usually only effective within four hours of eating a suspect plant, but it may be worth trying while you find medical help.

can rapidly become infected in warm, humid climates; wash any break in the skin carefully with soap and water or antiseptic solution (or an antiseptic wipe if you haven't got access to water) and keep it covered with a sterile, non-fluffy, non-adherent dressing (eg a sticking plaster if the wound is small). It's worth checking your child carefully at the end of each day for cuts, scratches and potentially problematic bites. Itchy insect bites are a common cause of infection – another reason for making a strenuous effort to avoid them in the first place.

HEAT & SUN

If your child is not used to strong sun and a hot climate, they will need time to get used to it. Babies and children can become dehydrated relatively easily and require a significant increase in their fluid intake, especially if they are not used to the heat. As a general rule you can double their fluid intake. Consider sprinkling a little extra salt on their food as salt can be lost through sweating, especially to start with. You could also encourage them to eat lots of juicy fruit and vegetables. Keep an eye on how much urine they are passing – small amounts of dark urine or dark urine stains on nappies in babies mean you need to increase their fluid intake.

Little ones can get sunburnt very quickly and need to be protected from the sun's harmful rays. Keep them covered up as much as possible (eg long-sleeved T shirt and long trousers or skirt and hat, or an all-over sunsuit – popular in Australia, but available elsewhere), apply liberal amounts of the highest factor sunscreen you can find on any exposed areas, and re-apply frequently, and avoid the sun during the middle of the day when it is at its fiercest. Beware the strong reflections of the sun from sand and water. Not only is sunburn miserably painful for your child, it's thought to be a major risk factor for skin cancer in later life.

! If you're carrying a child in a baby-carrier backpack, remember that they are exposed to the elements, and protect them against sunburn, heat exhaustion and the cold.

ALTITUDE

If you're planning on going to any of the high altitude areas in Asia (such as the Himalaya or the Karakoram), remember that children are as susceptible to the effects of altitude as adults, and they may not be able to tell you they have symptoms. Read the section on Altitude in the Climate, Altitude & Action chapter earlier for more details. The symptoms of altitude sickness (such as headache, nausea, vomiting) may be nonspecific, mimicking other childhood illnesses, so it is particularly important for you to be aware of the possibility, and to be confident you can recognise these symptoms in your child.

Children are at greater risk of the effects of the cold, especially if they are immobile (eg when they're being carried) so appropriate clothing and other layers is vital.

IF YOUR CHILD FALLS ILL

Children are at risk of the same diseases as you are when you are away, so unless otherwise indicated, you can follow the guidelines given in the main text. Because children can't always tell you what's wrong and in many cases don't show typical symptoms of diseases, it's even more important to seek medical help at the earliest opportunity, and always seek medical help urgently if you have any concerns about their condition. Local doctors and healthworkers will be very experienced in dealing with all common childhood problems, so getting reliable help shouldn't be a problem even in less-touristed areas.

IS MY BABY/CHILD UNWELL?

Children can quickly change from being well and active to becoming ill, sometimes seriously ill. In young children, especially, the signs can be quite subtle and difficult to interpret, which can be worrying.

As the parent you will know your child best of all and any change in their behaviour should be taken seriously – listen to your sixth sense. This is particularly true of young children. Babies up to six months may become quieter than usual, miserable and crying. They may not want to feed or drink or they may develop more specific signs, such as diarrhoea, a cough, vomiting or a rash.

Don't rely on a child's skin temperature as an indication of whether they have a fever or not. Always carry and use a thermometer, preferably a digital one, or a fever strip. It is important to have an actual reading of the temperature. A cold child to touch may have a raging temperature and the other way around.

Older babies and toddlers may just not 'perform' as well as you are used to. They may stop walking, stop sitting up, stop feeding themselves or being as generally developed as you are used to. Children of this age are unable to tell you what's wrong and this may be the only sign before a rash or a cough appears. If you have any cause for concern check the temperature and make sure your child is taking at least enough fluids to pass urine twice a day, even if they have gone off their food.

FEVER

This is very common in children wherever they are, and is always a cause for concern. In addition, a high temperature can sometimes cause a convulsion in babies and young children. Skin temperature is a confusing and unreliable sign. If you think your child has a fever, for example if she's flushed and irritable and obviously unwell:

- ▶ take her temperature (see p106 for how to do this) and take it again 30 minutes later as a check
- ▶ put your child to bed, remove most of her clothing (perhaps covering her up with a cotton sheet) and make her comfortable (under a mosquito net if necessary)
- ▶ wipe her face and body with a sponge or cloth soaked in tepid (not cold) water or place her in a tepid bath to help lower the temperature
- ▶ giving paracetamol (acetaminophen) syrup or tablets will also help to lower the temperature – you can give them every four to six hours
- ▶ prevent dehydration by giving small amounts of fluid often – make up oral rehydration salts with bottled or boiled water, or packet or fresh fruit juice diluted half and half with safe water; give 5mL every 15 minutes for the first hour

Remember that conditions like viral infections, colds, ear infections, urine infections and diarrhoea occur commonly, but always bear in mind the possibility of malaria or dengue fever if you've been travelling in risk areas.

Febrile Convulsion

If your child's temperature quickly rises high, she may have a fit, whatever the cause of the fever. This generally occurs in young children up to five years of age. If this occurs:

- try not to panic
- don't try to restrain your child's movements, but do remove any sharp objects from the area to prevent her injuring herself
- don't put anything in her mouth
- when the movements subside, roll her onto her side so that she can breathe freely
- comfort her when it has stopped, then take measures to cool her – fans, tepid spongeing, tepid baths, paracetamol
- seek medical help

Take steps to lower the temperature and seek medical help urgently in any of the following situations:

▶ if the temperature is over 37.7°C (100°F) in a baby of less than six months
▶ if the temperature is over 39°C (104°F) in any infant or child
▶ if your child has had fits in the past
▶ if it could be malaria; malaria should be suspected with ANY high fever if you are in a malarial area
▶ if the fever shows no sign of improving after 24 hours (take your child's temperature regularly to see if it's going up or down)

MALARIA

Children can rapidly become very ill with malaria, and it's easy to miss the diagnosis because the symptoms can be very vague. You need to suspect malaria if your child develops a fever with or without flu-like symptoms that persists for more than eight hours if you are in or have visited a malarial area within the last few months.

Seek medical help urgently for a blood test, and treatment if the test is positive. If you are in a remote area without access to medical help, you'll need to give your child emergency treatment for malaria while you seek medical help. Ideally this is something you will have discussed with your doctor before you left.

DIARRHOEA

Children, especially young children and babies, are more likely than adults to get diarrhoea when they are away. They also tend to get more severe symptoms, for longer. It's partly because children tend to be indiscriminate about what they put in their mouths and it's hard to keep them clean, but it may also be because they have less immunity than adults to disease-causing microorganisms.

Babies and children can become rapidly dehydrated through diarrhoea and vomiting, and it can be difficult to make sure they drink enough. The best fluids to give children are oral rehydration salts (ORS). You need to start giving them ORS as soon diarrhoea or vomiting appears – you can make this more palatable by adding flavours (eg juice of an orange) or different flavoured sachets may be available. Avoid food if they are actively vomiting.

You don't need to give your child ORS if you're breast-feeding, but make sure you're taking in enough fluid yourself. If your child is being fed a milk-based formula, you need to replace this with oral rehydration salts until the diarrhoea is better. As the diarrhoea improves, introduce diluted milk feeds, then solids.

For older children, follow the same dietary guidelines as for adults, avoiding milk and milk-based products until your child is on the mend. The World Health Organization gives the following guidelines for the quantity of fluid replacement:

- under two years – one-half to one-quarter cup per loose stool
- two to 10 years – one-half to one cup per loose stool
- over 10 years – as for adults (see p139 for more details)

If children are vomiting, allow the stomach to rest (eg for an hour) before trying to give fluids, then reintroduce fluids very slowly – 5ml every 15 minutes for the first hour, and building up from there. If your child is refusing to drink, try giving small amounts by teaspoon or syringe every few minutes.

Seek medical help earlier rather than later, especially if you notice any of the following symptoms developing:

- prolonged vomiting and diarrhoea
- refusal to take fluids
- listlessness
- fever
- blood or mucus in the diarrhoea

In children, faeces may take 10 to 14 days to return to normal, sometimes longer following an episode of diarrhoea. As long as the faeces are not too frequent parents should not worry about slightly loose faeces in an otherwise fit and recovered child.

!Note that antidiarrhoeal medications (especially ones that may be available locally) are not recommended in children and should be avoided (apart from ORS and the anti-biotics recommended in the diarrhoea section).

TUMMY ACHE

This is a very common complaint, as it is in adults. The causes are many and varied, some more serious than others. If your child is prone to tummy aches, the stress of travelling may make them more likely while you are away. Otherwise, situations when you should seek medical help include:

- any tummy ache with a fever (could be malaria, typhoid, bladder infection etc)
- severe tummy ache that is continuous for more than three hours (could be appendicitis)
- tummy ache with profuse vomiting and diarrhoea – the danger is dehydration
- tummy ache that's not normal for your child, especially if she's generally unwell

COLDS, COUGHS & EARACHE

Children are particularly likely to succumb to new germs in new places, so be prepared! Asthma (cough, wheezing) may occur for the first time while you are away, and can be frightening especially if you or your child have not experienced it before. You should seek medical advice if your child is having difficulty breathing, especially if you notice that their ribs are being drawn in with each breath.

Swimming can make ear infections more likely – see the Ears section in the Ears, Eyes & Teeth chapter for more details. Remember that if your child has grommets in their ears, they shouldn't swim.

HEAT

Children tend to acclimatise relatively easily, but remember that young children (with their greater surface area relative to their body mass) can lose fluid through sweating very rapidly and become dehydrated and vulnerable to heatstroke. Babies and young children may not be able to tell you how hot they're feeling, so be aware of this and make sure they're dressed appropriately. Discourage mobile youngsters from rushing around in the heat of the day.

PRICKLY HEAT & NAPPY RASH

Prickly heat tends to be more of a problem in children than in adults. Calamine cream can soothe the irritation, and you can help prevent the rash by dressing children in loose cotton clothing, bathing them often and drying them carefully, especially any skin folds and under their arms.

Nappy rash can be a lot worse in the heat. Take a good supply of barrier creams (for example petroleum jelly, zinc and castor oil cream or Sudocrem), and avoid plastic overpants. Wash the area with water after any bowel action, dry it well, apply barrier cream and try to keep the nappy off as much as possible. If the area is red and painful and doesn't go away with simple treatment, the rash may be due to a fungal infection. In this case, try treating it with an antifungal cream (eg clotrimazole, trade name Canesten, or with hydrocortisone eg Canesten HC if it is very red and painful) applied twice daily. Check their mouth, as they may have a fungal infection (thrush) there as well, indicated by white patches that are difficult to remove.

Treatment is with antifungal drops (such as nystatin). Remember to change rubber teats and feeding utensils as soon as treatment is started and halfway through.

INSECT STINGS

Children seem to attract bees and wasps like the proverbial honey pot, so be prepared with sting relief spray and lots of sympathy. Take plenty of insect repellent and sting relief sprays and cream. If you know your child is allergic to bee stings, discuss this with your doctor before you leave.

AFTER YOU GET BACK

Consider getting a checkup for you and your children if you've been on a long trip or have been travelling rough. Children are particularly likely to pick up intestinal parasites like worms, so a test for this is a good idea when you get back. This is a simple stool test, which your family doctor can arrange. If there's any chance your child may have swum in bilharzia-infected water, you'll need to get this checked out. Remember the possibility of malaria if your child gets an unexplained fever after you get back, particularly within the first month or so, but up to a year after. Tell your doctor if you have been travelling and where.

OLDER TRAVELLERS

We hardly need to tell you that age is no barrier to travelling. The thousands of older travellers (we're taking this to mean 60 plus) who go trekking in Nepal, sightseeing in India and relaxing in Thailand are ample proof of the increasing mobility of older people. More and more older travellers are opting for 'adventure' type holidays, as well as traditionally popular less active options like cruises.

BEFORE YOU GO

You don't have to be young and in perfect health to enjoy a trip to Asia, but good preparation helps to minimise the chances of problems while you are away.

SOURCES OF INFORMATION

Make sure you get reliable advice on current health risks and possible hazards at your destination, as well as the availability of adequate medical services at your destination. Good sources of information are specialist travel health clinics – see the Before You Go chapter for more details.

If you have an ongoing condition – such as heart or lung disorder, arthritis, diabetes or kidney dialysis – your specialist physician will be able to give you advice on travel hazards. For more information, see the section on Travellers with Special Needs in the Before You Go chapter earlier in this book.

IMMUNISATIONS & MALARIA PREVENTION

Being older doesn't mean you're immune – immunisations are just as important as for younger travellers, perhaps more so as older people are more susceptible to disease as immunity wanes with age. It's a good idea to get this checked out well in advance of travelling as you may need full courses of some immunisations. See the Before You Go chapter for more details of the travel-related immunisations you may need for your trip. In addition, if you are over 65, it's a good idea to be immunised against flu and possibly pneumococcal disease, if this is available, before you travel. You may be more at risk of the flu and pneumonia when you're travelling, and you don't want to waste your trip being ill.

If you need to take antimalarials, be aware that some antimalarials may interact with your regular medications (for example mefloquine should not be taken if you are taking beta blockers for a heart condition), if any, so it's a good idea to check this with your doctor.

MEDICAL CHECKUP

As well as getting travel health advice, it's probably a good idea to visit your doctor for a checkup before you go, especially if you are planning on doing anything strenuous like trekking, visiting extreme climates or going to altitude.

Preexisting Medical Conditions

It's not age itself that is a problem, it's that as you get older, you are more likely to have an ongoing medical condition. Although older travellers are less likely than their younger counterparts to get sick when travelling, the outcome is more likely to be serious. For older travellers, the most common cause of death is from preexisting conditions like heart disease.

Some medical conditions can affect your ability to cope with the physical and environmental challenges that travelling may involve; for example travellers with heart or lung conditions may find the heat more difficult to cope with.

It also means that you are more likely to be taking medications regularly. Travel-related diseases like diarrhoea and vomiting can affect the absorption of medications. The more medications you take, the more likely side effects are to occur.

It's important to find out before you go what the medical facilities are like at your destination. If you are on an organised tour or trek, find out what provisions they have for dealing with medical problems.

If you have any medical conditions like heart or lung problems, diabetes, kidney failure or recent medical or surgical treatment, check with your doctor that you are fit to travel. It's also a good opportunity to discuss any potential problems you may encounter while you are away and to clarify what to do about them if they do occur.

If you're intending to go scuba diving, you'll need to have a medical performed by a specialist diving doctor. This is particularly important as older divers and those with preexisting conditions are more likely to suffer serious problems. See also the section on Scuba Diving in the Water chapter.

DENTAL CHECKUP

This is a good idea if you are going away for more than a couple of weeks. If you wear dentures, have them checked before you leave home. Make sure you wear in a new pair of dentures before you go away, as adjustments may be required during the first month to make them comfortable. Consider taking a spare pair with you; you may have an old pair which your dentist could modify to make them useable in an emergency.

Getting a new set of dentures while you're away could be a major problem. However, simple temporary repairs may be carried out by a dentist or you can make a simple repair yourself, like sticking a tooth back on, or sticking a broken denture back together, using glue. If you use an epoxy glue, be careful not to put them back in your mouth before the glue has set ...

EYES

If you wear glasses, remember to take a spare pair with you, as well as the prescription in case you need to replace them. See the section on Eyes in the Ears, Eyes & Teeth chapter for more details.

FITNESS PREPARATION

You might want to consider starting a gentle exercise program well before you go, especially if you're out of the habit of doing much exercise. Travelling can involve a lot of standing around and lifting luggage on and off luggage racks, and negotiating your way around large airports and other transport terminals can involve a lot of walking, perhaps carrying heavy luggage. Sightseeing can also be surprisingly exhausting.

Obviously, if you're planning a trek or other strenuous exercise, you will want to prepare well in advance. Avoid activity-related injuries by warming up and stretching properly before you start and when you finish.

Finally, don't be overambitious with your travel itinerary – it's better to do less comfortably than to push yourself too hard and perhaps regret it.

TRAVEL INSURANCE

It's important for everyone to have travel health insurance, but it's particularly important for older travellers with preexisting illnesses. See the main section on Travel insurance in the Before you Go chapter for more details, but always check the small print carefully to see what the policy covers you for. Try to find a policy that provide a 24-hour hotline for assistance on the spot, finds hospitals or flies you out in an emergency situation.

MEDICAL KIT & MEDICATIONS

It's a good idea to take a well-stocked medical kit with you, including a plentiful supply of any regular medications plus a bit extra. You don't want to run out at an inopportune moment and replacements may not be easy to find. Always keep an adequate supply of your medications on you as well as in your luggage, in case you lose your luggage.

The What to Take section in the Before You Go chapter gives detailed guidance on what you might want to consider taking with you in a medical kit. In addition, if you suffer from severe prostate trouble, you might want to consider taking a sterile catheter set with you – discuss this with your doctor if necessary.

Medicines

If you're on any regular medications, remember that these can interact with medicines you may be prescribed for a travel-related problem.

- some medications can make very you sensitive to the effects of the sun – see p291 for more details
- pseudoephedrine hydrochloride (decongestant) don't take if you have raised blood pressure
- hyoscine (for travel sickness) – best avoided if you have glaucoma or prostate problems
- antimalarials and some drugs for heart problems

You could consider getting bracelets or tags engraved with any medical conditions, medications and drug allergies to carry on you. MedicAlert is an organisation that provides these, together with a toll-free number to call in emergencies – see Useful Organisations in the Before You Go chapter for contact details.

ON THE MOVE

Keep any regular or as-needed medications (eg for angina) in your hand luggage so you can access them readily if necessary.

Sitting immobile for long periods of time can make your feet and ankles swell and may possibly increase the risk of blood clotting in the legs, especially if this is something you are prone to. Wriggle your toes, flex your calves and get up and move around periodically if you can. Drink plenty of non-alcoholic fluids to prevent dehydration. Discuss this with your doctor, but it may be advisable to take low dose aspirin (75mg) before, during and after the flight. Alternatively, some doctors may suggest an injection of a blood-thinning agent like heparin. It's not all bad news – older travellers tend to suffer less from jet lag than younger travellers.

STAYING HEALTHY

All the general, common-sense measures suggested in the Staying Healthy chapter earlier in this book are just as relevant to older travellers.

Acclimatisation to hot climates shouldn't be much of a problem if you are normally physically fit and you take some sensible precautions like avoiding strenuous exercise and drinking plenty of fluids. As you get older, you tend to acclimatise less well and older travellers are more likely to faint in the heat. If you're overweight or have preexisting conditions like heart and lung problems or diabetes you may find it more difficult to acclimatise, and some medications may need to be adjusted in hot weather. Discuss this with your doctor before you leave. Remember that it's very easy to become dehydrated, especially if you're taking heart medicines that make you lose fluid or if you have diarrhoea. Drink plenty of cool safe fluids, don't over exert yourself and allow yourself lots of rest time.

Older travellers are less likely to suffer from diarrhoea while travelling, perhaps because they are more discerning about where and what to eat than younger travellers. If you do get diarrhoea and/or vomiting, remember that this may mean that your usual medications are absorbed less well. You are also at more risk of dehydration, so seek medical help earlier rather than later. On the other hand, constipation is a common complaint. Eat lots of fresh fruit (peeled) and vegetables (cooked) and keep up your fluid intake. If you are prone to constipation, take a supply of a remedy you know works for you.

Air pollution is a major issue in many large urban areas in Asia. You should probably avoid problem areas, especially at peak times like the winter months, if you suffer from heart or lung conditions.

If you're reasonably fit, altitude shouldn't pose any particular problems. In fact you may be safer because you're more likely to ascend slowly, allowing time for acclimatisation.

IF YOU GET ILL

Follow the guidelines given in the individual sections, but remember that many drugs interact with each other so if you are taking any medicines regularly, check this with your doctor or pharmacist.

CLIMATE, ALTITUDE & ACTION

○ For guidelines on safe sun exposure and acclimatisation, see the Staying Healthy chapter.
○ For advice on keeping feet happy and healthy, see the section on Feet (p199) in the Skin chapter.
○ Need guidance on fuelling up? See the Food for Action section on p101.

Part of the allure of Asia is its great environmental and climatic diversity, from the snows and mountain peaks of the Himalaya to the tropical beaches of southern Thailand. If you know what to expect and are well prepared, you should be able to cope with most environmental and climatic hazards.

SUN

SUNBURN

We'd like to think, of course, that after following all the advice about preventing sun damage on p72, you won't need to read this section, but just in case ...

The trouble with sunburn is that it comes on gradually, unlike burns from other causes, and you often don't notice it until it's too late. Sunburn can vary from just a mild redness with some soreness to more severe swelling with blistering.

For mild sunburn, take the heat out of the burn by using damp cloths and a fan, and try simple painkillers like aspirin or paracetamol (acetaminophen) if necessary. There are lots of skin treatments you could try – the best known are perhaps calamine cream (messy but effective) and aloe vera gel, but there's also a huge selection of commercial 'after sun' products. However, avoid greasy creams as these trap the heat and make further damage likely.

Natural remedies you might like to try include lavender essential oil applied undiluted to the area, comfrey cream or hypericum oil.

If the burn is more severe and has blistered, there's a risk of secondary infection. Take steps to avoid this by keeping the area clean and covered. For a smallish area of blistering sunburn, an antibacterial cream like silver sulphadiazine 1% (Flammazine) is useful – spread it on liberally and cover the whole area with a dry sterile dressing. You'll need to reapply the cream and change the dressing daily until it has healed up. For larger blisters, it's best to get medical attention.

Take care not to get burnt again, especially if peeling has left areas of unprotected new skin.

! Note that widespread severe sunburn is a serious condition that needs to be treated like any other extensive burn (see the First Aid appendix for more guidance) – you must get medical assistance urgently.

If the burn is more extensive, fluid and heat loss may make you feel feverish and perhaps cold, in spite of the burn, and you may have heatstroke (see later in this chapter). Get medical attention, and in the meantime, rest, drink plenty of fluids and try any of the measures suggested for mild sunburn.

SKIN CANCER

There are a few different types of skin cancers, but the two you need to keep a lookout for are malignant melanoma – the most dangerous one which can occur at any age, but typically affects people in their 30s and 40s – and something called a basal cell carcinoma (BCC) or rodent ulcer, which isn't life threatening as a rule, and usually occurs in older people. They look quite different. Sun-induced skin cancers are relatively rare if you're dark-skinned. Try to get into the habit of checking your skin for these, especially if you're at risk for them. Picking them up early greatly improves your chances of a full recovery.

Risk factors for melanoma include fair skin (especially if you live in tropical or subtropical areas of the world), short intense bursts of sun exposure as well as prolonged sun exposure, and getting sunburnt as a child (something else to blame your parents for).

Melanomas can occur anywhere, but they tend to be more common on the legs in women and on the upper back in men. Melanomas are often moles that have gone bad, so if you've got lots of moles, it's worth taking particular care to protect yourself from the sun. (Moles are raised freckles.)

Melanomas can vary quite a lot in appearance, but they often look like irregularly shaped and coloured moles. If you notice any of the following signs in a mole or freckle, see a doctor as soon as possible (it's the sort of thing you might want to cut your trip short for):

- rapid growth
- any change in shape or colour
- itching, oozing or bleeding
- any increase in thickness or change in the surface

BCCs are common skin cancers. They look unsightly, but don't spread throughout the body like melanomas and are much less dangerous. They're more common in older people and often occur on the face or head.

Be suspicious of any lump or rough patch that turns into a sore, with oozing or bleeding – seek medical advice as soon as you can for appropriate treatment and in case it's something worse.

OTHER EFFECTS OF THE SUN

The sun can affect your skin in other ways. Taking certain medicines can make you hypersensitive to the effects of the sun – you may find you burn more readily and badly than is normal for you. It's something that your doctor or pharmacist should warn you of when it's prescribed. If you are taking medicines for a preexisting condition, this is something you should check with your doctor before you leave. Medicines that can cause problems like this include:

- tetracycline antibiotics, including doxycycline (may be prescribed as a malaria preventive)
- ciprofloxacin (antibiotic that may be prescribed for diarrhoea)
- anti-inflammatory painkillers like ibuprofen and diclofenac
- the contraceptive pill (rarely)
- thiazides (diuretics often prescribed for blood pressure control and heart problems)
- nalidixic acid (antibiotic often prescribed for bladder infections)
- sulphonamide antibiotics eg co-trimoxazole (unlikely to be prescribed under normal circumstances)

The sun tends to make atopic dermatitis (eczema) worse, although it can improve psoriasis. Sunlight can trigger cold sores, if you get these.

HEAT

Generally, your body is able to adapt to the heat pretty well, although you need to give it time – full acclimatisation can take up to three weeks. The most important change that occurs with acclimatisation is that you sweat more readily and in larger quantities. Sweating helps cool you down as heat is lost when sweat evaporates off your skin. If the sweat pours off you without evaporating, it won't cool you down, which is why humid heat feels hotter than dry heat and why fanning helps cool you down by encouraging evaporation of sweat.

Some people are more vulnerable to the heat than others. Children are much more prone to heat illness than adults. Older travellers who are less fit may be at greater risk of heat illness (although if you're physically fit, you'll cope just as well as younger adults). People with heart or lung problems are vulnerable to heat stress because the heart has to work harder under hot conditions. If you're overweight, you may find it more difficult to lose heat.

Physical fitness makes you more able to cope with the heat and quicker to acclimatise, but don't be complacent as you can still get heat exhaustion and heatstroke if you don't take sensible precautions

! *If you're planning on doing physical activity in the heat, remember that your body has to work much harder to keep cool under these circumstances.*

Sweat contains water and salts. Your main requirement is to replace lost water. You can lose an astonishing 2L an hour in sweat, or more if you're doing strenuous physical activity. You need to drink a lot more than you would normally in a cool climate, even when you have acclimatised. Don't rely on feeling thirsty to prompt you to drink – by the time this kicks in, you'll probably already be dehydrated. How much urine you're passing is a much better indicator of how dry you are. If you're only passing a small amount of concentrated urine, you need to drink more.

! *As a rough guide, an adult needs to drink about 3L of fluid a day in a hot climate or 5L and more if you're doing strenuous physical activity like trekking or cycling.*

You generally lose more water than salt in sweat; as you acclimatise, your body learns to conserve salt. However, at first you can lose more salt than normal, but as long as you're not on a salt-reduced diet, you should still be able to make it up from your diet without adding salt or taking salt tablets. The current thinking is that you don't need to actively replace salt unless you experience symptoms indicating a relative lack of salt, mainly cramps in your muscles. As a rule, salt tablets are best avoided – our diets tend to be relatively high in salt anyway, and too much salt can cause kidney and heart problems in the long term.

Heat illness covers a spectrum of conditions ranging from uncomfortable heat cramps to potentially fatal heatstroke. Even if you don't feel too bad, heat and dehydration can affect your physical performance and mental judgement. This is especially important if you are relying on these, such as when you are on a trek or doing other strenuous physical activity.

HEAT CRAMPS

Heavy and prolonged sweating can cause painful cramps in your muscles. If you get these, you need to rest in a cool environment and replace salt and fluids – this is one time when it is appropriate to have extra salt. Make up oral rehydration salts from sachets (readily available throughout Asia) or make up your own – for more guidance on rehydration, turn to the section on treating diarrhoea (p139). But if nothing else is available, any fluid is better than none.

FAINTING

This is quite common if you've recently arrived in a hot climate as is more likely to affect older travellers. It occurs because heat causes the blood to pool in your legs when you're standing, meaning that less blood reaches your brain, causing you to feel dizzy and faint. Treat by raising the person's legs above their head, fanning them, spraying them with cool water and, when they are conscious, giving them fluids (safe water or diluted fruit juice) to sip.

HEAT EXHAUSTION & HEATSTROKE

These two conditions are different entities, but they overlap to a certain extent and, for practical purposes, you should treat any heat illness as heatstroke. Both are caused by heavy and prolonged sweating with inadequate fluid replacement and insufficient time for acclimatisation. In heatstroke, sweating stops and you get a dangerous rise in body temperature which can be fatal.

Symptoms to look out for are headache, dizziness, nausea and feeling weak and exhausted. You may notice that you're passing only small quantities of dark urine and you may have muscle aches or cramps. At this stage your temperature may

Dehydration

This can be caused by any condition that leads to an excessive loss of body fluids, including heat, fever, diarrhoea, vomiting and strenuous physical activity. Signs of dehydration are:

- nausea and dizziness
- headache, and dry eyes and mouth
- weakness and muscle cramps
- passing small quantities of dark urine
- raised temperature

Treatment is to drink lots of fluids: oral rehydration salts if available, but otherwise any fluid will do. For more guidance on fluid replacement, see the section on fluid replacement in diarrhoea (p139).

be normal. Treatment is aimed at cooling down and replacing fluids:

▸ rest in a cool environment (try fanning and cool water sprays)
▸ drink lots of fluids (water, oral rehydration salts or diluted fruit juice)

If untreated, heat exhaustion can progress to heatstroke. Signs (more likely to be noticed by your travel companions than yourself) include confusion, headache, lack of sweating and flushed and red appearance. The skin feels hot to touch and the person's temperature is raised. In addition, they may show lack of coordination, fits and finally coma (unconsciousness).

Heatstroke can be rapidly fatal, so you need to take immediate action to lower the person's temperature and to get medical help:

▸ move the person into the shade or a cool environment (get a fan going or use a room with air-con)
▸ give them cool water to sip (cool fluids are absorbed more rapidly than warm ones); intravenous fluid replacement may be needed once you get medical help

▶ seek medical help or evacuation urgently
▶ ice packs, sponging or spraying with cold water and fanning will all help; ice packs are most effective if you put them over the groin and under the arms, but wrap them up first

COLD

This isn't going to worry you much if you're going to tropical Asia, but the Himalaya and Karakoram range, much of China, Mongolia, Japan and Korea can all be on the chilly side of cold, so make sure you're prepared. Your body is pretty limited in what it can do to stay warm – shivering is just about the only thing in the short term – so it's up to you to minimise the dangers by wearing adequate clothing and avoiding temperature extremes (unless you're properly prepared). Remember that food equals heat – make sure you eat regularly and get sufficient calories in cold climates.

If you're out and about in the cold, the main problems cold causes are general body cooling (hypothermia) or localised cooling, usually affecting your hands and feet, called frostnip or frostbite. Travelling at speed – for example if you're skiing on Mt Fuji or cycling in northern India – causes you to get colder quicker. Other problems of cold climates are dehydration (because cold makes you urinate more, you may not feel thirsty and cold air is drying), constipation and sunburn, especially at altitude.

HYPOTHERMIA

This is when your body starts to lose the battle to maintain your body heat in cold conditions and your core body temperature starts to fall (officially, hypothermia is when your temperature, taken by the rectal method, falls below 35°C). Be aware that you don't need incredibly low temperatures to become hypothermic.

Because hypothermia can come on gradually and take a hold before you realise, it's important to recognise when it might be a risk and to take steps to prevent it. You're more at risk of hypothermia if you're thin (less body fat for insulation), tired, wet, or inadequately dressed or equipped (such as not having a sleeping bag). If it's windy, you get colder more easily as your body heat is removed by convection. Alcohol and other mind-altering substances also put you more at risk, as alcohol encourages heat loss and affects your judgement.

Children and older travellers are more vulnerable to the cold, especially if children are being carried (such as in a backpack child carrier). An added problem is that children may not let you know how they're feeling until it's too late.

Remember that immersion in cold water, for example if you fall in a mountain stream, can rapidly cause you to become hypothermic.

If you think cold might be an issue, take care to prepare well and minimise your risks:

▶ always be prepared for the worst possible weather, even if you're just passing through on a bus journey, for example, or spending a night in the hills on the way to somewhere else
▶ wear appropriate clothing – layers are best as you can adjust them easily to match changing weather conditions throughout the day, and make sure you include windproof and waterproof layers; lightweight polyester fleece clothing is ideal
▶ a surprising amount of heat is lost through radiation from your head, so wear a hat
▶ stay dry – adjust your layers to prevent your clothes getting wet through with sweat, and always carry an umbrella, waterproof layer or large plastic bag on you, even if there isn't a cloud in the sky when you set off
▶ don't let tiredness get a hold – have frequent rests
▶ carry plenty of fluids and carbohydrate-packed goodies and snack regularly throughout the day

Check regularly if you're feeling cold or if you have cold hands and toes. Watch for subtle early signs of hypothermia in

Buddy System

Many of the signs and symptoms associated with heat, cold and altitude illness are much more likely to be noticed by people you are with than by you. Because of this, it's vital to keep a regular watch on each other if you are in harsh environmental or climatic conditions. Never leave someone on their own if they're showing symptoms. It's also a good idea to self-check for aches, pains, cold areas, numbness and dizziness.

your travel companions. These are what Rick Curtis of the Princeton Outdoor Program calls the 'umbles' – stumbles, mumbles, fumbles and grumbles, as you get changes in mental function and coordination.

If hypothermia is allowed to progress, the person becomes more disorientated, may show poor judgement and reasoning, and is unable to make appropriate decisions about survival strategies. Finally, shivering stops, the person is unable to walk and loses consciousness.

Watch for and treat the early signs of hypothermia:

▶ remove any cold or wet clothes and replace with warm, dry ones, being careful to cover the head and extremities and insulate the sufferer from the ground
▶ find shelter for protection from wet, wind and cold
▶ rewarm using blankets, sleeping bags and body-to-body contact (zip two sleeping bags together and get in with the cold person to help warm them up)
▶ you can use hot packs or hot water bottles (or improvise), but remember to wrap these up first to prevent the risk of burns
▶ drink warm, sweet fluids (sweet milky tea is excellent and readily available)

'Space blankets' are a popular cold weather survival aid, but there are doubts about their effectiveness in the field, and you're probably better off using a sleeping bag or other thermal layers, depending what you have with you. Carry lots of plastic bags with you – covering yourself up with these prevents further heat loss through evaporation, and can double as protection from rain.

! *Severe hypothermia is a very serious condition – seek medical help or evacuation immediately. Handle the person carefully and don't rewarm them too fast as this can be dangerous.*

CHILBLAINS

These are the most common form of cold injury and the least dangerous. Chilblains can occur if your bare skin is repeatedly exposed to low temperatures (above freezing) and usually affect fingers and toes. You get red, swollen, itchy and tender areas which will heal up on their own in one to two weeks.

Prevent chilblains by wearing warm mittens (not gloves) and socks, and suitable footwear. There's no specific treatment, but remember that any open areas on your skin can get infected so keep them clean and covered.

Natural remedies that have been recommended include calendula or witch hazel tinctures for unbroken chilblains or hypericum ointment for broken chilblains. Comfrey ointment is soothing for any skin inflammation.

FROSTBITE

When your tissues get so cold they freeze, this is frostbite. It's not going to be a big risk for most travellers as it doesn't generally occur unless you're at temperatures below freezing for prolonged periods of time without adequate gloves or footwear. High winds, high altitude (usually above about 4000m) and badly fitting boots make frostbite more likely. Bear in mind that running shoes are not going to protect your feet from the cold if the weather suddenly changes and there's a fall of snow. Fingers, toes, ears, nose and face can all be affected. (There's an unforgettable report of a male jogger getting frostbite of the penis – don't say we didn't warn you.)

*!Prevent frostbite – cover all exposed skin with waterproof
 . and windproof layers in cold conditions and if you notice
your hands or feet turning numb, stop immediately and warm
them up by body to body contact if necessary.*

A frostbitten part looks white and waxy – keep a watch on
your companions for this – and is painless while it's frozen.
It's best to seek medical advice as soon as possible. Some
effects of frostbite, especially if it's mild, are reversible but
you will need expert advice.

What you do immediately depends on your situation. If
there is no risk of refreezing (ie you can be evacuated promptly or you are near medical facilities), you should thaw the
affected part, although this depends on whether you have
appropriate facilities at hand.

*!Never rub the affected part to warm it up as this can cause
 . further damage.*

Rewarm the part by immersing it for about half an hour in
water heated to 40°C. As it starts to warm up, the pain can be
pretty severe, and you'll need strong painkillers. The thawed
part will swell up so be sure to remove any rings from fingers
(or toes). Infection is a significant risk, so make sure you keep
the area clean and dry, and cover it with a dry dressing until
you reach medical help. If there is a risk of refreezing (ie you
are far from help), don't attempt to thaw the part until you
reach medical help.

ALTITUDE

If you're planning on travelling to any of Asia's high places,
you need to know how altitude can affect you. In Nepal, for
example, about three trekkers a year die from the effects of
altitude – don't let it be you! For more detailed information,
check out some of the information sources listed in the box.

Altitude & Outdoor Activities Resources

If you want to find out more about the effects of altitude and other related issues, you could check out some of the following web sites or some recommended books are listed under Books in the Before You Go chapter. The Wilderness Medical Society (☎ 317-631-1745, PO Box 2463, Indianapolis, IN 46206, USA) is an authoritative source of information on all aspects of wilderness safety.

Princeton University's Outdoor Action Program (www.princeton.edu/~oa/altitude.html). This excellent and comprehensive resource has detailed information on altitude, heat and cold and other wilderness safety issues, as well as lots of links to related sites on a wide variety of outdoor activities, including biking, hiking, caving and mountaineering.

The British Mountaineering Council (www.thebmc.co.uk) is another good resource, with information on altitude and related issues. They can also be contacted on ☎ 0161-445 4747, fax 0161-445 4500, info@thebmc.co.uk or by post: 177-79 Burton Rd, Manchester M20 2BB.

High Altitude Medicine Guide (www.gorge.net/hamg) is just that; it also has good information on water treatment and travellers diarrhoea (aimed at travellers to Nepal), an excellent books section and lots of useful links.

Himalaya Rescue Association (HRA; www.nepalonline.net/hra) is a voluntary organisation relying on donations that operates aid posts in Pheriche on the Everest trek and Manang on the trek around Annapurna. It has good basic health and safety advice for trekkers in Nepal. HRA (☎ 62746) can be contacted in Nepal at Thamel Mall Building, Jyatha Thamel, Kathmandu.

CIWEC Clinic (www.bena.com/ciwec) is a well-established travel medicine centre in Kathmandu has lots of good health and safety information if you're planning on going to Nepal. See the Medical Services appendix for contact details.

You're not usually at risk of altitude sickness until you reach about 2500m but it is possible to get symptoms from about 2000m upwards. You're very unlikely to get problems if you stay at altitude for less than about six hours. Going above 3500m, about 50% of trekkers experience symptoms of mild altitude illness, whereas about one in 20 have life-threatening severe altitude illness.

The problem with altitude is that the air is thinner and less oxygen is available to you. Your body adapts to having less oxygen available through various mechanisms. At first, you increase the rate and depth of your breathing; later you get an increase in heart rate and changes in red blood cells. Although you can acclimatise sufficiently in a couple of days to a particular altitude, full acclimatisation takes about three weeks.

WHO'S AT RISK?

Anyone can have problems at altitude, whatever your age or fitness level. The most important risk factor is how rapidly you ascend – if you reach a high altitude by trekking, acclimatisation takes place gradually and you are less likely to be affected than if you fly or drive straight to altitude, for example to Lhasa in Tibet (3658m) or Leh in northern India (3514m). Some people are naturally more prone to altitude sickness than others. Overexerting yourself before you are fully acclimatised increases your chances of getting altitude sickness. Children appear to be at the same risk of altitude sickness as adults, but they are less likely to be able to let you know if they have symptoms, which makes it more risky.

! *Check with your doctor before you go if you have any on-*
• going illness, especially heart or lung problems.

Note that there's a theoretical risk that the oral contraceptive pill or hormone replacement therapy will make altitude sickness worse in women taking these, although at altitudes below about

5500m there's little evidence to support this. It probably makes sense to discuss this issue with your doctor in advance if you fall into either of these categories. Some other points to bear in mind:

- you're not necessarily safer on an organised trek, in fact you may be at greater risk – there are lots of reasons for this, including a reluctance to hold up other members of your group
- fit people tend to climb too high too fast, and therefore put themselves at greater risk for altitude sickness
- you're more likely to get problems at altitude if you've had them before (60% likelihood for high altitude pulmonary oedema), so get expert advice in this situation

PREVENTION

The best way to prevent acute mountain sickness (AMS) is to ascend slowly and gradually, allowing time for acclimatisation to occur. In practice this means:

Warning

Madeline Frucht Wilks worked as a volunteer physician for the Himalaya Rescue Association at their post in Manang (Nepal). She wrote to us about her concerns for trekkers on the Annapurna circuit, but her words of warning hold good wherever you're planning to trek at altitude.

With increasing numbers of trekkers each year, we are seeing alarming numbers of people who are completely unprepared for trekking at altitude. Many people push themselves too fast because they don't plan on extra days for acclimatisation or unexpected illness. AMS can be precipitated by overexertion. People who have never trekked before think they can walk seven hours a day with no ill effects!

We have treated lacerations, ankle sprain and severe blisters from improper footwear. Properly broken-in hiking boots are a must. Snow blindness and severe sunburn from lack of sunglasses and sunscreen and hypothermia from insufficient warm clothes are all too common.

- having frequent rest days – plan to spend two to three nights at each rise of 1000m
- 'climb high, sleep low' – as far as possible, sleep at a lower altitude than the greatest height you reached during the day
- above 3000m don't increase your sleeping altitude by more than 300m per day
- if you have any symptoms of AMS, stop ascending until the symptoms have gone
- descend immediately if your symptoms persist or worsen in 30 to 60 minutes

Other general measures for preventing illness at altitude include the following:

- don't trek alone – you may not recognise the symptoms of AMS in yourself and you may not be able to get to safety
- if you plan to trek at altitude, make sure you know where the nearest medical facility is
- drink plenty of fluids to prevent dehydration (4L or 5L daily), as the air at high altitude is dry and you lose plenty of moisture through sweating and breathing
- don't overexert yourself, especially in the first week or so at high altitude
- eat light, high-carbohydrate meals to give you energy
- avoid alcohol, sedatives or any other mind-altering substances

Another option for preventing AMS is with drugs, but be aware that this is a highly controversial issue, and you will get different advice from different sources. Although there are some situations where drug treatment is useful, the bottom line is that if you follow the rules of gradual safe ascent, you shouldn't need drug treatment.

The most widely used drug for preventing AMS is currently acetazolamide (Diamox). This drug works on cellular biochemistry, resulting in increased breathing rates and improved oxygen supply to the body and brain. Diamox can be used to prevent mild AMS as well as to treat it, but it doesn't prevent or treat severe AMS, high altitude pulmonary or cerebral oedema. Side effects are common, usually tingling in the fingers, and it makes you pass more urine.

There is no evidence that Diamox masks the symptoms of AMS. However, if you decide to take it, you should realise that Diamox is not a replacement for acclimatisation – if you ascend too fast, even if you're taking Diamox, you'll get AMS. For more information about Diamox and other drugs used in altitude illness, check out the information sources listed in the boxed text earlier or talk to your doctor. Remember:

- the best treatment for AMS is descent
- you should never use drug treatment as a means of avoiding descent or to enable you to ascend further

MILD AMS

When you first arrive at altitudes over about 2000m (eg if you fly into Lhasa in Tibet), it's common to get mild symptoms of AMS, coming on gradually about six or so hours after arrival. Symptoms include:

- headache
- loss of appetite
- nausea and vomiting
- tiredness and irritability

You may also notice that you're a bit unsteady on your feet, and you may feel a little short of breath. Because symptoms of AMS are so nonspecific, it can be difficult to distinguish them from flu, colds or jet lag – if in doubt, assume it's AMS.

Having difficulty sleeping is very common at altitude – you may find it hard to get to sleep, have vivid dreams and wake up frequently. Your travel companions may notice you have periodic breathing, when your breathing slows and appears to stop. Periodic breathing can be very scary to witness, but it's not dangerous. Sometimes you can get swelling of your face, arm or leg (oedema). This doesn't mean that you are getting a more severe form of altitude sickness, and it usually settles without any treatment over the course of a couple of days.

Symptoms of mild AMS are unpleasant, but they usually disappear after two to three days, as long as you don't go any higher. The main concern with mild AMS is that it can progress to more severe forms if you ignore it or go higher.

SEVERE AMS

About one in 20 people will develop more severe forms of altitude illness, usually at 4000m and above, but sometimes lower. Severe AMS includes high altitude pulmonary oedema and high altitude cerebral oedema.

In high altitude pulmonary oedema (HAPE), fluid accumulates in your lungs, preventing you from breathing properly. It can follow from mild AMS or it can come on suddenly without any warning. The main symptoms are:

- breathlessness at rest or persistent cough (common early on)
- coughing up pink, frothy sputum
- tiredness and weakness

If fluid collects within your brain, you get high altitude cerebral oedema (HACE). This condition is rare, but is life-threatening, so you need to be know how to recognise it and what to do about it. Symptoms to look out for are:

- severe headache, unrelieved by simple painkillers
- change in behaviour, confusion and disorientation
- double vision
- unsteadiness
- drowsiness and coma (unconsciousness)

Early HACE causes a condition called ataxia (a form of incoordination) which can be picked up by the straight line test. To do this test, draw a line on the ground and get the person to walk heel to toe along it. If they can't do it without overbalancing or stepping off the line, assume they have HACE, especially if they have other signs of illness.

TREATMENT

We can't emphasise enough that descent is the best treatment for any form of AMS. Mild AMS can be treated with simple measures, but bear in mind some not-to-be-broken rules:

▶ never ascend with any symptoms of AMS
▶ always descend promptly if your symptoms are moderate to severe or getting worse, or there's no improvement in mild symptoms after two to three days
▶ seek medical advice if necessary, but don't let this delay descent
▶ rest up for a couple of days
▶ drink plenty of fluids as dehydration is common at altitude
▶ take simple painkillers or an anti-inflammatory like ibuprofen for the headache
▶ try a motion sickness remedy (p70) for nausea and vomiting
▶ if you have access to oxygen by mask, this can be helpful

Severe AMS, HAPE and HACE are all medical emergencies – you need to act immediately:

▶ seek medical advice if possible but don't let this delay descent
▶ descend immediately (even 500m can help)
▶ use oxygen by mask, if possible

Drug treatments are as follows, but remember these are powerful drugs that can be dangerous if used incorrectly. If you are carrying them, make sure you know all about how to use them before you go.

▶ Severe AMS or HACE – dexamethasone 8mg by mouth immediately, followed by 4mg every six hours until you are safely evacuated.
▶ HAPE – nifedipine 20mg by mouth immediately.

If necessary, if you're not sure what the problem is (as is often the case), you can take all treatments together.

Note that dexamethasone is a powerful steroid drug that should be used with extreme caution, and ideally only under medical supervision. Side effects include mood changes and an increased risk of indigestion and ulceration. Nifedipine is a drug used in the treatment of high blood pressure and heart problems.

Treatment in portable hyperbaric chambers (eg the Gamow bag) can simulate descent and may be available in some high risk areas, like the Himalaya Rescue Association posts in Nepal. It can be a useful first aid measure, but is no substitute for descent. It's possible to hire them in Nepal, but you'd need to be a pretty serious and experienced trekker to consider this.

OTHER HEALTH CONCERNS

Sunburn is common at high altitude because less sunlight is filtered out by the atmosphere, and if there is snow, this reflects sunlight much more than plain ground. Cover up and use a high protection factor sunblock (don't forget your lips), and wear good sunglasses to protect your eyes. Dehydration is common, so drink plenty of fluids, even if you don't feel thirsty. You still need to be careful about your drinking water. Most diarrhoea-causing bugs are resistant to cold temperatures, even freezing, and water from streams on popular routes is quite likely to be contaminated with faeces. Water from glacial streams can contain mineral salts, which may have a laxative effect.

Snow blindness is sunburn of the backs of the eyes and is caused by sunlight reflected off snow. Prevent it by wearing goggles or sunglasses with UV protection. Symptoms are a gritty feeling in your eyes, extreme sensitivity to light, redness and temporary blindness several hours after exposure. There's no specific treatment apart from relieving the pain (for example by putting cold cloths on your closed eyes), and it usually heals completely in a couple of days. Anaesthetic eye drops (eg amethocaine) are sometimes used but they may slow the healing process and make your eyes more vulnerable to other injuries. Antibiotic eye drops are not necessary. You can make emergency eye protection by cutting slits in cardboard or cloth.

ACTION SAFETY

TREKKING SAFELY

There are plenty of opportunities for short and longer treks in Asia. If you decide to do a trek of any length, here's a quick health and safety checklist.

Preparation

If you are going on a trek of any length, you should inform someone reliable of your route and estimated arrival date so that if you do run into difficulties, the alarm can be raised. You could consider letting the folks back home know via a brief phone call; alternatively, leave the information with your hotel or other travellers. This system will only work if you let people know when you get back, so that unnecessary rescues aren't initiated.

- Fitness – trekking can be a strenuous activity, particularly if you're not in peak physical condition, so make sure what you are planning is within your capabilities and that there is some flexibility built into your plans in case you find you need to bail out at any stage.
- Training – if you can, some pre-trek fitness training is a good idea, and will reduce the likelihood of sprains, falls and overuse injuries.
- Equipment – make sure you are fully prepared for the environmental conditions you're likely to encounter and take a well-stocked medical kit (see the Before You Go chapter earlier in this book).
- Footwear – running shoes and sandals are not much use on a trek in rough terrain, so unless you can get hold of a decent pair of walking boots, consider changing your plans.
- High altitude trekking – make sure you know what to look for and what to do if you develop signs of altitude illness.
- Map and compass – a reasonable map of the area is vital, especially if you are going without a guide and probably a good idea anyway), but it's no good if you can't follow it.
- Insurance – check that your insurance covers you for trekking, and consider joining a local emergency rescue organisation.

On the Trek

Consider hiring porters to carry the heavy equipment (and help the local economy), and a guide if you're unsure of the route.

- Water – don't assume there will be water along the way unless you find out that there is from a reliable source; otherwise you'll need to carry all your water requirements with you (remember if it's hot, you will need a minimum of 5L of water each per day).
- Food – again, you shouldn't rely on food being available along the way; take plenty of food with you, including energy-giving snacks like chocolate and dried fruit, and remember that a trekker marches on his/her stomach ...
- Tiredness – this makes injuries more likely so eat properly throughout the day, take regular rests and don't push yourself too hard, especially towards the end of the day.
- Blisters – avoid these by wearing well worn-in walking boots and socks that fit snugly with no seams; if you do get one, follow the guidelines on p200.
- Protect yourself against insect bites and leeches (p83).

Rescue & Evacuation

If someone in your group is injured or falls ill, leave someone with them and go for help. If there are only two of you, leave the person in a sheltered position with as much warm clothing, food and water as you can sensibly spare, as well as some means of attracting attention (like a whistle or torch). Mark the position with something conspicuous, for example a brightly coloured bag or a large stone cross on the ground.

Note that this is the accepted strategy for rescue, but when you're travelling in remote areas in Asia, self-evacuation is going to be your only and best option, especially as rescue may be delayed or difficult due to transport problems and communication difficulties.

CYCLING SAFELY

Cycling is a great way to see parts of Asia you would otherwise miss. If you're considering a short or longer cycle tour, here are some basic health and safety tips; you might also like to check out Lonely Planet's cycling guides.

Health & Fitness

It's a good idea to get fit on a bike if you plan on doing more than a couple of days of cycle touring – practise riding an average daily distance two or three days in a row. Before you set off, be sure to warm up and stretch properly. On the ride:

- take regular breaks during the day
- consider having a massage in the evening
- avoid sore hands from gripping the handlebar on rough roads for long periods by changing hand position (if possible), relaxing your grip on the handlebars and taking frequent rests
- be prepared for climatic extremes
- remember to drink plenty of fluids, especially if it's hot, and avoid cycling during the hottest part of the day
- take snack food with you for any ride that's more than about an hour long

Equipment & Cycling Technique

This can make a big difference to your enjoyment and comfort, as well as safety on the ride.

- If you're hiring a bike, check it over carefully – make sure the brakes work and check the wheels and tyres.
- Wear safety gear – helmet (essential), sunglasses, cycling gloves and two layers of clothing (helps prevent road rash if you come off your bike) and check your bike on a daily basis.
- Learn the local road rules, ride single file and ride defensively.
- Make sure your bike is adjusted for you – check that the seat and handlebar height are comfortable and the seat is parallel to the ground.
- Take lights with you if you're intending to ride at night.
- Balance the load on your bike and keep the weight low to the ground, preferably with panniers.
- Learn to spin the gears (70 to 90 revs per minute) not push them – this way you'll avoid sore knees from pushing big gears.

For more information, you could try *The Bicycle Touring Manual* (Bicycle Books) by Rob van der Plas, or check out either of these two recommended web sites: www.cyclery.com or www.ctc.org.uk.

CAVING HAZARDS

South-East Asia has some of the longest cave systems in the world, for example the Clearwater Cave system in Sarawak. There are some hazards associated with caves that you should be aware of, although you're unlikely to be at any great risks from these on most standard guided tours. Caves are dark, so you'll want to take a good torch with you and, even in hot climates, they can be cold so be prepared. Flash floods are always a risk.

- Leptospirosis is a risk as this bacterial disease can be transmitted through rat or bat urine, and you can get infected if you scrape yourself against the cave walls; you can also acquire it by swimming in contaminated water – see p333 for more details.
- You can get a fungal chest infection, histoplasmosis, by inhaling dried bat droppings, but this is a risk mainly in small confined spaces; you get a fever, headache, chest pains and cough about two weeks after you've been exposed – there's no specific treatment, but you should seek medical advice, as it can make some people very ill.
- Rabies can be carried by bats and rats, as well as animals like cats and dogs – although you normally acquire the disease through bites, there have been cases in cavers from inhaling dried bat droppings, so if you are planning on any serious caving, you should make sure you get immunised against rabies before you leave (see p35 for more details).
- Scorpions and snakes live in caves, so be wary of where you put your hands.
- Various small biters (including sandflies, mosquitoes, ticks and leeches) live in and around the entrance to caves – cover up and apply insect repellent to prevent bites and the diseases they carry.

MISCELLANEOUS OUTDOOR HAZARDS

Monsoons are an obvious hazard to be aware of when you're travelling in tropical Asia. Find out when these are likely to occur and plan around them.

Tropical storms can be fantastic spectacles, but you probably don't want to get caught out in the open during one of these. Lightning has a penchant for crests, lone trees, gullies, caves and cabin entrances, as well as wet ground. If you are caught out in the open, try to curl up as tight as possible, with your feet together, and a layer of insulation between you and the ground. Make sure you're not sitting next to metal objects like walking poles or metal-frame backpacks – place them a short distance away from you.

If you have to cross any fast-flowing rivers, remember to take one arm out of your pack, and unbuckle it so that if you feel yourself getting swept away, you can slip out of it easily. Use a stick to feel the river bed before putting your feet down, and walk side-on to the direction of flow so that the water can flow more easily round your body. Snowmelt is cold, so beware of hypothermia and muscle cramps.

Leeches, ticks and animal bites are also hazards, and are covered in the chapter on Bites & Stings later in this book.

WATER

Safe water for drinking is vital if you want to stay healthy (see the section on Safe Drinking Water in the Staying Healthy chapter for the complete lowdown on this), but contact with water through swimming, paddling and water sports has its hazards too.

○ See the inside backcover for guidelines on emergency resuscitation in near-drowning.

WATER IN EYES & EARS

You can easily get eye infections (conjunctivitis) from a not-too-clean swimming pool, and you can get chemical irritation of your eyes from poorly maintained swimming pools.

Take care not to get water in your eyes, especially if you have any doubts about the cleanliness of the swimming pool, or wear swimming goggles. If you do get an eye infection, bathe your eyes with clean water and avoid swimming until they are better. Water in the ears commonly causes infection and irritation Using ear plugs helps to keep ears dry and healthy.

For more guidance on what to do if you think you have an eye or ear infection, see the relevant sections in the Ears, Eyes & Teeth chapter earlier.

WATER & SKIN INFECTIONS

Not drying your skin properly between swims, especially if it's hot and humid, can make fungal infections of your skin more likely – see the section on Fungal Infections in the Skin chapter for more details. If spa baths are not well-maintained, bacteria multiply and can cause infection of the hair follicles, which appears as a rash of boils. Sea water contains all sorts of sea bacteria, which can infect cuts and scrapes, turning them into persistent sores if you don't clean them promptly and thoroughly.

SWIMMING & SNORKELLING

Sunburn is a big risk at the beach or pool, especially for children, so you need to be aware of the risk and take measures to protect yourself – see the Safe Sun section of the Staying Healthy chapter for the complete lowdown on this. Sunscreen works off easily when you're in and out of the water. Use a waterproof sunscreen and apply it liberally and often. Remember to drink plenty of fluids (and encourage your children to as well) to prevent dehydration (see the Heat section in the Climate, Altitude and Action chapter).

It's unlikely you'll want to sit on a beach that's littered with animal faeces, but if you do, be aware that you can get a skin rash, geography worm (p198), caused by a worm that may be present in dog and cat faeces.

Most of the diseases you can get through drinking contaminated water can also be caught through swimming or bathing in unsafe water (by swallowing small amounts). Sea water isn't necessarily safer than fresh water from this point of view, as sewage is often emptied into the sea, especially around urban settlements. It's not just bugs, though – you need to be wary of chemical and industrial pollutants that get washed or dumped in the water at beaches near big cities. They can cause an itchy skin rash or more serious toxicity.

Chlorinated pools that are well maintained should be safe, although some diarrhoea-causing parasites (like *Giardia*) are able to survive chlorination. You can't get diseases like HIV from swimming in pools.

If you're doing any water sports, use your common sense and don't take unnecessary risks. Check the quality of any equipment you hire, as safety standards in many Asian countries are generally less stringent than you may be expecting.

Tides & Currents

Always ask around locally about currents, tides and any other marine hazards you should be aware of. Be especially wary of rips, as these strong currents are a common cause of beach drownings. A rip is where the water that's brought to the beach by breaking waves runs back out. It tends to take you out to sea, not down under the water.

Telltale signs of a rip current include colour (it may be darker than the water on either side), a rippled effect on the surface of the water, and a trail of surf extending beyond the surf zone. Rips can be very difficult to spot, even if you're looking for them.

Watch out for side shore currents, which flow parallel to the shore, and can wash you quite a way down the beach, where conditions may be less safe. Don't stray too far from the shore in this situation, and watch the shoreline to make sure you don't drift too far down. Swim in to the shore before you float too far away from your starting point.

Getting out of a Rip

If you do get into a rip, you may feel yourself being dragged out to sea, or you may be sucked underwater if it passes through a rocky passage. To avoid getting into serious trouble, do the following:

- don't panic – this will tire you out quicker
- get out of the rip current by swimming parallel to the shore, then catching the waves back in; don't swim against the current as you'll just exhaust yourself

If you are unsure of your swimming abilities and there are people on the beach, raise an arm above your head to indicate that you are in trouble, and tread water (you can stay afloat for a surprisingly long time) until you are rescued. Alternatively you could try conserving your energy while you wait for rescue by allowing yourself to float motionless face down in the water, raising your head just when you need to take a breath.

Riding the Waves

Surfers and windsurfers should study water, wind and weather conditions especially waves, currents, tides and storms. Watch for submerged rocks, logs, coral, hazardous animals and floating debris. Learn survival and self-rescue techniques. Check and recheck your gear before heading out. Always stay in shape and avoid heading out in conditions too difficult for your skills.

Since surfers and windsurfers are exposed to the elements for long periods, sunburn (and hypothermia in some places) are real dangers. To prevent exposure, wear a wetsuit and consider neoprene gloves and booties. A helmet is now recommended by many experts. Consider using surf goggles to protect your eyes from water and sun. Earplugs will keep your ears clear of water as well. Finally, wear waterproof sunscreen.

Injuries you're most likely to suffer if you're surfing or windsurfing are sprains, strains, cuts and bruises. Take good care of any wounds you get.

Christopher Van Tilburg

Cramps

These are caused by a muscle going into spasm because of dehydration and alterations in blood flow or salt composition, often as a result of poor acclimatisation to the heat. Cramps can also be caused by cold water, tiredness, overexertion or if you're unwell for any reason. You get a twinge at first, often in your calf, then the pain builds up and is only relieved when you stop using the muscle. Massaging and stretching the muscle, such as by pulling on your toes while straightening your leg, can help. Cramps can be very painful, and are potentially dangerous if you are in rough seas or you're a weak swimmer. Try to rest the muscle then use it gently.

Prevent cramps by warming up well before starting any activity. Remember to warm down too, and stretch before and after strenuous activity.

AQUATIC LIFE

The tropical waters around Asia are home to a fascinating variety of creatures, some of which can be a danger to you. Learn to recognise and avoid the villains (see the following pages), but the risks are fairly small, so long as you use a bit of common sense:

‣ seek out and heed advice on local dangers
‣ don't walk along reefs in shallow water
‣ don't go diving or snorkelling when the waters are murky (this may attract predators and you won't be able to see them coming)
‣ unless you're a marine biologist, don't touch or feed any creature you come across underwater

CORAL CUTS

Coral is sharp stuff, and if you brush against it you're likely to get a scratch or graze or a more severe laceration. It may not seem like much at the time, but the consequences of coral cuts can be as serious as those of much more impressive marine creature injuries. Coral wounds are notoriously troublesome, often because people don't bother to clean them properly at the start. Coral is covered in a layer of slime that is full of marine microorganisms which can infect the wound, and small particles of coral, including its stinging cells, are often left in the wound.

If you ignore a coral wound, there's a high chance it will get infected and develop into a sore you can't get rid of. It's worth taking a bit of trouble to prevent this. For any coral cut:

‣ rinse the wound with plenty of water (eg bottled water), perhaps using a small brush or a syringe (with or without a needle) to dislodge any small particles
‣ apply an antiseptic solution (like povidone-iodine)
‣ apply an antibiotic cream or powder (eg mupirocin 2%) to the area
‣ cover it with a dressing
‣ watch for signs of infection (p400)

You can cause irreparable damage to the coral when you come into contact with it, so it's mutually beneficial to avoid getting cut by coral in the first place. Try to avoid walking on or swimming over reefs and maintain correct buoyancy and control when you're diving. It's a good rule never to put your hands or feet somewhere you can't see first. Always wear shoes in the water, especially if you are walking in the shallows – flip flops (thongs) or sports sandals work well.

BITES

Sharks are probably your number one concern, but you shouldn't worry unduly about shark attack – there are many tastier and more convenient foods for sharks than you. However, you may catch a glimpse of one (often a tiger, hammerhead or whale shark) if you are diving in South-East Asia. Obviously, if you know the waters are shark-infested, it makes sense to avoid swimming. Here are some tips for minimising your risks of shark attack:

▸ don't swim or dive where fishermen are cleaning their catches (why would you want to anyway?)
▸ avoid swimming with an open wound or abrasion in risk areas
▸ be careful at dusk, as this is when sharks feed
▸ if you see a shark, don't panic: try to move away slowly – sharks have poor eyesight and are attracted by movement and smell

Electric rays (similar to sting rays but they discharge an electric current into you), eels (can inflict pretty severe bites), octopuses (can bite) and some fish (including the surgeonfish and the triggerfish) may be a risk if you get too close.

Crocodiles

The chances of a traveller being attacked by a crocodile in Asia are fairly remote, it should be said. Species here include the ominously named Indian mugger crocodile that has been known to attack humans if provoked, and the saltwater crocodile which occurs in India and parts of South-East Asia and is an infamous attacker of humans. Crocodiles tend to be found along waterways and estuaries. Your best bet is to ask around locally for reliable advice on the risks, and to keep your wits about you if you are walking along or camping near waterways or rafting on rivers.

Treatment

Treatment for bites and other injuries inflicted by marine creatures is basic first aid:

▶ get out of the water
▶ stop any bleeding by applying pressure to the bleeding spots
▶ clean the wound with plenty of pure water and soap; apply disinfectant and a sterile dressing
▶ look out for signs of poisoning, and get help if necessary

STINGS

Many marine creatures use venom to protect themselves from attack or to kill their prey. Although most venoms have little or no effect on humans, there are some notable exceptions you should be aware of – read on.

! Remember: most marine creatures are not aggressive – if you don't threaten them, most will leave you alone.

Sea Snakes

These beautiful creatures are found throughout coastal Asia. They're often very inquisitive, although not usually aggressive. However, their venom is extremely toxic, so you should give them a wide berth. Symptoms of poisoning may not appear for several hours, and include anxiety and restlessness, dry throat, nausea and, eventually, paralysis.

Treatment You'll need to get help urgently. While you're waiting:

■ keep the casualty calm
■ apply a pressure bandage (NOT a tourniquet)

- immobilise the limb by splinting it (this reduces circulation of the toxin)
- be ready to perform emergency resuscitation (see inside backcover) if necessary

Jellyfish

Despite their ethereal appearance, jellyfish are carnivorous animals. They occur in all tropical and sub-tropical waters, and you need to treat them with appropriate respect. They catch their prey by discharging venom into it from special stinging cells called nematocysts. If you come into contact with these stinging cells, you can get a variety of symptoms ranging from just a mild itch or pain and blistering to a severe, potentially fatal reaction. Children tend to be more severely affected by jellyfish stings.

Sea lice may be a problem in tropical waters. They are thought to be the tiny larvae of thimble jellyfish, and they can cause an uncomfortable rash (sometimes called 'sea bather's eruption'), especially if they get caught in your swimming costume. Shower thoroughly after getting out of the sea; calamine cream may help relieve the discomfort.

There are two potentially lethal species of jellyfish you need to keep a lookout for in Asian waters (and other parts of the world): the Portuguese man-of-war or bluebottle (right) and the box jellyfish or sea wasp (top right). Dead man-of-wars are often washed up on shore and they may still be able to sting – never touch any jellyfish lying on the beach, just in case it's a poisonous one.

Box jellyfish are often unnoticed until it's too late. They have long, white string-like tentacles which can get wrapped around you, leaving multiple, interlacing whiplash marks on your skin. Box jellyfish stings are excruciatingly painful, and can be lethal, although an antivenin is available. They can cause extensive scarring.

Man-of-war stings feel like a severe burn, and can produce general symptoms including nausea, vomiting and muscle pains. Rarely man-of-war stings can result in breathing difficulties and collapse..

Treatment Basic first aid for any jellyfish sting is with the following measures:

▶ get out of the water
▶ remove any bits of tentacle with tweezers or a gloved hand
▶ pour vinegar on the affected area (this doesn't help the pain, but it will prevent any stinging cells left in the wound from firing)
▶ man-of-war sting: put ice packs or local anaesthetic sprays, creams or ointments to help the pain, although severe pain may need to be treated with strong painkilling injections
▶ seek medical advice for severe stings, especially box jellyfish stings, as antivenin may be available
▶ be prepared to start emergency resuscitation if necessary – see inside backcover

!Don't wash a jellyfish sting with water or rub it, as it may make the pain worse.

Sting Rays & other Venomous Fish

Most venomous fish are found in salt water, although there is a species of catfish that lives in fresh water in Thailand and can produce a nasty sting if you come into contact with it. Saltwater species that can be a hazard to you in Asian waters include sting rays, stonefish and scorpionfish (butterfly cod), usually through stepping on them by accident. Sting rays (right) like to lie half-submerged in mud or sand in the shallows and are usually invisible unless you're looking out for them. You'll know if you step on one – they whip their tails up in defence. This can cause a nasty ragged wound, but they also have venomous spines which can sometimes produce fatal poisoning.

Scorpionfish (left) and stonefish (below right) occur throughout the Indian Ocean and the Indo-Pacific region. Stonefish are reef dwellers but can also be found in the shallows of estuaries. They have the dubious distinction of being the most dangerous of all venomous fish. Both stonefish and scorpionfish have sharp dorsal spines through which they inject a venom.

Stonefish are as ugly as scorpionfish are beautiful, and they are masters of disguise, as their name suggests. They lie half-submerged in sand, mud or coral debris, looking exactly like (you've guessed it) a stone. If you step on one by accident, you'll certainly know – stonefish stings are extremely painful and may lead to collapse and coma. There is a stonefish antivenin which should be given as soon as possible after the sting.

Scorpionfish are very distinctive and much easier to avoid, and the chances of you being stung by one is pretty remote. There's no antivenin available.

!Shuffle along in the shallows to give sting rays and stonefish plenty of warning to get out of your way.

Treatment Hot (nonscalding) water can help break down the toxins in fish venom and can be surprisingly effective at relieving pain from stings.

The procedure is as follows:

- if any spines are poking out, try to remove them gently (be sure to protect your own hands)
- wash any surface venom off with water
- bathe the wound in hot (nonscalding) water for up to 90 minutes or until the pain has gone, or apply hot packs
- if the pain is very severe, strong injected painkillers or a local anaesthetic injection may be needed
- wash the wound thoroughly once the pain is under control and apply a clean dressing
- rest with the limb raised
- seek medical help for antivenin if necessary eg for a stonefish sting

Blue-Ringed Octopus

Keep a lookout for these in rock pools at low tide. They are quite small, varying in size from 2cm to 20cm. The ringed marks, normally a yellowish brown, turn bright blue when they are angry. Their venom is highly dangerous, causing paralysis and possibly death.

Treatment You must get help urgently. While you are waiting for help:

- wash the wound out with any water or antiseptic available
- apply a compression bandage to the affected limb and immobilise it (to help prevent the poison from entering the circulation)

Cone Shell

However pretty a shell looks, unless you're sure you know what it is, it's best not to pick it up in case it is venomous. Cone shells are probably the worst-case scenario, and they are found in the tropical waters of the Indo-Pacific, as well as further north, around Japan. The y can be found buried in rock crevices or under sand in shallow waters. Fish-eating cones kill their prey by harpooning them with a poisonous barb, which has been known to cause death in humans. The pain from a sting can be excruciating, and may be followed very quickly by paralysis.

Treatment is as for a blue-ringed octopus sting: get help urgently; in the meantime, apply compression bandaging and immobilise the limb.

Crown of Thorns

These impressive reef creatures can cause immense pain if you tread on them by accident or brush against them while diving. They inject venom from the base of their spines which can break of and remain embedded in you. If the spines are not all removed, they can cause pain, swelling and generally make you feel unwell for several weeks or months.

Remove any spines that you can see, making sure not to break them. Immerse the affected area in hot (nonscalding) water, which will help ease the pain, and then immobilise the limb. Seek medical advice as soon as possible.

Sea Urchins & Other Stingers

Avoid stepping on sea urchins as their spines can break off and become embedded, causing pain and irritation. Some species occurring in the Indo-Pacific region have poisonous spines and can cause a severe reaction that may result in paralysis and breathing difficulties. Sometimes you can get an itchy skin rash for several months after. If you do step on one, remove any spines you can, taking care not to break them off. Run hot (nonscalding) water over the wound. Applying meat tenderiser, made from the flesh of the paw paw fruit, to the area may be helpful. Watch out for breathing difficulties, and seek medical help immediately if they appear.

Various other marine creatures can cause problems if you come into contact with them. Some sponges can cause severe itching, fire coral or feathery stinging hydroid can cause a painful sting and prolonged itching, and anemones can also give you a painful sting, so don't touch!

SCUBA DIVING

Indonesia, Malaysia, the Maldives, the Philippines and Thailand offer excellent diving for first timers or old hands. If you're a first timer, bear in mind that diving safely needs some knowledge and care.

It's absolutely vital that you have specific diver insurance that covers evacuation to a hospital or recompression chamber and subsequent treatment, something that will otherwise cost you thousands of dollars. Divers Alert Network (DAN – see the boxed text for more details) offers this, as do some other organisations, like PADI. Note that some dive operators won't let you dive unless you have this insurance. If you do get into an emergency situation, you should contact your insurer as soon as possible.

You should always make sure you know where the nearest hyperbaric chamber is, especially if you are planning on div-

Divers Alert Network (DAN)

DAN is an international nonprofit organisation providing expert medical information and advice for the benefit of the diving public. It operates a 24-hour diving emergency hotline in the US at ☎ 919-684-8111; alternatively ☎ 919-684-4DAN (4326) accepts collect calls in a dive emergency.

DAN emergency hotlines for the Asian region include DAN Japan (☎ 03-3812-4999), DAN South-East Asia-Pacific region (DES Australia; ☎ 08-8212 9242), Singapore Naval Medicine & Hyperbaric Center (☎ 750 5546) or DAN SEAP Philippines (☎ 02-815 9911).

DAN does not directly provide medical care, but it does provide advice on early treatment, evacuation and hyperbaric treatment of diving-related injuries.

For general queries and information about diving health and safety, contact DAN in the US on ☎ 919-684-2948 (or toll-free ☎ 800-446-2671 from within North America) or check out their web site (www.dan.ycg.org).

ing somewhere remote. You should be able to find this information through DAN before you leave.

If you are going to be doing even a limited amount of diving, it's important to know how it can affect your body and how to prevent potentially serious problems such as decompression sickness ('the bends').

DIVING CERTIFICATE & MEDICAL CHECKUP

If you want to dive, you're going to need a diving certificate issued by a major diving organisation (PADI, NAUI etc) – it's a bit like a driving licence when you're hiring a car. To get a certificate you need to complete a diving course. You can either do this before you go or at a dive centre in Asia (Thailand for example offers plenty of low-cost courses). Once you've got your diver's card, you can dive anywhere you want.

As a prerequisite to doing a course you need to have a diving medical checkup to show that you are fit to dive. Some dive centres may just want you to fill in a questionnaire, but ideally you should get a proper medical checkup before you leave. Age is no barrier in itself, but conditions that may make diving unsuitable for you are heart or lung disease (including asthma), ear or sinus problems, and any fits or dizzy spells.

INFORMATION SOURCES

If you contact DAN (see the boxed text), they will be able to answer any specific diving-related health queries you may have.

You'll find lots of good books on all aspects of diving, including health and safety. Some recommended titles include *Encyclopaedia of Recreational Diving*, a basic text produced by PADI and *The Diver's Handbook* by Alan Mountain, which is a comprehensive, well-thought out guide covering most aspects of diving. Another good book is *Scuba Diving Explained: Questions and Answers on Physiology and Medical Aspects of Diving* by Martin Lawrence. Lonely Planet's new Pisces series has specialised diving guides, including Asian sites.

Diving Safely

Basic rules for safe diving are:

- don't dive if you're feeling physically or mentally below par
- avoid going in if you are uncertain about the water or weather conditions
- check rental equipment carefully before using it
- never dive after taking alcohol or any mind-altering substances
- always follow your dive leader's instructions – but be aware that there are good and less good divemasters and ask around beforehand
- be aware of your limitations and stick within them
- never dive in murky water – you won't be able to see and avoid hazards
- stop diving if you feel cold or tired, even if it's not the end of the dive
- try not to panic if you find yourself in difficulties – instead take some slow deep breaths and think through what you need to do
- avoid touching or picking up things underwater – they may be harmful to you and you may cause harm to a fragile environment

DECOMPRESSION SICKNESS

Also known as the 'bends', decompression sickness is probably the best known hazard of diving. It's also one of the most serious, so you should make sure you know what it is and how to avoid it.

Breathing air under pressure (when you're diving) forces quantities of nitrogen (a major component of air) to dissolve in your blood and body tissues. If the pressure is later released too quickly (ie you ascend too fast), nitrogen can't be eliminated in the usual way and bubbles of gas form in the blood stream and body tissue.

Symptoms depend on where the bubbles are. Bubbles in the bloodstream can block circulation and cause stroke-like symptoms, such as blackouts and weakness of one side of the body. The most common form of decompression sickness is where bubbles form in large joints (joint bends) like the shoulder and elbow, giving you pain that increases to a peak some hours after the dive, then gradually subsides. Skin bends can occur, giving you itches and a rash over your body. In spinal bends you get back pain that typically circles your abdomen, followed by pins and needles in your legs, unsteadiness and paralysis. Inner ear bends make you dizzy and unable to balance.

Treatment of the bends is by recompression in a hyperbaric chamber which causes any bubbles to dissolve again, followed by slow, controlled decompression. This allows all the dissolved nitrogen to be eliminated without forming bubbles. Treatment is usually effective, but you need to get to a recompression chamber as soon as possible, because any delay could result in further damage which may be irreversible.

You can never guarantee that you won't get the bends, but you can do a lot to make it very unlikely. Dive tables are available to give you guidance on safe dives, but they obviously don't take your individual condition into account.

! Never dive if you are feeling unwell in any way, avoid strenuous activity before you dive, and drink plenty of fluids to prevent dehydration.

Be particularly careful to avoid diving if you're dehydrated, as this can slow down the rate at which nitrogen is eliminated from the blood. Sea sickness, alcohol the previous evening, and heat can all make you dehydrated.

Nitrogen build-up can be a problem if you're on a diving holiday, doing multiple dives a day or diving on consecutive days, and is the most common cause of decompression sickness at diving resorts. Taking a day off can allow any nitrogen that has built up to be eliminated.

BAROTRAUMA

The increased ambient pressure under water can cause problems if pressure is not equalised within the various air-filled cavities of the body, including the lungs, ears, teeth cavities, sinuses, and gut. Lung barotrauma is a very serious condition, often caused by not breathing out on ascent from a dive. Symptoms are variable, but include chest pain, dizziness and unconsciousness. Treatment is by recompression in a hyperbaric chamber.

Ear and sinus pain can be quite severe, and you should avoid diving if you have a middle ear infection, sinus trouble, a cold or hay fever. If you get dental pain while diving, it may be due to cavities in your teeth (eg dental decay), and you should see a dentist as soon as is convenient.

DIVING & ANTIMALARIALS

If you're taking mefloquine (Lariam) for protection against malaria, you need to be aware that it's not recommended to

Diving & Flying

If you fly too soon after diving – even a single dive – you can get decompression sickness, as the cabin pressure is set to a lower level than the pressure at sea level which encourages nitrogen bubbles to form. If you are planning to dive before you fly, discuss it with a reliable diving instructor, but basic guidelines are as follows:

- don't fly within 12 hours of a single no-decompression-stop dive (ie you didn't need to stop or descend to relieve pressure effects) and not within 24 hours of multiple dives (no-decompression-stop)
- wait 24 to 48 hours before flying after any dive which required decompression stops
- if you required recompression therapy, you need a medical certificate to say you are fit to fly

dive while you are taking it. This is because mefloquine can cause dizziness and balance problems, especially in the first few weeks of taking it, and it can make fits more likely in susceptible people. If you are planning on going diving and think you may need to take an antimalarial, mention this to your doctor before you leave so you can be prescribed an alternative if necessary.

FRESHWATER HAZARDS

SCHISTOSOMIASIS

You can get this disease, also known as bilharzia, by bathing, swimming or showering in fresh water in some parts of Asia, including China (mainly the Yangzi River basin – successful eradication programs have eliminated it from other areas), the Mekong Delta (Vietnam), the southern Philippines, central Sulawesi (Indonesia) and a very limited focus in Maharashtra state in India. As a result of a very successful eradication program, no human cases of the disease have been reported in Japan since 1978. There's currently no vaccine and none is likely in the near future.

Schistosomiasis is caused by a minute worm that lives its early life in a species of freshwater snail. When you enter the water, the worms head for you and make their way through your skin (you don't need to have an open cut, they can penetrate intact skin). There are two main types of the disease, which can either affect your bladder or your intestines. In Asia, you're at risk of the intestinal type, which is a more severe form of the disease. The worms don't multiply once they're inside you, but their eggs can remain in your tissues and this is what causes damage. Although chronic schistosomiasis is a major public health problem in risk areas, it's extremely unlikely that the disease would reach this stage in you.

Schistosomiasis is passed on when eggs in urine or faeces from a sufferer find their way back to water, which is why it is a problem in areas with inadequate sewage disposal systems.

Avoiding Schistosomiasis

In risk areas, it's worth taking care to avoid infection:

- check if the area you're going to is in a risk zone (see map); you can get schistosomiasis if you swim, wade, paddle, wash or do water sports in fresh water in these areas
- there's no risk of schistosomiasis from sea water, but beware of estuaries where freshwater rivers empty into the sea
- you don't just have to swim in the water to be at risk – paddling, crossing streams and water sports that involve immersion in water are risky
- wear waterproof footwear
- although infection is less likely, you are still at risk further offshore, for example if you swim from a boat
- if you do get wet, dry off quickly as the disease-causing worms can't survive long out of water
- stagnant water is especially dangerous (eg the lake behind a dam)
- if you're using water to wash in, either boil and chlorinate it or keep it (in a snail-free container) for at least two days (the infective worms die off in 48 hours if they don't reach a host)
- boil, treat or purify all drinking water

Schistosomiasis doesn't generally cause an acute illness like, say, malaria, but if left untreated it can cause serious long-term problems. It's best to avoid infection in the first place, but if there's a chance you may have been infected while you were away, be sure to get it checked out when you get back home.

Symptoms

A few hours after you've been in contact with infected water, you may get itching all over, known as 'swimmer's itch', and perhaps a rash as the worms penetrate your skin, but this does not last long (a day or two), and you may not even notice it. You may notice a cough or wheezing about a week to 10 days later as the worms pass through your lungs.

Sometimes you can get an acute illness (called Katayama fever) four weeks or so after infection, which is thought to be an allergic response to the eggs. You get a fever, itchy rash, diarrhoea, aches and pains, cough and wheeze and weight loss.

After several months you may get abdominal pain and blood in your urine or faeces. Often this is the first indication that there is a problem.

Diagnosis & Treatment

Infection can be diagnosed by a blood test (but not until at least three months after you were infected) or by a urine or faeces test. Effective treatment is available, with a single dose of a drug called praziquantel, which has few side effects.

LEPTOSPIROSIS (WEIL'S DISEASE)

This is another reason to be wary of swimming in fresh water. Leptospirosis is a bacterial disease that you can get from contact with water contaminated by animal urine (eg dogs, rats). You're probably at greatest risk of this if you're swimming or doing water sports (canoeing, rafting or caving) in affected water. Rice paddy fields are quite likely to be affected. The bacteria enter your body through breaks in your skin or through your nose or eyes.

You can get just mild flu-like symptoms, about 10 days after infection, but sometimes it can be more severe with high fever, vomiting, diarrhoea and red, irritated eyes. The illness can occasionally progress to jaundice and severe liver failure and even death in about one in 100 affected people.

You should seek medical help as soon as possible if you think you have leptospirosis. After the diagnosis is confirmed, treatment is with antibiotics (penicillin or doxycycline).

BITES & STINGS

Bites and stings from insects and other small beasties are the most likely hazard you face travelling in Asia. In contrast, you're much less likely to be at risk from higher profile dangers like snakes and tigers.

FLYING INSECTS

MOSQUITOES

These bloodsuckers (right) are likely to pose more of a hazard to your health – and sanity – than all the rest of the beasties discussed in this chapter. Mosquitoes have an astonishingly important role in the health of populations in tropical and subtropical regions of the world, mainly because they are carriers for serious diseases like malaria, dengue, yellow fever and lymphatic filariasis (elephantiasis).

It's not just the diseases mosquitoes carry, their bites itch like mad, and you run the very real risk of infection if you scratch them open. Insects inject a small amount of saliva when they bite and this sets up a local reaction. Bites are usually worst when you first arrive but, in theory at least, you develop a measure of immunity to the itch with time. If you're particularly sensitive to insect bites, they can develop into quite large swellings with a blister in the centre.

If you do get bitten, try not to scratch – if you break the skin, infection is likely and can be troublesome to get rid of. Calamine cream, tea-tree lotion, lavender oil or hydrocortisone cream applied to the bite can all be soothing. Antihistamine creams or sprays are widely available without a prescription, but they are probably best avoided as they are no better than calamine, and may cause an allergic reaction. If the itching is driving you mad, try taking an antihistamine tablet.

SANDFLIES

Sandflies (see below) are tiny (2mm to 3mm long) flies that are found throughout temperate and tropical regions, including Asia where they are found in drier areas. They cause an initially painful, and later itchy, bite and are responsible for transmitting a parasitic disease called leishmaniasis (see the Rarities chapter) and a viral infection, sandfly fever (see later in this section).

Sandflies breed in dark, moist habitats (such as cracks in walls, caves, long drops etc). They have a short flight range, and they don't fly very high; they rarely bite people sleeping on the first floor of a building. They usually bite at dawn, dusk and during darkness.

Because they are small they can get through most standard mosquito netting. You can get special sandfly netting, but this is probably going to be too suffocating for most people. A permethrin-treated net is effective at keeping sandflies out. Use DEET-containing insect repellents on any exposed skin to prevent bites.

Sandfly Fever

This viral disease can be transmitted through the bite of an infected sandfly and is a possibility wherever there are sandflies. Symptoms appear three to four days after a bite and include fever, chills, headache, joint pains, backache, nausea and vomiting, and sore throat. It generally clears up spontaneously without any specific treatment, usually within a few days.

OTHER BLOODSUCKERS

LEECHES

Leeches live just about anywhere that's damp, which covers a lot of Asia. They live on land (particularly during monsoon conditions) or in fresh water and vary in size, but are usually about a couple of centimetres long. They look like thin black worms before they fill up with your blood. They can drop into your boots or find gaps in your clothing as you pass through, or they can attach themselves to you if you swim in infested waters. Leeches usually attach themselves to your skin, but they have been known to reach the inside of the nose, lungs and bladder (don't even think about it).

Once a leech has attached itself to you, it produces a substance which prevents the blood clotting where it has attached and then it drinks its fill. A leech can suck up to 10 times its weight in blood within half an hour, and it drops off when it's full. Leech bites cause only minor irritation and don't spread any disease, but it can take a while for the bleeding to stop and there's a risk of secondary infection.

It has to be said that leeches tend to inspire a reaction in their victims quite out of proportion to their potential for harm. The sight of a couple of these bloodsuckers nuzzling your ankles can reduce even the most avid nature lover to a state of blind hysteria. Avoid getting grossed out by leeches with a few basic measures:

‣ check all over for them if you've been walking in infested areas
‣ avoid swimming in rainforest pools or streams
‣ insect repellent (DEET-containing) will discourage them
‣ tuck your trousers into your socks or wear gaiters to prevent them dropping down your boots
‣ consider soaking your clothes in permethrin, an insect repellent

Although leeches will drop off spontaneously if you leave them alone, unless you have nerves of steel you'll probably want to remove them before this. You need to encourage them to let go – if you try to pull them off directly their mouthparts may get left behind, increasing the risk of infection. Tried and tested methods for getting leeches to drop off include applying vinegar, salt or, cruel but possibly the simplest, putting a lit match to their unattached end.

After the leech has dropped off, clean the wound carefully with antiseptic and apply pressure through a non-stick dressing to stop the bleeding. It can take some time – keep applying a steady pressure, raise your limb and don't keep removing the bandage to see if the bleeding has stopped.

TICKS & MITES

The problem with these little biters is that they transmit a surprising number of rather peculiar diseases, so you'll want to do your best to avoid contact with them, although you're generally at low risk of these diseases. Illnesses can be spread directly via bites, body fluids of the creature or through inhaling their faeces in dust.

Ticks and mites occur worldwide and prefer woodland, scrub and long grass, where they hang around waiting for a meal to pass through. They are basically animal parasites and are found on animals and in places animals live. You often don't notice them until you get undressed. Ticks tend to be slow feeders and can remain attached, unnoticed by you, for some time. Take the following precautions where necessary:

- seek reliable local advice on likely problem areas (usually scrubland or pastures with long grass)
- wear long trousers and boots, and tuck your trousers into your boots
- use DEET-containing insect repellent on any exposed areas and consider soaking your clothes in the insect repellent permethrin if you are planning a trek in tick or mite country
- check your body regularly all over for ticks and mites if you have been walking in infested areas
- use a sleeping net at night, and sleep as high off the ground as possible
- remember that animals may be a source of ticks, so avoid close contact

If you find a tick attached to you, resist the impulse to pull it off directly, as its body will just separate from the mouth-piece, which makes infection much more likely. Remember that tick body fluids can be infective to you, so avoid handling it with your bare hands as far as possible. If you do, remember to wash your hands thoroughly as soon as possible.

The idea is to induce the tick to let go – various methods have been advocated in the past, including burning the tick off or applying chemicals to it, but these are no longer recommended as they can be harmful to you and may make the tick's contents more likely to contaminate you.

The most effective and safest method of removing a tick is to use a pair of tweezers to grasp the head (not the body or this will squeeze the contents into the wound and make matters worse) and pull gently. After the tick has dropped off, clean the wound thoroughly and apply an antiseptic solution like povidone-iodine. If tick parts get left behind, either try scraping them out (under sterile conditions as far as possible) or get medical help to do this.

Tick-Borne Diseases

These include various tick fevers with names you may recognise, like Q fever, tick paralysis, Lyme disease and typhus. You'd be pretty unlucky to get any of these diseases, but they are a possibility if you've been trekking or camping in tick-infested areas. If you get sick after you've been bitten by a tick or mite, it's sensible to seek medical advice.

Some tick-borne diseases like Lyme disease can cause long-term problems, including arthritis and meningitis, but they can generally be treated effectively with antibiotics if they're caught early enough. Most tick-borne diseases cause a skin rash, fever (often recurring), headache, vomiting, tiredness and aching muscles and joints. Tick paralysis is extremely rare, but if you experience any breathing difficulties after a tick bite, seek medical help immediately.

If you think you may have been at risk of tick bites, seek medical attention if you develop any of the following:

- red skin rash spreading from the initial bite
- fever, headache, muscle and joint pains
- neck stiffness
- deterioration and collapse – this is an emergency

Typhus There are several different varieties of typhus, which can be spread by ticks, lice and mites. The varieties all cause a similar disease, but differ in severity. There are no vaccines against any form of typhus, but they respond rapidly to appropriate antibiotic treatment without any long-term effects.

Scrub typhus, transmitted by a small red mite, is widely distributed throughout Asia and is common in newly cleared areas. The mites don't cause any itching when they bite, so check for passengers when you take your clothes off at night.

Scrub typhus is the most severe form of typhus, and can make you pretty sick. You get a swelling at the site of the tick bite which enlarges and later forms a black scarred area. Anything from four days to two weeks after the bite you get fever, headache and swelling of the glands near the bite. You also often get a skin rash that spreads over your body, cough, sensitive eyes and abdominal pain. In its most severe form it can be fatal, but it is unlikely to reach this stage in you. Seek medical advice as soon as possible for appropriate antibiotic treatment (usually a 10-day course of tetracycline 500mg four times daily).

FLEAS

These can be a problem in low-budget accommodation. Neither human nor animal fleas can live on you, but they do like to visit for a meal. You may notice itchy bites, usually in groups around the ankles or at the margin of clothing, and secondary infection is common. Kill the fleas with an insecticide and wash yourself and your clothes. Find another hotel if you can. Although fleas are widespread, they very rarely cause disease. However, as every self-respecting hypochondriac knows, fleas are capable of transmitting at least one serious disease – plague. The other disease certain fleas can transmit is a type of typhus. Both diseases are extremely rare, and no cases of plague have ever been reported in travellers.

Plague

As a traveller, even to affected areas, you're at a minuscule risk of this most famous of diseases, but it's worth knowing a bit about it because outbreaks always receive a huge amount of publicity and you'll want to know how it might affect you.

Plague exists in most parts of Asia (cases have been reported in China, Myanmar, Mongolia and Vietnam), with occasional outbreaks occurring – the most recent being in India in 1994. A vaccine is available, but it's only indicated for people like zoologists who could be at high risk of infection.

Plague is the Black Death of medieval Europe. It's caused by a bacterial microorganism that primarily infects rodents and it's transmitted to humans via the bite of certain species of flea that live on the rodents. You can also get it by direct contact with infected animals, and via coughs and sneezes from an infected person. The dry summer months encourage spread of the disease and the occurrence of epidemics.

The disease occurs quite soon after the infecting bite or contact (two to seven days), with a sudden onset of high fever, severe headache, chills and muscular pains, with pain in the groin or armpit (from inflamed lymph nodes called 'bubos', hence the name 'bubonic plague'). Untreated, the illness progresses rapidly, and sufferers are highly contagious. The risk of dying from untreated plague is high – 60% to 65%, but it's very unlikely to get to this stage. If caught early, treatment with antibiotics (ideally streptomycin or tetracycline) is very effective.

You should obviously seek medical advice as soon as possible if you think you have plague.

Plague is essentially a disease of poor living conditions, so you are unlikely to be at risk under normal circumstances. You're most at risk if you're a naturalist handling animals, hunter or camper in affected areas. Sensible precautions in these circumstances are:

▶ avoid handling live or dead rodents (including rats, rabbits and squirrels)
▶ use insect repellents to prevent flea bites
▶ avoid flea-infested hang-outs

VENOMOUS STINGS & BITES

BEES, WASPS & ANTS

Most stings are not dangerous, they're just painful. Children often get stung, especially if they're eating outdoors. Rarely you can have a severe allergic reaction to stings, which is a medical emergency.

Stings – When to Worry

You should seek medical help in the following situations:

■ if you've been stung in the mouth or throat, especially if the area swells rapidly
■ if you get rapid swelling from a sting anywhere
■ if it's followed by breathing difficulties or signs of shock – rapid pulse, pale clammy skin, breathlessness, sweating or faintness

In an emergency, such as a severe allergic reaction, and no medical help is available, treatment is as follows:

■ lie flat, with your feet elevated
■ give adrenaline injection (1 in 1000) 0.3mL into the top of your arm or thigh
■ get medical help urgently

If you know that you are allergic to stings, you should take an emergency kit with you containing antihistamines and adrenaline (epinephrine), to be used if you are stung – discuss this with your doctor before you leave.

Bee, wasp and ant stings puncture the skin; bees leave their stings behind, but wasps don't usually. If the sting is still visible, remove it with a pair of tweezers. You can relieve the pain and swelling with an ice pack or a cloth soaked in cold water. A sting relief spray (eg aluminium sulphate), calamine lotion, tea tree or lavender oils or the ubiquitous Tiger Balm can also be soothing. If the sting is in the mouth or throat, try to remove it and suck on an ice cube before seeking medical help.

SCORPIONS

These fascinating creatures are found throughout the tropics and subtropics, especially in dry desert areas. Scorpions grip their prey with their front pincers, finishing them off by injecting a poison through their tail. Before you get too alarmed, most scorpion stings are only painful. Some species can cause severe poisoning, which is heralded by vomiting, sweating, breathing difficulties, muscle spasms and abdominal pain – seek advice locally on the risks of scorpions.

Scorpions are nocturnal creatures, so you're very unlikely to see them, but sensible precautions include the following:

▸ always check your shoes before putting them on in the morning
▸ take care when lifting or moving boulders
▸ if you're camping, clear your camp site of rocks and other debris

We can't resist telling you that the largest scorpion in the world, growing to over 18cm long, is found in India. Check it out at the Mumbai Natural History Society.

SPIDERS

Although most spiders are venomous, only a few have powerful enough jaws to penetrate human skin and cause you harm.

There are a few venomous spiders in Asia, the most notorious of which is probably the black widow spider, which occurs worldwide in warm climates. They're small, dark spiders, usually with characteristic coloured markings on the abdomen. Bites can be painful, and may cause nausea, vomiting and muscle cramps. Orb web spiders, which are often exquisitely patterned, aren't generally harmful to you.

If you get bitten, put ice on the bite and, if you think it might be a poisonous spider (get advice from a reliable source locally), immobilise the limb and apply a compression bandage (not a tourniquet) to prevent the venom from spreading while you seek medical help. Antivenin (for severe black widow bites) should be available locally if necessary.

SNAKES

Asia has its fair share of venomous snakes, including many pitvipers, several species of cobras and kraits and some vipers. The deadly tiger snake occurs in Japan and much of China. Snakes don't usually occur at altitudes above about 4000m. Don't be too paranoid about snakes – although snake bites are an important cause of illness and death in local people, especially in rural areas, they are a very small risk to you. Having said that, you should be aware of the dangers, especially if you are going to be camping or trekking in rural areas.

If provoked, snakes may bite – or spit – in self defence. However, even bites from venomous snakes don't always inject enough venom to be dangerous. Some venoms cause mainly local effects around the bite, whereas others can cause severe poisoning, with paralysis or uncontrolled bleeding. Don't be too alarmed, though, as effective antidotes to snake bites are generally available locally in high risk areas.

Indian spitting cobras can project their venom a surprising distance, aiming for the eyes of their victim. If you do get struck in the eyes by cobra venom, seek medical help urgently, as there is a risk of permanent damage to your eyesight.

Prevention

It obviously makes sense to avoid getting bitten by a snake in the first place:

▶ never handle, threaten or chase after a snake

▶ wear socks and strong boots if you are walking through grass-lands or undergrowth, and give snakes plenty of chance to hear you coming

▶ use a torch if you are walking at night in rural, snake-infested areas

▶ be careful if you're climbing foliage-covered rocks or trees, or swimming in lakes or rivers surrounded by thick vegetation

▶ take care if you're collecting firewood or moving logs, boulders or other debris, as these may shelter sleeping snakes

Treatment

If you or someone you are with gets bitten by a snake:

▶ reassure them and try to keep them calm – they will probably be very frightened, and moving around may encourage further absorption of the venom

▶ immobilise the bitten limb with a sling or splint (see the First Aid appendix p411); this will help prevent the venom from being absorbed

▶ it's probably best not to apply pressure bandaging if you get bit-ten by a snake in Asia, unless you know that you were bitten by a snake with a neurotoxic venom, as it may worsen the damage caused by viper and some cobra bites

▶ seek medical help urgently for antivenin treatment, if appropri-ate, and other supportive measures

▶ make a note of what the snake looked like, but don't endanger yourself and others by trying to catch it

▶ watch for signs of shock and breathing difficulty and be prepared to start cardiopulmonary resuscitation (see inside backcover) if necessary

! Note that traditional first aid methods, like tourniquets or cutting into the bite and sucking the poison out, are poten-tially dangerous and you should avoid them, whatever you are told locally.

Antivenins are antibodies from horses or sheep, and although they are very effective at preventing the harmful effects of snake venom, they can cause severe allergic reactions in some people. This means that they should not be given without medical supervision except in extreme emergency.

ANIMAL BITES

Animal bites are a significant risk if you're travelling through Asia, as domestic and stray dogs and monkeys are everywhere, especially around temples. Animal bites are important as they carry a high risk of secondary bacterial infection (mouths harbour many bacteria and animals don't brush their teeth) and also because they carry a significant risk of rabies.

!Note that human bites are potentially as dangerous as animal bites from an infection point of view – they must be cleaned thoroughly and you'll need antibiotics to prevent infection.

RABIES

Rabies is a disease caused by a virus found in the saliva of infected animals. It's transmitted to humans by bites, but also potentially by contact between animal saliva and an open cut or graze on your skin. Rabies occurs throughout Asia, with the exception of Japan and Taiwan which are both currently rabies-free. Particular hot spots are the Indian subcontinent,

Rabies Prevention
Take care to avoid animal bites: be aware of animals around you in the street, never pet any animal and try not to surprise a sleeping animal. Monkeys can be very aggressive, especially the ones around temples which are used to being fed. Don't walk around eating as they may try to grab the food from you, and don't try to feed them.

where it is an under-rated and huge problem (in India latest figures are 30,000 deaths from rabies, compared with 16 in Europe), and parts of South-East Asia, including Thailand.

Rabies Risk

Practically any warm-blooded animal can be infected, although infected dogs and monkeys are probably the greatest risk to you as a traveller in Asia. Other potentially infected animals include rats, bats, cats, foxes and wolves. Note that you can get rabies from bats by inhaling infected bat faeces (particularly if you are caving). Domestic pets are less likely to be infected, but you can't assume they are risk-free.

You can't get rabies from touching an infected animal. You can get it from a bite (ie your skin is punctured) or if an infected animal licks a cut or graze on your skin. Rabid dogs may not show any signs of illness when they bite you, although if they do, they usually rush around, biting things and people at random, salivating excessively. An infected dog will usually be dead within 10 days, so if a dog that bit you is still alive after this time, there's a small risk that it would have been infected – but this is assuming you can find the animal and observe it for 10 days.

Rabies Information Sources

Before you go, it's a good idea to find out the current status of rabies in the areas you're planning to visit, and which animals are most likely to be rabies carriers, especially if you will be travelling off the beaten track in remote areas. Reliable sources of information include specialist travel health clinics, the US Centers for Disease Control & Prevention, the World Health Organization (contact details are given in the Infomation Sources section of the Before You Go chapter) and embassies of the countries you are planning to visit. If you are ultra-interested you could check out the WHO's online rabies resource, RABNET (http://oms.b3e.jussieu.fr/rabnetS).

Symptoms

The rabies virus attacks your central nervous system, causing extremely unpleasant symptoms. Once symptoms have appeared, the disease can't be cured and a painful death is inevitable. However, the infection can be stopped during the incubation period (ie before symptoms appear, anything from about five days to a year or more), by vaccination against rabies and, if you haven't been vaccinated before, a special injection of rabies immunoglobulin.

Symptoms of rabies infection include fever, headache, sore throat and nausea. This is followed by pain and burning around the bite, extreme sensitivity to light and sound, and anxiety. Hydrophobia or fear of water is a classic symptom of rabies, which is a result of painful throat spasms on drinking, and foaming at the mouth does occur (because of overproduction of saliva). Convulsions and coma then lead to death.

What to Do

If you are bitten by any animal, immediately clean the bite or scratch thoroughly. This is important even if the animal is not rabid because animal teeth harbour all sorts of bugs. If the animal is rabid, this can help kill the rabies virus before it has time to enter your body.

- Use lots of soap and water to flush the wound out, and then apply an antiseptic solution like povidone-iodine directly to the wound.
- Strong alcohol will also kill the rabies virus, and in an emergency you can apply spirits directly to the wound.
- Don't attempt to close the wound with stitches.
- Seek medical help as soon as possible.

You'll need to get advice on rabies prevention (you can wait until the next day if necessary). Bites to the head and neck area carry a higher risk of rabies. You will also need a course of antibiotics if it is a deep wound and a tetanus booster if you're not up to date with this. If no medical help is available, a suitable antibiotic course to take is co-amoxiclav 250mg three times daily (erythromycin 500mg twice daily if allergic to penicillin), while you find reliable advice on rabies prevention.

Postexposure Rabies Treatment

See also the section on rabies immunisation (p35) under Immunisations in the main Before You Go chapter.

After a potentially rabid bite, you will need a course of rabies immunisation to prevent the disease whether or not you were immunised before you left. If you weren't vaccinated before, in addition you will need a rabies immunoglobulin injection.

There are a couple of issues to be aware of with postexposure rabies treatment. For a start, both the vaccine and the immunoglobulin are expensive. Secondly, both are often in short supply, particularly in rural areas. Even when it is available, you need to avoid locally made vaccine and immunoglobulin as they are usually derived from non-human tissue, and carry a high risk of serious reactions. You need to find imported human vaccine, which should be available in most major cities. Try a university-affiliated health department, your embassy or members of the expatriate community for reliable advice on your risks of rabies and where to get antirabies treatment. Unfortunately, even if you wanted to, taking rabies vaccine with you is not an option, partly because it's often in short supply, but mainly because it needs to be kept at fridge temperature to remain effective.

TRADITIONAL ASIAN MEDICINE——

All over Asia, traditional healing systems, evolved over hundreds of years, are practised alongside 'western' (or, more accurately, 'international') medicine – the relative newcomer. The fundamental difference between traditional Asian medical systems and western medicine is that the eastern systems are holistic – ie they emphasise the interaction between mind, body and spirit and their relationship with the environment; by contrast, western medicine typically focuses on a specific disease process.

If you're travelling in Asia, you may want to sample some of the huge range of traditional healing therapies available in the region. In most places, you shouldn't have any trouble accessing practitioners. You don't necessarily have to be ill – most traditional therapies are used to promote general wellbeing as well as to treat specific illnesses.

The two most influential and widely practised traditional medical systems in Asia are traditional Chinese medicine (TCM) and Ayurveda (the traditional medical system of India and Sri Lanka). These two systems are complete and separate, but have a great deal in common with each other. Over the centuries, they have influenced each other as well as traditional medical practices in Pakistan, Nepal, Tibet, South-East Asia and Japan.

Following is a brief guide to the philosophy and practice of traditional medical systems in Asia, using the two main systems, TCM and Ayurveda, to illustrate principles common to all the systems. You should bear in mind that traditional therapies are not without their dangers – under Some Cautions later in this chapter we've given some basic guidelines for using traditional therapies safely.

If this brief guide stimulates your interest in traditional Asian medical systems, you might want to find out more from the many sources available. Under Further Information at the end of this chapter, we've listed some resources to get you started.

PHILOSOPHY

One reason why traditional Asian medical systems have sparked such an explosion of interest in the west is the 'mystic East' allure of their underlying philosophies. It's also the aspect that can be hardest for westerners to understand, as Asian medicine is based on ideas about the body, health and disease that seem very different from modern western notions of anatomy and disease. One major difference is that in traditional Asian healing systems, spirituality is seen as intrinsic to wellbeing.

TCM is based on Taoist philosophy, which is concerned with the balance of opposites in the universe: yin and yang, cold and hot, dark and light, winter and summer, female and male. These two forces interact constantly, pulling in opposite directions. Ayurveda is based on the ancient Hindu scripts, the Vedas. The word 'Ayurveda' comes from two Sanskrit words, *ayus* meaning life and *veda*, meaning knowledge: the knowledge of life.

All traditional Asian systems identify a vital force which is essential for life: in TCM this is called *qi*, in ayurveda, *ojas*, in Japanese medicine, *ki*, in yoga, *prana* and in Tibetan medicine, *rlung*. This vital life force or energy flows through and around the body, acting as a mediator between the various organs in the body, the mind, the spirit and the environment. Most systems have complex theories about how this energy and its various components circulate. Ill health results if the free flow of this vital force is blocked or unbalanced. Treatment is aimed at restoring balance by unblocking the flow of energy.

TCM and Ayurveda both have organ systems, but these refer to function rather than specific anatomical organs. TCM and Ayurveda share the belief that the human body is a reflection of the universe in miniature. The Five Organs in TCM, for example, reflect the Five Elements or Phases that in Chinese thought make up everything in the universe. Each

Organ (Heart, Liver, Spleen, Lungs and Kidneys) is linked to one of the Elements (Fire, Wood, Earth, Metal and Water, respectively) and has all the associated qualities and affinities of that Element.

In Ayurveda, the basic belief is that our constitutions are determined by the balance of three vital energies, the *doshas*: *vata*, *pitta* and *kapha*. These are composed of combinations of the Five Elements that make up everything in the universe: Space, Air, Fire, Water and Earth. The doshas affect all aspects of our lives. We all have one or maybe two dominant doshas; for example, a vata (Air and Space) person tends to be thin, highly active, mentally restless and often insecure. Interestingly, karma from previous lives can also determine the balance of doshas – a belief not found in TCM.

Various factors, including your emotional or spiritual state and diet, as well as external factors like the change of seasons, can disturb the balance of the doshas, which leads to illness. Correcting the balance of the doshas with therapies tailored to your individual constitution restores health.

PREVENTIVE

Both TCM and Ayurveda encompass much more than curing disease. They prescribe a way of life that aims to maintain health and wellbeing. A good doctor is seen as one who prevents a patient from becoming ill in the first place, which makes good sense. Balance or harmony between body, mind, spirit and environment is achieved through diet, exercise and meditation. For example, you need to change your diet to keep in harmony with the changing seasons. Various forms of meditative exercise are practised, which are seen as an important means of strengthening the vital energies. These include yoga in the Indian tradition and qigong or tai chi in the Chinese tradition.

An important component of Ayurvedic preventive medicine is a set of five 'purification' or detoxification therapies called *panchkarma*. These traditionally include enemas, purgation, therapeutic vomiting, nasal snuff and bloodletting (with leeches). If this sounds vaguely familiar to you, it's probably because the same techniques, with the same reasoning, were widely used in the west in the 18th and 19th centuries.

DIAGNOSIS

The initial consultation is generally the longest, and can last about an hour. Traditional practitioners are trained to assess the balance of the vital energies in an individual and any interaction with the environment, and to identify the cause of any disharmony. They can then prescribe therapies aimed at restoring the balance. Many of the diagnostic techniques used (eg taking your pulse) will be familiar to you, although the practitioner will be putting a very different interpretation on the information gained in this way.

In order to gain as much insight as possible into your constitution, the practitioner will ask you lots of questions about all aspects of your life, including areas that don't appear to have anything to do with your present illness. For example, you may be asked about your sex drive, whether you prefer hot or cold drinks and the colour of any discharges you have.

The practitioner also relies on their senses to gain information: they will look to see if you have dry skin or shiny hair and assess whether you have a particular odour. These all provide vital clues to the state of your health, the balance of elements within you and your normal constitution.

Another important part of the diagnostic process in both TCM and Ayurveda is examination of the pulse and tongue. In TCM, the pulse of each of the Five Organs can be read at the wrist, while in Ayurveda, this provides vital clues about the doshas. The practitioner will probably also want to feel your abdomen to check on your internal organs. In Tibetan medicine, which is an interesting amalgam of ayurvedic theory and TCM therapies, urine analysis is an important diagnostic tool.

THERAPIES

Once an imbalance has been identified and the reasons under-lying it explored, you'll be prescribed an appropriate therapy. These aim to restore balance or strengthen the energy flow, and can be internal or external.

Internal therapies include all forms of herbal remedies, which are used extensively in traditional Asian healing. External therapies include a wide variety of techniques, including acupuncture, moxibustion, various forms of mas-sage and the application of pastes and compresses.

Herbal Remedies

You'll find herbal remedies for sale in Asia in markets, road-side stalls and pharmacies, often alongside western medi-cines. In traditional Asian medical systems, use of herbal remedies is extremely well developed and draws from exten-sive lists of remedies, many of which have been used to treat the same disorders for centuries.

Asian medicines are not just derived from herbal sources, as a wander through any market will show you. Two other important sources are animals and minerals. Animal-based remedies include substances like rhino horn, cow urine, bull's testes and tiger bones. The rationale behind the use of these substances varies. For example, because the cow is a sacred animal to Hindus, any substance derived from it is inherently beneficial. In TCM, tiger bones are used because the tiger's strength is supposed to be passed on in this way. Neither rhino horn nor tiger bones appear to have any pharmacological action, and responsible practitioners are now trying to per-suade people to use alternatives.

Minerals used in remedies include salt, sulphur, gold, lead, mercury and silver. Gold has a special place in TCM and Ayurveda because of its incorruptibility. Some of these sub-stances are recognised to be toxic, and are generally only used to treat serious or otherwise untreatable diseases. Some of

Traditional Remedies

Some common remedies include the following, although there are many more remedies available. Remember that it's safest to follow the advice of a reliable practitioner on which remedies to take.

Ayurvedic Remedies

You'll find a huge range of remedies on offer; here are some you might like to keep a lookout for.

- Guggul is a herb that has received a lot of interest in the west in the treatment of inflammatory arthritis. It's a good anti-infective and anti-inflammatory.
- Cyavana prasam is a tonic for general health and bronchial complaints.
- Liv 52 is for hepatitis and liver problems.
- Varishtam is for coughs and bronchitis.
- Chandanasava is used in the treatment of cystitis.
- Maha Yograj Guggal is useful for arthritis and joint aches.
- Paspanguwa and peyava are used in Sri Lanka for colds.

Chinese Herbal Remedies

If you go into a Chinese pharmacy, you'll see walls of little drawers containing herbal remedies in various forms.

- Ginseng is probably the best known Chinese herbal remedy. It is thought to aid digestion, increase energy, benefit the heart, calm the spirit and benefit yin. Note that you shouldn't take it if you have blood pressure or heart problems as it can raise blood pressure. Korean ginseng is the hottest type.
- Dong quai is sometimes called the woman's herb as it helps to regulate the menstrual cycle.
- Wu wei zu, or five-flavoured seed, helps to stop coughs and wheezing, and is a sex tonic.

these metals have been used in western medicine, such as gold to treat rheumatoid arthritis.

You'll find that remedies come in a variety of forms, including raw herbs, freeze-dried herbs, powders, pills and tonics. Remedies for massage and external application are available in oil form or prepared in ghee. Although single herbs are sometimes used, you will more usually be prescribed a combination of many different herbs specially formulated for your particular problem. For example, most Ayurvedic medicines contain between five and 25 ingredients, including a mixture of herbs and minerals.

Acupuncture

Acupuncture is an ancient therapy (thought to date back to 1200 BC) and is practised throughout China, Japan, Korea, Taiwan and Tibet, as well as other parts of Asia. In China, it's even used to provide anaesthesia for certain operations, although not for emergencies or trauma. Legend has it that it arose because of the observation by wounded soldiers that a new wound made the pain of old ones diminish.

Acupuncture is based on the theory that the channels or meridians through which qi (the vital energy) flows make contact with the surface of the body at various points, called *xue*. The flow of qi can be manipulated at these points – in acupuncture by the insertion of needles. Acupuncture points are found all over the body, but most practitioners only use about 150 or so of the possible 500.

The needles are usually stainless steel and very fine. Most people don't find the needles painful when they are inserted, although a pulling sensation is said to be show that the needle is connecting with the qi. The needles are usually left in place for 20 minutes or so and, especially in China, the practitioner may manipulate them, which can feel a bit uncomfortable.

An acupuncture microsystem has been developed by a Korean acupuncturist. This system, called the Koryo System, allows conditions to be treated through body points on the hand, and is claimed to be as effective as normal acupuncture. The needles used for this type of acupuncture are tiny.

In China, moxibustion is often performed in conjunction with acupuncture. This involves burning a pellet of dried moxa (mugwort) or other herbs on the skin near acupuncture points. A variation on this is to wave a burning moxa stick over the point.

Cupping is another technique that uses acupuncture points. Bamboo or glass cups are placed at strategic points and herb is burnt inside, creating a suction effect. It leaves a purple bruise which looks unsightly, but fades in a couple of days.

If you don't like the thought of needles, there are other possibilities: acupressure uses manual pressure on acu-points, or there's electro-acupuncture, which is a relatively new development using electrodes instead of needles – an interesting example of the way this ancient technique is evolving. Shiatsu also uses acupuncture points.

Shiatsu

This technique was developed in Japan at the beginning of the 20th century, but has its origins in TCM. It's extremely popular in Japan where it's widely practised. It's a form of massage that uses manual stimulation as a way of manipulating acupuncture points, called *tsubos*. There's no pushing, pressing or squeezing as only natural body weight, not muscular effort, is used to apply pressure. Shiatsu is usually given on the floor (you lie on a futon mattress). You wear light clothing and oils are not used. It can produce a profound sense of wellbeing.

Massage

'Medicine is the art of rubbing' said Hippocrates. Don't let the slightly seedy image of massage in many western countries put you off; traditional Asian massage is in a different league altogether. Massage is an integral part of traditional Asian medical systems and, together with acupuncture, probably the best known form of Asian medical therapy in the west. You'll probably be offered an Ayurvedic massage at some point in your travels if you are on the tourist trail in South India, and it's hard to escape offers of a massage on the tourist trail in Thailand. If you're in Japan, you shouldn't find it hard to track down a shiatsu practitioner.

Traditional Asian massage usually works on acupressure or marma points (Ayurveda), and oils are usually used (ie it usually involves contact with bare skin, although shiatsu is an exception to this – see earlier). Traditional Chinese massage is called *tuina* and is one of the oldest forms of therapy, said

Reiki

This healing modality uses the transfer of universal energy via hands-on treatment, rediscovered in the early 1900s by a Japanese Buddhist monk called Mikao Usui.

Using symbols to harness varying frequencies of vibrational resonance, the Reiki practitioner is able to direct energy into the body via the chakra system (chakras are the seven major energy centres in the body). Each symbol has many uses and varying frequencies to cleanse, balance, ground, centre and transmute diseased energy from the human electromagnetic field into higher energies. Symbols may also be used to transcend time and space and send energy to distant people or places.

During a standard treatment or healing, the Reiki practitioner will channel energy by placing the hands in various positions on the body. The patient may perceive energy in many ways, such as warm, cold, tingling, throbbing or vibrating sensations, leaving them relaxed and revitalised.

There are many Reiki associations all over the world, using different symbols or hand positions depending on their lineage, but it is the same universal life energy.

Bernadette Saulenier

to predate acupuncture. There are many different styles of tuina, and regional variations. All techniques are used to manipulate acupressure points and channels, and particular combinations of techniques have been identified as beneficial for certain conditions when applied to particular channels. Tuina generally involves bare skin contact and the use of oils.

Ayurvedic massage takes several different forms, but always involves the use of oil. It's usually quite a vigorous affair, with tapping, kneading, rubbing and squeezing. One type of Ayurvedic massage involves the therapist hanging from the ceiling and carrying out the massage with their feet!

Internationally, massage is probably the best known aspect of traditional Thai medicine (which owes much to both Ayurveda and TCM). It's an extensive and highly refined system of massage, combining techniques like kneading and stroking with manipulation of joints and acupressure.

TRADITIONAL VERSUS WESTERN MEDICINE
In general, traditional medical practices are enjoying a revival in most parts of Asia. In Japan, for example, traditional Japanese medicine or *kampo* (which is based on TCM) was banned at the beginning of the 20th century, but today herbal remedies and therapies like shiatsu and reiki have never been so popular. Ayurveda, discouraged under colonial rule, has bounced back since then, and now the two systems coexist. There have been attempts to integrate TCM and western medicine, with limited success, but now the two systems are encouraged to exist side by side.

In places like India, Sri Lanka and China, traditional medicine and western medicine are often used to complement each other. For example, you may receive conventional surgery for a broken bone, followed by traditional massage and dietary advice aimed at promoting recovery. In these places, there are colleges and universities of TCM and Ayurveda, and dedicated hospitals and clinics in traditional medicine.

Traditional Asian Medicine

In many parts of Asia, western medicine has the same novelty value and 'magical' power that traditional Asian medicine has in the west, whereas traditional medicine is seen as boring and familiar. In many rural areas across the region, the majority of people only have access to traditional healers, and can't in any case afford western medicine.

WHAT THEY'RE GOOD FOR

Because TCM and Ayurveda are complete medical systems, they can in theory be used to treat any condition. However, most practitioners would agree that they are best for more chronic conditions as they don't generally have an immediate effect. So it's probably best to stick to western medicines for acute infections and trauma, but you could use traditional remedies in the recovery period to help you get over the illness.

Traditional Asian medicine is particularly valuable for migraine, chronic fatigue, arthritis and joint aches, irritable bowel syndrome, asthma, skin conditions like eczema and psoriasis, menstrual disorders and stress. The World Health Organization (WHO) has even compiled a list of conditions that it officially recognises as treatable by acupuncture.

Remember that although traditional Asian medicine can be used to treat specific disorders, it's good if you just want advice on optimising your health because it is very much concerned with preventive strategies and the maintenance of good health.

FINDING A PRACTITIONER

It's just as important with traditional medicine as it is with western medicine to make sure you see a reputable, well-qualified practitioner – this is not always easy as a traveller in a foreign country, especially if you are unfamiliar with the culture and language. There are no failsafe guidelines, but personal recommendation is probably the best criterion. You can try scrutinising your practitioners' qualifications if you like: TCM

359

and Ayurvedic practitioners have to train for five or six years at college or university in China, India or Sri Lanka.

During the consultation, trust your intuition – do you feel comfortable with them? Do you trust them? It's always a good idea to settle the cost of the consultation and any therapies beforehand.

SOME CAUTIONS

If you are prescribed therapies, don't be afraid to ask if there are any side effects or potential problems from the therapy – and use your common sense. Just because a treatment is traditional doesn't automatically mean it's safe. Also, be aware that there is a difference between 'folk' remedies and traditional Asian medicine. Folk remedies are probably best avoided as they may not work and they may actually be harmful. For example, there's a belief in Cambodia that paraplegics can be 'cured' by suspending them over fire. And most experts would agree that psychic surgery, famous in the Philippines, is probably little more than a confidence trick.

Always let the practitioner know of any health problems you have and any medicines you are on, as interactions between herbal remedies and drugs are possible. As a general rule, if you take any 'western' medications regularly (eg for a chronic heart condition), it's best not to stop them suddenly.

Herbal remedies can contain potentially toxic ingredients if taken in the wrong dose or for the wrong reasons. Some basic guidelines are as follows:

- ▸ avoid substances derived from endangered species (eg rhino horn) for obvious reasons
- ▸ follow the instructions carefully for any remedies you are prescribed (check the dose, how often and the best time to take it, how to make them up)
- ▸ stop taking it immediately if you experience any adverse effects
- ▸ herbal remedies can be unsafe in pregnancy, so are probably best avoided

▶ some conditions like kidney or liver disease can make toxic effects more likely, so make sure you discuss this fully with your practitioner

▶ combination remedies containing traditional herbs and western medicines are generally best avoided as they have a greater potential for harm

Acupuncturists have been known to puncture the wrong thing (eg the lung), but this comes back to the importance of finding a good practitioner. If acupuncture needles are re-used and not adequately sterilised, there is a theoretical risk of transmission of hepatitis B and HIV. If you're at all concerned, buy your own acupuncture needles or choose a therapy like acupressure that doesn't involve needles.

Massage is basically safe in the hands of an experienced practitioner, although it's best avoided in certain situations:

- if you have varicose veins
- if you have severe back pain
- if you've had blood clots in your leg veins
- fever
- in the first three months of pregnancy

Bear in mind that, especially in tourist resorts, you may get more than you bargained for with a massage – take care to choose the type you want.

FURTHER INFORMATION

Because of the explosion of interest internationally in traditional Asian medicine, you are spoilt for choice when it comes to finding more about them. Go to any good bookshop and you'll find plenty of literature on eastern therapies, or do a search on the web. However, it's not always easy to get information on the practice of traditional therapies within Asia, and it can be difficult to find information about the genuine article and not just the western populist notion of traditional Asian medicine. Do your own search on the web, or try these recommended web sites to get you started:

www.ayurveda.com – a good, easy to follow and seemingly authoritative introduction to the principles and practice of Ayurveda by Dr Vasant Lad of the New Mexico-based Ayurvedic Institute.

www.healthy.net/library – this site has a good range of informative extracts from books and articles on acupuncture, TCM and Ayurveda.

www.tibet.com – this is the official web site of the government of Tibet in exile, and it has a comprehensive introduction to the principles and practice of traditional Tibetan medicine.

Here's a very small selection of the many books available on traditional Asian medicine that you might like to try.

Traditional Chinese Medicine by Rey Tiquia – an excellent, clear and readable account of the principles behind TCM and TCM treatments.

Chinese Medicine: The Web That Has No Weaver by Ted J Kaptchuk – the classic text on all aspects of TCM presented clearly and sympathetically and in detail.

Ayurveda: The Ancient Indian Healing Tradition by Gopi Warrier & Deepak Gunawant – an extensively illustrated, detailed and authoritative guide.

Ayurveda: Life, Health & Longevity by Robert Svoboda – one of a number of useful texts on Ayurveda by this prolific and sympathetic author.

In Exile in the Land of Snows by John Avedon has a very readable chapter on Tibetan medicine.

Back to Balance: A Self-Help Encyclopaedia of Eastern Holistic Remedies by Dylana Accolla with Peter Yates – this book is just what it says it is, and it's full of practical advice for lifestyle changes (including recipes) and remedies for a range of common conditions.

HOSPITALS, COLLEGES & INSTITUTES

In most parts of Asia, you shouldn't find it hard to track down dedicated traditional medicine hospitals, clinics and institutes, especially in China, India and Sri Lanka. Here are a few suggestions to get you started.

Ayurvedic Hospitals

You'll find these all over India (especially in South India) and Sri Lanka, or you could ask at branches of the India tourist board. If you have access to the web, you could check out the section on Ayurveda on the India Tourist Board site (www.india-tourism.de), which has an extensive list of colleges, hospitals and resorts offering Ayurvedic treatments.

Arya Vaidya Clinic & College (☎ 0422 213188, fax 0422 214953), 1382 Trichy Rd, Coimbatore 600 045, Tamil Nadu, India

Arya Vaidya Sala Hopsital (☎ 04934 2216) Kottakal 676503, Malappuran, Kerala, India

Ayurveda Centre (☎ 0834 513291), Sarovar Park Plaza Resort, Bogmalo 403806, India

Siddhalepa Hospital (☎ 738622) 106A Templers Rd, Mt Lavinia, Colombo, Sri Lanka

Tibetan Medicine

If you want to find out more about this fascinating healing system, you could try either the Tibetan Medical & Astrological Institute, Gangchen Kyishong in the home of the Dalai Lama in exile, Dharamsala in Himachal Pradesh, India, or in Lhasa in Tibet you could check out the Tibetan Traditional Hospital.

TCM

Most provincial capitals in China have institutes and hospitals of traditional medicine, so you should have no trouble getting traditional treatment here. Some institutes offer courses in acupuncture and herbal medicine for foreigners: in Guangzhou, try the Traditional Chinese Medicine Hospital (☎ 8188 6504, 16 Zhuji Lu) or, in Beijing, the Beijing Institute of Traditional Medicine.

AFTER YOU GET BACK

Some illnesses can show themselves for the first time when you get back, and illnesses that started while you were away may persist or get worse after you return. Before you rush off to make an appointment, remember that unless you are worried for some reason, you don't automatically need a health check when you get back. In some situations, however, a post-travel health check is advisable:

- if you develop any of the symptoms listed in the following section (What to Look Out For)
- if you have any persistent symptoms (eg diarrhoea, recurrent fevers, generally under the weather, weight loss)
- if you were bitten by an animal, whether or not you received a rabies injection
- if you were on a long trip or you spent some time in rural areas or living rough
- if you're worried you might have something
- if you were ill when you were away (unless it was just a brief episode of traveller's diarrhoea)
- if you received medical or dental care while you were away
- if you had unprotected intercourse with a new partner

You can go to your usual doctor, a travel health clinic or, if you're concerned you may have something exotic, a doctor specialising in tropical medicine. The advantage of a travel health or tropical medicine specialist is that they may be more alert to symptoms of tropical diseases. On the other hand, your doctor will be familiar with your health history.

See the section on Post-Travel Blues later in this chapter, but you should consider seeing your doctor or arranging counselling if you experience significant stress, anxiety or depression after you return.

If you had medical or dental treatment while you were away, remember to claim for it as soon as possible on your travel insurance.

WHAT TO LOOK OUT FOR

You should see your doctor, a specialist travel health expert or tropical medicine specialist if you develop any symptoms in the days or weeks after you get back.

!Remember that doctors at home may not think of tropical diseases as a cause for your symptoms unless you tell them. Be sure to mention that you have been travelling, where you went and any risk situations you were in.

The time between getting infected and symptoms appearing varies with different diseases, but it can be weeks or even months, so if you were on a short trip they may not appear until after you get back. In addition, some aspects of travelling (such as exposure to the sun) can make conditions, such as skin cancer, more likely in the longer term.

Fever

This is especially important if there's any risk that you may have malaria. You should suspect malaria if you develop any fever or flu-like symptoms after you return, especially in the first four weeks. Although the most serious form of malaria (falciparum) is most likely to occur in the first four weeks after you return, other forms of malaria (more likely if you were travelling on the Indian subcontinent than in South-East Asia) can occur several months after you were infected. In some circumstances you may need to have a course of an antimalarial, called primaquine, which clears persistent liver forms of the parasite.

Malaria deaths have occurred in returned travellers because the infection was not suspected by doctors at home, so it's important to tell anyone treating you if you have been to a malarial area, even if you were taking antimalarials.

!Don't forget that you need to continue taking your antimalarials for four weeks after you leave a malarial area or you will be at higher risk of getting malaria.

There are lots of other causes of fever in returned travellers, including dengue fever, hepatitis, typhoid and tuberculosis.

Diarrhoea

Gastrointestinal problems can persist or appear for the first time after you get back – see the section on Prolonged Diarrhoea in the Digestive System chapter for more details. Bacterial dysenteries, giardiasis and amoebiasis are all possibilities, and even malaria, the great mimic, can cause diarrhoea. You often find that diarrhoea clears up spontaneously once you get back to your usual routines and lifestyle. You need to see your doctor if your symptoms persist for longer than a week after you get back or there's any blood or mucus in your faeces.

Worms are often symptomless, so it's probably a good idea to get a check for these if you've been on a long trip or you've been travelling rough. If you know you ate something dodgy like raw meat or seafood you may have picked up tapeworm or liver flukes so you should get this checked out.

Travelling can make you more likely to develop noninfectious conditions such as irritable bowel syndrome or milk intolerance (usually temporary), so bear this in mind if you develop any gut disturbances that are not normal for you. Some gut problems may be unrelated to travelling, you may have got them anyway, so get any symptoms checked out.

! Be aware that diarrhoea can be contagious and this may affect whether you can go back to work when you return (eg if you work with young children or in the food industry).

Schistosomiasis

Although this occurs only in limited areas in Asia (see p330), it can cause long-term problems if it's not picked up and treated early. If you have been swimming in fresh water in risk areas, you may have become infected – but bear in mind that infections are regularly picked up in travellers who didn't think they had been at risk. It can appear with fever and other symptoms a few weeks or months after you were exposed or you may get no symptoms for several months, then you may notice blood in your urine or faeces. Infection can be confirmed by a test on your faeces or by blood test. The blood test needs to be done at least three months after you were exposed to the risk.

Skin

If you've got any infected cuts, persistent ulcers or rashes or any weird skin blemish that you're not sure about, you should get these checked out as soon as possible. Mention if tick bites or any other nasties were a possibility. Fungal infections like athlete's foot are common while you're away, but they may clear up once you get back.

Another thing to look out for is any change in a mole or freckle (see p290 for more details), especially if you've been scorching yourself in the tropical sunshine.

Animal Bites

If you were bitten by any animal while you were away and you didn't get rabies injections, it's a good idea to discuss with your doctor whether you should take any action now. It may be advisable, for example, to have a course of rabies injections.

Sexual Health Checkup

This is definitely a good idea if you had unprotected intercourse with a new partner while you were away, or you experience any symptoms. Hepatitis B, HIV and other sexually transmitted infections (STIs) are all a possibility. STIs can be symptomless but can still have serious effects on your fertility so it's worth getting this checked out early if you think it may be a possibility.

Other Symptoms

It's worth reporting any unusual symptoms, such as weight

loss, night sweats, recurrent fevers or if you're simply not feeling right and you don't know why. Tuberculosis can sometimes appear after you get back, and may be a cause of weight loss, fevers and night sweats. Consider this possibility if you spent several months living with members of the host community. Some more exotic diseases may not show up until after you get back.

POST-TRAVEL BLUES

It's a sad fact that everyone has to return home eventually. You may be glad to get back to familiar faces, culture and your old haunts. On the other hand you may be reluctant to exchange the exciting, challenging, temporary world of travelling for a return to a life that may seem at first less enjoyable and less meaningful.

If you've been away for a while, you may experience reverse culture shock when you return. Have a read of the section on culture shock in the Mental Wellbeing chapter, and see if you recognise any of the feelings described.

Added to this is the big change in lifestyle that coming home usually involves – trying to pick up where you left off, maybe trying to find a job, coping with dreary weather and a (comparatively) dreary environment can be stressful. Friends and family may be surprisingly uninterested in hearing about all the experiences you had while you were away (but can you blame them?).

Be prepared for at least some emotional turmoil after you get back, as you try to match up your expectations of life with the realities. Talking through experiences you have had may help, especially if those experiences were particularly life-altering or traumatic. Try talking to other travellers to see how they coped, or to a sympathetic friends or a trained counsellor. Activity and a purpose in life can help enormously. On the other hand, if you feel persistently low and lose interest in life, you may be depressed and you should seek medical help.

BUYING & USING MEDICINES——

○ For guidelines on medicines in children see p266.
○ See also the Medical Kit section on p56.

All medicines have side effects, but the trick is to balance up the possible risks of using a medicine against the probable benefits – something most of us are usually happy leaving to our doctors to work out. When you're travelling, expert advice may not be available and there may be occasions when you need to self-treat with medicines – either ones you have with you or ones you have bought locally. In this chapter we give general guidelines on how to use prescribed drugs safely and how to avoid dangerous medications. Although these guidelines are primarily for western-style medicines, the general safety points also apply if you're buying traditional medicines.

DRUG NAMES

We've highlighted this issue in the boxed text 'Drug Names' (p56) in the Before You Go chapter, where you'll also find guidelines on finding out the generic name of a drug. As you'll no doubt be aware, drug names is one of those sticky issues that can have a big impact on travellers and to which there is as yet no satisfactory answer. We've used the generic (chemical) name for drugs throughout this book because these are the same the world over, and will be understood in any language (you may need to point this out).

You can consider different brands of drugs as basically interchangeable (although different brands can differ in the way they are absorbed and how convenient they are to take). Some common drugs that have been around for ages are available under the generic name (eg paracetamol/acetaminophen) as well as various brand names. To confuse the issue further, some medicines that are made up of a combination of generic substances may be given a new generic name. For example, the painkiller co-codamol is a combination of paracetamol (acetaminophen) and codeine.

MEDICINES

BUYING MEDICINES IN ASIA

You need to take a bit of care if you're buying western-style (or traditional medicines) in Asia. Generally, western countries have rigorous safety standards for medicines, as well as well-regulated medical and pharmaceutical professions, but the situation can be very different elsewhere. In addition, drugs made by local companies may be substandard (ie less effective) or even fake, especially in South-East Asia.

As well as different safety standards, you may find there are very different attitudes towards medicines and their use – in many Asian countries medicines are sold in roadside stalls and corner shops without prescription, just like any other commodity. If you need to buy medicines while you are away, take some basic safety measures:

- if possible, buy from a trustworthy doctor or large pharmacy
- check if the drugs have been kept in suboptimal conditions eg in direct sunlight or without refrigeration
- check the expiry date – very few drugs (tetracycline is a notable exception) are actually harmful if they are kept too long, but they may well be ineffective
- if possible, look for drugs made by local branches of international drug companies and look out for fakes (although these can be difficult to spot)
- check the label and safety seal – if either look dodgy, avoid it

In many Asian countries, injections are seen as the best and most effective way to administer medicines. As a rule it's best to avoid injections because there is an increased risk of serious side effects from the drug, as well as the risk of an abscess at the injection site or infection with HIV or hepatitis B if the needle has not been sterilised properly since it was last used. Try asking if a tablet form is available instead.

Remember that in some countries, for example China and Cambodia, western-style medicines may be in short supply and difficult to obtain.

Medicines

MEDICINES

MEDICINES TO AVOID

One safety concern you should be aware of is that drugs now considered dangerous in many developed countries because of unacceptable side effects may still be available in Asia; safer alternatives are given later in the relevant sections of this book. Combination drugs tend to be popular in Asia and India – try to avoid these because it's best not to take any unnecessary medications and the added ingredients may be harmful

Some medicines to be wary of include the following (we've used the generic name unless indicated).

- steroids – these powerful drugs are used to treat a variety of conditions (eg asthma and dermatitis), usually to suppress inflammation. They have some pretty powerful side effects too, and should not be used except under medical supervision. Combination medications available in Asia and India may contain steroids. Look out for the following generic names (but be aware that this is not a complete list): prednisolone, betamethasone, cortisone, dexamethasone, hydrocortisone, methylprednisolone. Never use eyedrops containing steroids except under medical supervision.
- chloramphenicol – an antibiotic that may be prescribed for tonsillitis or traveller's diarrhoea. It can have a very serious effect on the blood system in some people and should only be used for life-threatening infections (eg sometimes for typhoid fever). Note that this does not apply to chloramphenicol eyedrops and eardrops, which can be used safely.
- clioquinol – an antidiarrhoeal drug; you should avoid this because it can have serious side effects on the nervous system – see p143 for more details on antidiarrhoeal remedies to avoid.
- opium tincture – widely available in Asia for treatment of diarrhoea and other ailments; best avoided for obvious reasons.
- phenylbutazone – an anti-inflammatory painkiller with potentially serious side effects
- sulphonamide antibiotics – these will work if no alternatives are available, but are best avoided if possible because of potential side effects.
- Fansidar (pyrimethamine/sulphadoxine) – this antimalarial is no

longer used for prevention in most western countries because of side effects, although it is still used to treat malaria; if you are offered it as a preventive, try to find an alternative.

SIDE EFFECTS & ALLERGIES

Any drug may produce unwanted or unexpected effects, so be on the lookout for these when you take any medicine. You may need to stop taking that particular drug and take a different one. If you know you're allergic to a drug, you should avoid it.

Fake Medicines

According to a recent *Time* magazine article, up to one-tenth of all medicines on the market in Asia are fakes. These vary from small-scale operations, like the Pakistani doctor who allegedly sold a heroin addiction treatment containing chicken feed, to organised criminal organisations who specialise in putting near-perfect imitations of common drugs on the market. There's big money in this, as profit margins for fakes are huge. China, Indonesia, Malaysia and Thailand appear to be at the heart of the trade, but all countries in the region are affected.

The human cost is likely to be much greater than official figures estimate. It's not just that the fake may be ineffective, which is bad enough, but in many cases it may actually be harmful, as several horrific stories testify. For example, in 1986, 14 Mumbai hospital patients died after being given eye drops containing diethylene glycol – a component of antifreeze.

As usual, the most vulnerable members of society suffer the most. In rural communities, people tend not to see a doctor first (for social and economic reasons), but usually buy drugs from small village shops. They often buy them by the handful, without packaging, making it easy for fakes to be passed off. Even when the packaging is intact, many local people will not be able to read and are in any case unlikely to recognise a misspelt name.

Some drugs produce well-recognised side effects that your doctor or pharmacist should warn you about. Familiar drugs that have been around for many years are unlikely to have any unexpected effects, although new drugs may still be capable of causing a few surprises. Sometimes it can be difficult to work out if it's the drug or the actual illness process causing the problems, especially when you're treating diarrhoea; all antibiotics can cause stomach upsets.

Allergies are one serious type of side effect, but not all side effects are allergies. Mild symptoms of headache, diarrhoea, nausea and maybe vomiting are not signs of allergy. Signs of allergy usually appear soon after taking the medicine and include:

- a red, raised itchy rash (common)
- breathing difficulties and swelling of the face
- fainting or collapsing

Note that a severe allergic reaction is always a medical emergency, and you will need to seek medical help urgently.

Make sure you record any drug allergies that you know you have, and carry this information on you at all times. Some companies specialise in making engraved bracelets with these details on – see the Useful Organisations section in the Before You Go chapter at the start of this book for more details. Always tell anyone treating you of any drug allergies you think you have.

Medicines that commonly cause allergies include aspirin and antibiotics like penicillin and sulpha (sulphonamide) drugs. Remember that if you are allergic to one drug, you should avoid any related drugs too.

DOSES, TIMING & SPECIAL INSTRUCTIONS

Ideally, for any medicine, you should be clear about what dose to take at what interval and follow any special instructions on the label. In practice, you may find that the dosage of the brand available locally may differ from the one we've suggested in this book. This is usually because the drug has been formulated slightly differently or possibly the dose may have been expressed in different units.

If you're not sure what dose to take, either ask the pharmacist or doctor, read the information leaflet carefully or try to find another brand of the drug that causes less confusion. Remember that a single extra dose of most drugs is unlikely to cause problems.

Note that usually 'every six hours' means in practice to take the dose four times a day during waking hours; 'every eight hours' means take it three times a day.

Alcohol is best avoided because it can affect the absorption of drugs and may have an additive effect on drugs that are sedative (make you drowsy), such as some antihistamines. Alcohol should not be taken with metronidazole (an antibiotic that you may take for some types of diarrhoea) as it causes a particularly bad reaction, making you feel stupendously dreadful.

If you're taking several different drugs together, they can interact to make adverse effects more likely or reduce effectiveness. Similarly, medical conditions can affect how well a drug works and how likely it is to cause unwanted effects; for example, you should not take the contraceptive pill if you have hepatitis.

COMMONLY USED MEDICINES

We've summarised here details about doses, side effects and cautions for some common medicines you may find you need to use while you're away. Details about other medicines used for specific conditions are described in the relevant sections:

○ drugs for preventing (p39) and treating (p121) malaria
○ drugs for motion sickness (p70)
○ ear (p173) and eyedrops (p179)
○ drugs for vaginal thrush (p241)

MEDICINES

Can You Help Me Please?

What do you do when a local person asks you for treatment? It's a dilemma you'll almost certainly be faced with if you're travelling in a less developed country. In most situations it's probably better to avoid immediately diving for your medical kit – short term gratitude may lead to longer term harm. If the question arises, consider the following: do you know what is wrong with the person and the appropriate treatment? Do you know enough about that person to be reasonably confident that they will not react adversely to the treatment? Are they on any other medication that would interact badly with your treatment? Could they be allergic to your treatment? Can you communicate well enough with them to find all this out and explain the dosage regime? Even if you're a doctor, answers to these questions are not always straightforward.

If you're feeling guilty about not helping, a simple explanation that you are not a doctor and do not know how to treat them will usually be met with understanding. It is almost always better to encourage people to seek help from a local health centre. Don't forget that simple advice may be more helpful than you appreciate. It is common to be shown a dirty open wound. A suggestion to bathe the wound in boiled and cooled water regularly and to keep it as clean as possible will hopefully be heeded, and is far more useful than any tablets.

Corinne Else

Where the brand name tends to be better known than the generic name, we've listed some common brands, but be aware that these brands may not be available in Asia.

PAIN & FEVER

Simple painkillers include aspirin and paracetamol (called acetaminophen in the US); these are also good for reducing fever.

Paracetamol has very few side effects, except nausea, although it can cause liver damage in overdose. Aspirin is more problematic and should be avoided if you are hypersensitive to it, asthmatic or suffer from indigestion or stomach ulcers. It can also cause heartburn and stomach irritation.

Aspirin is not suitable for children under 12 years, but paracetamol is fine in infants and children.

Stronger painkillers include codeine phosphate, which

drug	dose – adult	dose – children
aspirin	one to two 300mg tablets every four to six hours when necessary (maximum 4g in 24 hours)	avoid in children under 12 years
paracetmol (aceta-minophen)	one to two 500mg tablets every four to six hours (maximum 4g in 24 hours)	three months to one year: 60 to 120mg; one to five years: 120 to 250mg; six to 12 years: 250 to 500mg; over 12 years: adult dose; (maximum four doses in 24 hours)
codeine phosphate	two to four 15mg-tablets every four , hours maximum 240mg in 24 hours	one to 12 years: 1mg/kg every six hours
ibuprofen	two 200mg tablets every six hours, as necessary	suspension (100mg/5mL) available for children; six months to one year: 2.5mL; one to two years: 2.5mL; three to seven years: 5mL, eight to 12 years: 10mL; all doses given three to four times daily

will also stop up diarrhoea. Side effects include constipation and drowsiness. Some customs officials may be a bit suspicious of codeine, because of its potential for abuse, so you may need a letter from your doctor if you are taking it with you. Other painkillers include a combination of paracetamol with codeine (eg co-codamol). Codeine can be given to children, but is best avoided if possible.

Ibuprofen (eg Nurofen and other brand names, also forms suitable for children) is an anti-inflammatory drug that is good for fever, pain (including period pain) and inflammation (eg painful joint). Avoid it if you have had stomach ulcers or a hypersensitivity to aspirin. Stronger anti-inflammatory drugs include **naproxen** and **indomethacin**, which are useful for treating sprains, strains, sports injuries and joint pains.

ANTIBIOTICS

Many travel-related illnesses are caused by infections, and you may find you need to take antibiotics to treat them while you're away. Antibiotics work against bacterial infections, but don't have any effect on viral or fungal infections. This means they won't be any good against common viral infections like colds and flu, as well as many throat and gastro infections.

Different antibiotics are effective against different bacteria. We give antibiotic recommendations in this book based on the likeliest cause of infection; however, the best way to find out if an antibiotic will be effective against an infection is to have a laboratory test to identify the bacteria causing it.

Antibiotics should stop most infections within a few days. Because they work to stop the infection and not the symptoms, you may need to treat symptoms (such as pain and fever) with other medications until the antibiotics kick in.

If an antibiotic appears not to be working (it needs at least two days to do its stuff), you may be taking the wrong dose (check) OR it's the wrong antibiotic (the bacteria are resistant or they aren't affected by this particular antibiotic) OR the illness is not what you think it is. In this case, it's always best to seek medical advice (after you've checked that the dose is correct).

Antibiotics can cause problems, which is why they need to be treated with respect. They commonly cause nausea and diarrhoea and, because they disrupt the normal balance of organisms in the body, can make women more likely to get thrush (vaginal candidiasis). They can cause severe allergic reactions, especially penicillins and cephalosporins, so you should always carry a record of any allergic reactions with you.

! If rashes and swelling of the throat and face occur, stop taking the drug immediately and seek medical advice. Always carry a record of any allergic reactions with you.

Antibiotic Resistance
This is a growing problem worldwide, and is one reason why you should always finish the whole course of antibiotics

---

Antibiotic Guide
Here's a quick guide to which antibiotics are suitable for what. Read the details about the antibiotics to find out if they are suitable for your age group, and avoid any antibiotics (including related antibiotics) you are allergic to.

- diarrhoea – ciprofloxacin (and related antibiotics), co-trimoxazole, metronidazole, tinidazole
- chest infection – co-trimoxazole, amoxycillin, co-amoxiclav, erythromycin/clarithromycin
- throat infection – phenoxymethylpenicillin or co-amoxiclav
- ear infection – amoxycillin, co-amoxiclav or co-trimoxazole
- urinary infection (cystitis) – amoxycillin or co-trimoxazole
- skin infection – phenoxymethylpenicillin, flucloxacillin or co-amoxiclav

Note: clarithromycin/erythromycin can be used if you are allergic to penicillin.

(unless you experience severe adverse reactions). Antibiotic resistance is more likely to occur if the infection is not quickly and completely eliminated. In many countries, antibiotics are readily available without prescription and are often taken indiscriminately and perhaps inappropriately. People may not be able to afford to buy a whole course and are often not aware of the importance of doing so anyway. The use of antibiotics in livestock rearing has also been an important factor.

You can help by only using antibiotics if really necessary, choosing the most effective antibiotic and completing the full course of antibiotics – this way there aren't any bacteria left hanging around with nothing better to do than work out ways of fighting back.

The Details

Suggested lengths of courses of antibiotics are indicated in the relevant sections. Note that all the antibiotics described in this section can cause nausea and stomach upsets.

Co-amoxiclav (Augmentin) is a combination of amoxycillin (a penicillin drug) and clavulanic acid (which makes it more effective against some bacteria than plain amoxyclllin). It's a useful 'broad spectrum' antibiotic, and is effective against bladder, ear, chest and sinus infections. It's also good for skin infections and animal bites. Although amoxycillin (Amoxil) is less reliable generally, it is useful if you can't get co-amoxiclav. Both drugs can sometimes cause skin rashes, and should be avoided if you are allergic to penicillin.

Trimethoprim is useful for treating bladder and ear infections, and for diarrhoea in children. There are concerns over potentially serious but rare side effects including severe skin rash and blood disorders. It should be avoided in pregnancy. Note that co-trimoxazole is a combination drug that contains a sulphonamide antibiotic plus trimethoprim – it's best avoided if possible as there is a slightly higher risk of serious side effects.

Ciprofloxacin is effective against most bacterial causes of travellers diarrhoea, cystitis (bladder infection) and chest

drug	dose (adult)	dose (children)
ciprofloxacin	500mg twice daily	not recommended in children under 12 years
amoxycillin	250mg three times daily (double dose if infection is severe)	up to 10 years: 125mg three times daily; 10 years and over: adult dose
co-amoxiclav	250mg three times daily	up to 10 years: 125mg three times daily
trimethoprim	200mg twice daily	two to five months: 25mg; six months to five years: 50mg; six to 12 years: 100mg; all doses twice daily
flucloxacillin	250mg four times daily (double dose if infection is severe)	under two years: 75mg; two to 10 years: 125mg; all doses four times daily
erythromycin	500mg to 1g twice daily	up to two years: 125mg; two to eight years: 250mg all doses twice daily
metronida-zole	500mg three times daily	7.5mg/kg three times daily

infection. Ciprofloxacin can occasionally cause kidney problems, which is why you should drink plenty of fluids when you take it. Similar drugs that can be used as alternatives include norfloxacin, nalidixic acid and ofloxacin. Ciprofloxacin should be avoided in pregnancy and it is not generally recommended for children under the age of 12 years because of potential side effects. Suitable alternatives for children are suggested in the relevant sections.

Flucloxacillin (eg Floxapen) is a penicillin drug that is effective for skin infections, although co-amoxiclav is usually used as the first choice. It can cause rashes and allergic reactions, and you should avoid it if you are allergic to penicillin.

Erythromycin (eg Erymax) or clarithromycin can be used as

an alternative to penicillin drugs if you are allergic to penicillin. Clarithromycin is less likely to cause side effects such as nausea and vomiting.

Metronidazole (eg Flagyl) is effective against infections causing diarrhoea, especially with a fever and abdominal pain, for example giardiasis and amoebic dysentery. It is also effective against bacterial vaginosis. You should avoid alcohol when you are taking it as it causes a severe reaction (flushing, headache, palpitations). **Tinidazole** (eg Fasigyn) is similar and can be used as an alternative.

ANTIHISTAMINES

These are useful for hay fever, allergies, itchy rashes, insect bites and motion sickness. There are many different ones available, mostly without prescription, and they vary in what side effects they cause (mainly drowsiness).

Antihistamines that are more likely to cause drowsiness include **promethazine**, **chlorpheniramine** and **cyclizine**. Non (or at least less) sedating ones include **astemizole**, **cetirizine** and **loratidine**. Ask your pharmacist for guidance on brands available to you, and follow the dosing instructions on the packet. They can be given to children.

Side effects are more common in children and older people and include drowsiness, headache, dry mouth and blurred vision. Because drowsiness can occur, you shouldn't drive, dive or drink alcohol in large quantities after you take antihistamines.

NAUSEA & VOMITING

○ For information on drugs to prevent and treat motion sickness, see p70.

Metoclopramide (eg Maxolon) is useful for nausea and vomiting associated with diarrhoea or food poisoning. The adult dose is 10mg three times daily. It's best avoided in children – if necessary, try an antihistamine instead. Some are available in suppository form (ie you insert it in the rectum) which might sound uninviting, but is a useful option if you're vomiting.

ANTIDIARRHOEALS

Drugs that help reduce the number of times you have to visit the little room include **loperamide** (eg Imodium and other brand names), probably the most useful, **diphenoxylate** with atropine (eg Lomotil) and **bismuth subsalicylate** (Pepto-Bismol).

The dose of loperamide is two 2mg tablets initially, followed by one 2mg tablet after each loose motion, to a maximum of eight tablets in 24 hours. It commonly causes constipation; other possible side effects include abdominal cramps, bloating and, rarely, paralysis of the gut. The dose of diphenoxylate is four tablets initially followed by two tablets every six hours until the diarrhoea is under control. Neither drug is recommended for children, and you should avoid them if you have a fever, or blood in your diarrhoea.

Bismuth subsalicylate is available in tablet or liquid form, but tablets are more convenient if you're travelling: take two tablets four times daily. It's not suitable for children (as it contains aspirin). It can cause blackening of the tongue and faeces, and ringing in the ears. You shouldn't use it for more than three weeks at these doses.

MEDICAL SERVICES

○ See the Help ... chapter for more guidelines on how to go about finding medical help.

The standard of medical services varies across the region, according to the political and economic climate. In general, medical care in Bangkok, Hong Kong, Japan, South Korea, Singapore and Taiwan is of a high standard, and if you needed to be evacuated for medical reasons, these would be good places to go. However, medical care in all these places is very expensive, so you will need to have good health insurance.

Elsewhere, you will generally find both public and private hospitals and clinics in provincial capitals and large towns, although rural areas may not be as well served. In many rural areas, the only care available is provided by healthworkers or traditional medical practitioners. In general, public hospitals tend to be under-financed and overstretched, and are probably best avoided unless they are affiliated to a university, or you can get a private ward. Private clinics or hospitals are generally better, although they can be expensive. Mission hospitals or those run by charitable organisations are often of extremely high standard, and may be the only option in more remote areas. In some countries military hospitals are good for emergencies.

In all countries in the region, traditional medicine is practised alongside 'western' medicine, and people often use both. In China and India, for example, you'll find colleges and hospitals dedicated to traditional medicine, as well as private practitioners.

WHAT TO EXPECT

Depending where you are, medical care may be very different from what you are used to back home, and this is often exacerbated by language and cultural differences. As a rule, standards of nursing care are very different from those you may be used to – attitudes towards basic hygiene can be alarmingly casual. If you have to stay overnight in hospital (best avoided if possible), you are often expected to have someone to bring you food and look after you.

In particular, attitudes towards the use of medicines can be very much more cavalier than you may be used to. Western medicines tend to be prescribed very readily, often when there is no need, so be prepared to try a few simple measures first. If you do have to take a medicine while you are away, make sure you know what it is and what it has been prescribed for.

Traditional remedies are widely available all over Asia. They are often herbal remedies, but this doesn't necessarily mean that they are harmless. For a more detailed discussion of this issue, see the chapter on Traditional Asian Medicine earlier in this book.

PAYMENT
In many parts of Asia, with some notable exceptions, fees for medical treatment can seem ridiculously cheap. However, you will generally have to pay upfront for all consultations and treatment. Remember that medical evacuation from anywhere costs thousands of dollars so it's vital that you have travel insurance, although you will probably need to come up with

In an Emergency
Unless you're travelling in one of the more developed countries in Asia, you can't rely on fast-reaction emergency services coming to your rescue eg in a road traffic accident. If you are in an emergency situation:

- don't wait for emergency services to arrive – if you can, get a taxi or flag down some transport, and ask them to take you to the nearest doctor or hospital
- contact your embassy for advice
- phone your travel insurance hotline as soon as possible

the money yourself at the time, and claim it back later. Keep an emergency stash with you just in case, and ask for and keep any receipts.

DIRECTORY

The information listed here is intended as a guide only. Although we have done all we can to ensure the accuracy of the information listed here, contact details change and places disappear. Note that listing here does not imply any endorsement or recommendation by Lonely Planet of the services provided.

BANGLADESH

Health facilities are very limited here. Your best bet is probably Dhaka; there are also hospitals in Chittagong, Sylhet and Rajshahi.

▸▸ *Dhaka Medical College Hospital* (☎ 318 202), Dhaka

BHUTAN

Health facilities are limited. There are hospitals in most of the district headquarters towns, but no private medical care. Your best bet is the National Referral Hospital in Thimphu; otherwise it's worth going to Bangkok for anything serious. Medical services are free to Bhutanese citizens.

▸▸ *Jigme Dorji Wangchuck National Referral Hospital* (☎ 22496, 22497), Thimphu

BRUNEI

Medical care is generally of a high standard here, although it may not be readily available in rural or remote areas of the country. The RIPAS hospital in the capital is the largest hospital, and is modern and fully equipped.

▸▸ *Raja Isteri Pengiran Anak Saleha (RIPAS) Hospital* (☎ 242424), Bandar Seri Begawan

CAMBODIA

Health care services here are basic and limited; in rural areas they may be nonexistent. If necessary, you should consider going to Bangkok for treatment.

▶▶*AEA International SOS Clinic* (☎ 216 911), 83 Mao Tse Tung Blvd, Phnom Penh – has 24 hour emergency service and can arrange evacuation

▶▶*Calmette Hospital* (☎ 426 948), Monivong Blvd, Phnom Penh – French-run

CHINA

Medical services in China are reasonable and relatively cheap (although you may get charged more than Chinese nationals). However, health services in more remote areas like Mongolia, Tibet and Xinjiang are few and far between, and western medicines may be hard to find wherever you go, so take a good supply with you. Hong Kong has excellent health care facilities but they are expensive, particularly if you use private care. For a comprehensive overview of Hong Kong's hospitals, including contact details, and other health services, check out the Hong Kong Health Authority web site (www.ha.org.hk).

Beijing

▶▶*Asia International Clinic* (☎ 6462 912, fax 6462 9111), Building C Bitic Leasing Center, No 1 North Rd, Xing Fu San Cun, Chaoyang District, Beijing – also offers emergency evacuation service

▶▶*Beijing Toronto International Hospital* (☎ 6554 1728, fax 6554 1734), 6th Floor, Fu Hua Plaza

▶▶*Capital Hospital (Peking Union Medical College Hospital)* (☎ 6513 2266), Foreigners Section, 53 Dongdan bei Dajie, Wangfujing

▶▶*International Medical Centre* (☎ 6465 1561, fax 6465 1984), Lufthansa Centre, 50 Liangmaqiao Lu

Hong Kong (Public Hospitals)

▸▸ *Prince of Wales Hospital* (☎ 2632 2415, fax 2637 8244), 30-32 Ngan Shing St, Sha Tin, New Territories

▸▸ *Princess Margaret Hospital* (☎ 2990 1111, fax 2786 3629), Lai Chi Kok, Kowloon

▸▸ *Queen Elizabeth Hospital* (☎ 2958 8428, fax 2958 8950), 30 Gascoigne Rd, Kowloon

▸▸ *Queen Mary Hospital* (☎ 2819 2111), Pok Fu Lam Rd, Pok Fu Lam

Hong Kong (Private Hospitals)

▸▸ *Adventist Hospital* (☎ 2574 6211), 40 Stubbs Rd, Wan Chai, Hong Kong Island

▸▸ *Baptist Hospital* (☎ 2339 8888), 222 Waterloo Rd, Kowloon Tong

▸▸ *Matilda & War Memorial Hospital* (☎ 2849 0111), 41 Mt Kellett Rd, The Peak, Hong Kong Island

Macau

▸▸ *Hospital Kiang Vu* (☎ 371333), Rua de Kiang

Guangzhou

▸▸ *Guangzhou General Hospital* (☎ 666 2266), 111 Liuhua Rd

Shanghai

▸▸ *Hua Shan Foreigners Clinic* (☎ 6248 3986), Hua Shan Hospital, 19th Floor, 12 Wumuluchi Zhang Lu

▸▸ *Shanghai Emergency Centre* (☎ 6324 4010), 68 Haining Lu

▸▸ *Shangahi No 1 People's Hospital* (☎ 6306 9478), 585 Jiulong Lu, Hongqiao

Tibet

▸▸ *Tibet No 1 People's Hospital* (☎ 633 2462, fax 633 3478), Lingkhor Shar Lam, Lhasa

INDIA

Health care facilities are generally limited, although the major centres have reasonably good medical facilities. There are state-run hospitals throughout the country, as well as private clinics and hospitals in most major towns. There are also hospitals run by western missionary societies, which often have very good facilities and are probably the best places to head for in an emergency. Most doctors speak English, as medicine is taught in English at universitites.

Calcutta

▸▸ *Medical Office* (☎ 249 2323), The Oberoi Grand, 15 JL Nehru Rd (Esplanade)

Chennai

▸▸ *Apollo Hospital* (☎ 827 6566), 21 Greams Lane

Goa

▸▸ *Goa Medical College Hospital* (☎ 225727), Damboline

Mumbai

▸▸ *Breach Candy Hospital* (☎ 363 2657), 60 Bhulabhai Desai Rd, Cumballa Hill

New Delhi

▸▸ *All India Institute of Medical Sciences* (☎ 661123, 6864581), Ansari Nagar

▸▸ *East West Medical Centre* (☎ 462 3738, 469 9229), 38 Golf Links Rd

Vellore

▸▸ *Christian Medical College Hospital,* Ida Scudder St

INDONESIA

Medical care is generally adequate in major cities, but may be nonexistent in rural areas. Jakarta has the best medical facilities in the country. Medical costs are generally cheap, although drugs can be expensive. If you need more specialist care, Singapore has excellent facilities or Darwin (Australia) may be closer if you are in eastern Indonesia.

Jakarta

▸▸ *AEA International Clinic* (☎ 7505980, fax 750 6002), Jl Puri Sakti No 10, Cipete, Jakarta Selatan

▸▸ *Medical Scheme* (☎ 5255367), Setiabudi Building II, Jl H Rasuna Said, Kuningan

▸▸ *Pondok Indah* (☎ 7500157), Jl Metro Duta Kav UE

▸▸ *Rumah Sakit Cipto Mangunkusuma* (☎ 330808), Jl Diponegoro 71

▸▸ *Sentra Medica International* (☎ 3157747), Jl Hos Cokroaminoto No 16, Menteng, Jakarta-Pusat

▸▸ *St Carolus Hospital* (☎ 3904441), Jl Salemba Raya 41

Bali

▸▸ *Gatotkaca Klinik* (☎ 223555), Gatotkaca 21

▸▸ *Manuaba Clinic* (☎ 426393), Jl Cokroaminoto

▸▸ *Rumah Sakit Umum Propinsi* (☎ 227912), Sanglah, Denpasar – the island's main hospital

▸▸ *Surya Husadha Clinic* (☎ 233786), Jl Pulau Serangan 1-3

JAPAN

The standard of medical care here is very high, but expensive.

The Tourist Information Centre has lists of English-speaking hospitals and dentists in the large cities. Note that most drugs are supplied by doctors rather than pharmacists.

▶▶ *International Clinic* (☎ 3583-7831), 5-9 Azabudai 1-chome, Minato-ku, Tokyo

▶▶ *Tokyo Medical & Surgical Clinic* (☎ 3436-3028), 32 Mori Bldg, 4-30 Shiba-koen 3-chome, Minato-ku, Tokyo

KOREA (NORTH)
Medical resources are very limited and there are shortages of basic western medicines.

▶▶ *Medical University Hospital*, P'yongyang

KOREA (SOUTH)
Emergency medical care is excellent and reasonably cheap, and most doctors in the main hospitals speak English (but not all nurses and receptionists). All the following are in Seoul.

▶▶ *Asia Emergency Assistance* (☎ 790 7561) – provides 24-hour emergency service for foreigners, and acts as a link between you and Korean hospitals (for a fee)

▶▶ *Seoul National University Hospital* (☎ 762-5171), 28 Yon-gon-dong, Chongno-gu

▶▶ *Severance Hospital* (☎ 361-6540; go to the International Clinic), 134 Shinch'on-dong, Sodaemun-gu

LAOS
Medical care is very limited and is mainly found in major towns and the capital. Evacuation to Thailand is your best option if you need anything more than basic care.

▶▶ *Mahasot Hospital*, (☎ 214018), Vientiane – has a Diplomatic Clinic for foreigners

▶▶ *Hôpital de l'Amitie* (☎ 413306), Phonthong Rd, Ban

Chommani, Vientiane – a French-run centre for trauma and orthopaedics

or go across the border to

▸▸ *Wattana General Hospital* (☎ 241031), 70/7-8 Suphakidjanya Rd, Udon Thani, Thailand

MALAYSIA

Health services are generally good and medical staff usually speak English. Government hospitals are free or make just a nominal charge. There are also private clinics and many private practitioners, who generally speak English.

▸▸ *General Hospital* (☎ 292 1044, fax 298 9845), Jalan Pahang, Kuala Lumpur

▸▸ *Queen Elizabeth Hospital* (☎ 223 185), Jalan Penampang, Kota Kinabalu

▸▸ *Sarawak General Hospital* (☎ 257 555), Jalang Ong Kee Hui, Kuching

MALDIVES

Health services are limited, although first aid facilities are available on all the resort islands. Emergency evacuation from resorts are coordinated by the National Coast Guard and Hummingbird Helicopters; alternatively you can call on the Maldivian Air Taxi seaplanes. If you need any serious medical or surgical care, you should get yourself to Colombo (Sri Lanka) or Singapore.

▸▸ *ADK Private Hospital* (☎ 324331), Sosun Magu

▸▸ *AMDC Clinic* (☎ 325979, private), Dharmavantha Magu

▸▸ *Indira Gandhi Memorial Hospital* (☎ 316647), Male

MONGOLIA

Health care facilities are limited and most drugs and medical equipment are in very short supply. If you need medical care, it's probably best to get yourself to Beijing or Hong Kong. International rescue organisations should be able to fly you out if necessary, but you'll definitely need that travel insurance. English is unlikely to be spoken in most hospitals.

▸▸ **Yonsei Friendship Hospital** (☎ 310 945), Enkh Taivny Orgon Choloo; Ulaan Baatar

▸▸ **Russian Hospital** No 2 (☎ 358 191), Enkh Taivny Orgon Choloo; Ulaan Baatar

MYANMAR
Medical facilities are pretty limited here, especially in rural areas, although there are decent private clinics in Yangon, Mandalay and Pathein. For serious conditions, you'll want to fly to Bangkok or Singapore.

▸▸ **AEA International Clinic** (☎ 667 879, fax 667 866), The New World Inya Lake Hotel, 37 Kaba Aye Pagoda Rd, Yangon – also provides air ambulance facilities

▸▸ **Kandawgyi Hospital** (☎ 01-542486), Natmauk Rd, Yangon

▸▸ **Pacific Medical Centre & Dental Surgery** (☎ 01-548022), 81 Kaba Aye Pagoda Rd, Yangon

NEPAL
Medical facilities are very limited, so for serious illnesses you will need to fly out to Bangkok or Singapore. Most doctors speak English.

▸▸ **CIWEC Clinic Travel Medicine Centre** (☎ 228531, www.bena.com/ciwec, email advice@ciwec.mos.com.np), Durbar Marg, Kathmandu

▸▸ **Nepal International Clinic** (☎ 412842), near Jaya Nepal cinema, Kathmandu

▸▸ **Patan Hospital** (☎ 521333), Langankhel, Patan

PAKISTAN
Medical facilities are very limited here. Consider flying to

Delhi in India or home for more serious conditions.

▸▸ *Karachi Adventist Hospital* (7218021, fax 7227010), 91 Depot Lines, MA Jinnah Rd, Karachi

▸▸ *Aga Khan Hospital* (☎ 493 0051), Stadium Rd, Karachi

▸▸ *Sheikkh Zaid* (☎ 586 5731), Canal Bank Rd, Lahore

PHILIPPINES

Public hospitals lack equipment and resources and are probably best avoided, although private practitioners provide a reasonable level of service.

▸▸ *Makati Medical Center* (☎ 815 9911), 2 Amorsolo St, Makati

▸▸ *Manila Doctors Hospital* (☎ 503011), 667 United Nations Ave, Ermita, Manila

▸▸ *Manila Medical Center* (☎ 591661), 1122 General Luna St, Ermita, Manila

SINGAPORE

Medical services are of a high standard and there are lots of private practitioners as well as government hospitals. It's expensive, so you'll definitely need that travel insurance.

▸▸ *National University Hospital* (☎ 1-800-772 5555, fax 779 5678), 5 Lower Kent Ridge Rd

▸▸ *Singapore General Hospital* (☎ 222 3322, fax 222 1720), Outram Rd

▸▸ *TMVC Singapore* (☎ 733 4440), International Medical Clinic, Tanglin Shopping Centre #04-20, 19 Tanglin Rd

SRI LANKA

Health care is adequate, but as in most countries in the region you're probably better off using the private sector. Public and private hospitals and clinics are listed in the *Official Tourist Handbook* and *Travel Lanka*.

MEDICAL SERVICES

▶▶ *National Hospital of Sri Lanka* (☎ 691111), Regent St, Colombo 8

▶▶ *Lakeside Adventist Hospital* (☎ 08-223 466), 40 Sri Sangaraja Mawatha, Kandy

▶▶ *Nawaloka Hospital* (☎ 544444, fax 541521), 23 Sri Saugathodaya Mawatha (off Union Place), Colombo 2

TAIWAN

The health service here is good and most doctors should be able to understand English or speak a little. Private hospitals are excellent, but expensive.

▶▶ *Adventist Hospital* (☎ 2771 8151), 424 Pateh Rd, Section 2, Taipei

▶▶ *National Taiwan University Hospital* (☎ 2397 0800), 7 Chungshan S Rd, Taipei

THAILAND

Standards of medical care here are generally good in the main centres, although they are variable elsewhere. Bangkok is the best place for medical care; elsewhere, you can get decent medical care in Chiang Mai, Khon Kaen and Hat Yai or Phuket.

Bangkok

▶▶ *Bangkok Adventist (Mission) Hospital* (☎ 281 1422, 282 1100), 430 Phitsanulok Rd

▶▶ *Bangkok General Hospital* (☎ 318 0066; emergency ☎ 310 3456), 2 Soi Soonvijai 7, New Phetburi Rd

▶▶ *TMVC Clinic* (☎ 655 1024, email bkk@tmvc.com.au), 8th Floor, Alma link Building, 25 Soi Chidlom

Chiang Mai

▶▶ *McCormick Hospital* (☎ 241107), Kaew Nawarat Rd

▶▶ *Chiang Puek Hospital* (☎ 220022, fax 218120), 1/7 Chang Pheuak Rd Soi 2

Phuket

▶▶ *Bangkok Phuket Hospital* (☎ 254421), Yonngyok Uthit Rd

▶▶ *Phuket Adventist Hospital* (☎212386, fax 212149), 4/1 Tepasatri Rd

VIETNAM

Medical care is pretty limited here, especially in rural areas where it may be practically nonexistent. You'll need to get to either Ho Chi Minh City or Hanoi, and if you have anything serious, it's probably best to go to somewhere like Bangkok (Thailand) or Hong Kong.

Ho Chi Minh City

▶▶ *Bach Mai Hospital* (☎ 852-2004, 852-2083), Giai Phong St

▶▶ *OSCAT/AEA International Clinic* (☎ 829 8424, fax 829 8551), 65 Nguyen Du Street, District 1

▶▶ *OSCAT/AEA International Clinic* (An Phu) (☎ 899 5080, 899 5084), Riverside Apartments, Block 8 Unit 1C, 670 Vo Truong Toa, Thao Dien Ward District 2

Hanoi

▶▶ *OSCAT/AEA International Clinic* (☎ 934 0555, fax 934 0556), Central Building, 31 Hai Ba Trung, Hoan Kiem District

Vung Tau

▶▶ *OSCAT/AEA International Clinic-Swedish Clinic* (☎ 845 2464, fax 823 0042), 358 Van Phuc Road, Vung Tau

▶▶ *OSCAT/AEA International Clinic* (☎ 858 776, 858 779), 1 Thanh Thai St, Vung Tau

FIRST AID

Although we give guidance on basic first aid procedures here remember that, unless you're an experienced first aider and confident you know what you're doing, it's possible to do more harm than good. Always seek medical help if it is available, but if you are far from any help, follow the guidelines given in this chapter.

! See the inside backcover for guidelines on responding to an emergency situation, dealing with near drowning and how to perform emergency (cardiopulmonary) resuscitation.

CUTS & OTHER WOUNDS

This includes any break in the skin – it could be an insect bite you've scratched, sunburn that's blistered, a raw area that your sandals have rubbed, a small graze or cut or a larger open wound from a fall or coming off a motorbike. If you're travelling in areas with poor environmental cleanliness and lack of clean water, there's a high risk of infection, especially in the hot, humid climates of the tropics and subtropics.

Carry a few antiseptic wipes on you to use as an immediate measure, especially if no water is available. A small wound can be cleaned with an antiseptic wipe (but remember to wipe across the wound just once). Deep or dirty wounds need to be cleaned thoroughly, as follows:

▶ make sure your hands are clean before you start
▶ wear gloves if you are cleaning somebody else's wound
▶ use bottled or boiled water (allowed to cool) or an antiseptic solution like povidone-iodine
▶ use plenty of water – pour it on the wound from a container
▶ embedded dirt and other particles can be removed with tweezers or flushed out using a syringe to squirt water (you can get more pressure if you use a needle as well)
▶ dry wounds heal best, so avoid using antiseptic creams which keep the wound moist, but you could apply antiseptic powder or spray

▶ dry the wound with clean gauze before applying a dressing from your medical kit – alternatively, any clean material will do as long as it's not fluffy (avoid cotton wool) because this will stick

! *Any break in the skin makes you vulnerable to tetanus infection – if you didn't have a tetanus injection before you left, you'll need one now.*

A dressing will protect the wound from dirt, dust and flies. Alternatively, if the wound is small and you are confident you can keep it clean, leave it uncovered. Change the dressing regularly (eg once a day to start with), especially if the wound is oozing, and watch for signs of infection (see later in this chapter). Antibiotic powders are best avoided as a rule (although antiseptic powders are fine) because they can give you sensitivity reactions. Alcohol can be used if you have been bitten by an animal (p347) as it can help kill the rabies virus, but otherwise avoid using it on wounds. In general, it's best to avoid poultices and other local remedies if they seem likely to introduce infection.

If you have any swelling around the wound, raising the affected limb can help the swelling settle and the wound to heal (eg sit with your foot up on your pack, or fashion a sling for your arm – see later in this chapter).

It's best to seek medical advice for any wound that fails to heal after a week or so. If a wound is taking a long time to heal, consider improving your diet, especially your protein intake, to aid healing – see the Eating For Health section at the end of the Staying Healthy chapter.

DRESSINGS & BANDAGES

If you're wondering how and when to use all those mysterious-looking packages in your first aid kit, here's a quick rundown:

- small adhesive dressings (ie sticking plasters or Band-Aids) are useful for small wounds (although they can cause skin irritation in people who are allergic to them, especially in hot climates because they block sweating)

- nonadhesive dressings are usually plain gauze pads or sterile padded dressings; fix in place with tape or a crepe bandage
- use nonstick dressings (eg Melolin or paraffin gauze) for open, oozing wounds

Bear in mind the following if you are bandaging something:

▶ remove any rings from fingers (or toes) in case your hand swells
▶ keep fresh bandages rolled and unroll them as you put them on – this makes it easier to put them on smoothly and evenly
▶ start from the extremity and bandage in (ie for an ankle, start bandaging from the toes upward)
▶ don't just bandage the painful bit, you need to bandage from the joint below the injured area to the joint above (ie from toes to knee for an ankle)
▶ make sure the bandage is firm enough to prevent it from slipping, but not tight enough to cut into your flesh or stop the circulation – if your fingers or toes start going numb and cold, it's too tight

PRESSURE IMMOBILISATION BANDAGE

This is used for bites and stings from some venomous creatures: some snakes, blue-ringed octopus, box jellyfish and cone shell. It's not a tourniquet, but applies pressure over a wide area of the limb and delays the rate at which venom enters the circulation. Use a roller bandage, and apply it from the fingers or toes as far up the limb as possible. It should be as firm as for a sprained ankle. Use a splint to immobilise the limb.

SIGNS OF WOUND INFECTION

Infected wounds take much longer to heal, which is not only a nuisance when you're travelling, it can also be debilitating. When they eventually heal, they're more likely to scar. If a wound gets infected, the infection can spread into your blood to give you blood poisoning, which makes you seriously ill. If you suspect you have an infected wound, it's best to seek medical advice for an appropriate course of antibiotics. However, if medical help is not available, you should self-treat with antibiotics if you have any of the following signs of (mild) infection:

- pain (throbbing)
- redness, heat and swelling in the area around the wound
- pus (thick yellow discharge) in the wound
- red streaks going away from the wound

Any of the following signs indicates a more serious infection:

- swelling of the involved limb
- swelling of the nearest glands eg in the armpit for a wound in the hand, or in the groin for a leg or foot wound
- fever and feeling unwell

Start a course of antibiotics and get medical help as soon as possible. Suitable antibiotics are: flucloxacillin 250mg four times daily OR co-amoxiclav 250mg three times daily OR erythromycin (if you're allergic to penicillin) 250mg four times daily. Double these doses for serious infections while you're getting to medical help.

Some bacteria in the tropics cause ulcers (sores); treatment is with specific antibiotics.

WOUND CLOSURE

If a wound is deep or gaping, it may need to be closed to help it heal better. If you think you need stitches, the sooner it's done the better. However, it's probably best not to close them yourself unless you feel confident and able to do so. An alternative to stitching is to close small clean cuts with special sticky strips (such as steristrips) or butterfly dressings. Note that some wounds should never be closed:

- wounds that are dirty and can't be cleaned adequately
- animal or human bites
- infected wounds

For small clean cuts, you can apply wound closure strips or butterfly dressings as follows:

▶ see if the edges of the cut come together easi- 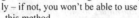 ly – if not, you won't be able to use this method

▶ clean the wound thoroughly, apply antiseptic and dry it with sterile gauze

▶ make sure any bleeding has stopped and that the area around the wound is clean and dry so that the dressings can stick

▶ put the dressings across the wound (see diagram) so that the edges of the wound are held together, taking care not to touch the side of the dressing that is to go on the wound

▶ space the dressings a few millimetres apart, and work from the middle of the wound outwards

▶ leave the dressings in place for about seven to 10 days, even if they start to look a bit worse for wear

Wound closure dressings can't be applied to hairy skin like the scalp, but scalp wounds can sometimes be closed by tying hair across them.

BLEEDING WOUNDS

Most cuts will stop bleeding on their own, but if a blood vessel of any size has been cut, it may continue bleeding for some time. Head and hand wounds, also wounds at joint creases, tend to be particularly bloody. To stop bleeding from a wound:

▶ wear gloves if you are stopping bleeding on a travel companion

- use your fingers or the palm of your hand to apply direct pressure to the wound, preferably over a sterile dressing or clean pad
- apply steady pressure for at least five minutes before looking to see if the bleeding has stopped
- raise the injured limb above the level of your heart
- lie down if possible
- put a sterile dressing over the original pad (don't move this) and bandage it in place
- check the bandage regularly in case bleeding restarts

Get medical help urgently if much blood has been lost.

! Never use a tourniquet to stop bleeding as this may cause gangrene – the only situation in which this may be appropriate is if the limb has been completely amputated.

BOILS & ABSCESSES

Don't try to burst these, however tempting it may seem, because this encourages the infection to spread. Instead:

- wash them with an antiseptic and keep them clean and dry as far as possible
- hot (clean) cloths may be soothing on the boil
- antibiotics don't usually help much with boils unless the infection spreads

SPLINTERS

Treat as follows:

- wash the area thoroughly with soap and water
- sterilise the tips of a pair of tweezers by boiling them for a few seconds
- grasp the splinter as close to the skin as possible and remove it carefully
- squeeze the wound to make it bleed (flushes out any remaining dirt)
- clean the area with antiseptic and cover it with a sticking plaster

If you're not up to date with your tetanus injections, you'll need a booster.

BURNS & SCALDS

There are two main dangers with burns:

- fluid loss through damage to blood vessels leading to shock – the amount of fluid lost from a burn is directly proportional to the area affected by the burn
- infection because of damage to the skin's natural barrier

Burns are classified according to how deep the damage to the skin is:

- painful area of redness – mild or first degree burn, usually heals well
- blisters form later, feels painful – moderate or second degree burn, usually heals well
- white or charred area, feels painless except around the edge – severe or third-degree burn, may result in extensive scarring

You need to seek medical attention for:

- any burn involving the hands, feet, armpits, face, neck or crotch
- any second or third degree burn
- any burn over 1cm to 2cm
- any burn in children

Mild burns or scalds (caused by hot fluid or steam) don't need medical attention unless they are extensive. Treat as follows:

- immediately pour cold water over the burn area for about 10 minutes or immerse it in cold water for about five minutes
- remove any jewellery such as rings, watches or tight clothing from the area before it swells up
- cover with a sterile nonstick dressing or paraffin gauze and bandage loosely in place
- don't burst any blisters, but if they burst anyway, cover with a nonadhesive sterile dressing
- apply antibiotic cream (eg silver sulphadiazine 1%), but avoid any other creams, ointments or greases
- take simple painkillers if necessary

FAINTING

This can occur in many different situations: pain or fright, standing still in the heat, emotional upset, exhaustion or lack of food. It's a brief loss of consciousness due to a temporary reduction in blood flow to the brain. Faints don't usually last long, but you may injure yourself as you fall. If you feel you are about to faint, or you notice someone you are with is about to (usually because they go as white as a sheet and start to sway), lie down before you fall. If someone faints:

- ▸ raise their legs (this helps to improve the blood flow to the brain)
- ▸ make sure they have plenty of fresh air
- ▸ as they recover, allow them to sit up gradually
- ▸ check for and treat any injury caused by falling

CONVULSIONS

A convulsion, or fit, is caused by a disturbance in brain function resulting in involuntary contractions of the muscles of the body and leading to loss of consciousness. Fits can occur for lots of reasons, including head injury, diseases affecting the brain, shortage of oxygen to the brain, some poisons and epilepsy. In babies and children, fits can be caused by a high temperature. If someone has a fit:

- ▸ ease their fall if possible
- ▸ loosen any clothing round the neck and protect their head by placing something soft under their head and shoulders if you can
- ▸ remove any sharp objects or other potential hazards from the vicinity
- ▸ don't try to restrain them or put anything in their mouth
- ▸ once the convulsions have stopped, put them in the recovery position (see inside backcover)
- ▸ get medical help

NOSEBLEED

This can be caused by blowing your nose vigorously or after a particularly earth-shattering sneeze. It's more likely when you have a cold. It occurs when blood vessels on the inner surface of your nose burst. Nosebleeds can look very dramatic, but most will stop quite quickly. If you get a nosebleed, do the following:

▶ sit down and put your head forward
▶ pinch your nose firmly just below the bridge (the bony bit) and keep a steady pressure for 10 minutes or until the bleeding has stopped
▶ rest quietly after it has stopped, and don't blow your nose or pick it for at least three hours or the bleeding may start again

An ice pack over the bridge of the nose can help. Putting your head back will allow blood to drip down your throat, which can cause irritation to your stomach and possibly vomiting.

! If you can't stop the bleeding after about half an hour OR the bleeding is torrential and you start to feel dizzy, get medical help.

Note that if you get a nosebleed after a head injury, it may indicate a skull fracture, and you need to seek medical help urgently.

SPRAINS & STRAINS

! If you're not sure if your injury is a sprain or a broken bone, treat as a broken bone (see Broken Bones later in this chapter).

These soft tissue injuries affect ligaments and muscles and are common if you're doing any sort of vigorous activity like walking over rough terrain. They often occur as a result of a sudden wrench or twist. Sprains are injuries to a ligament near a joint, usually the ankle or knee joint. You get pain and swelling, with bruising often appearing 12 to 24 hours later. Strains are damage to the muscle caused by sudden violent movements, and are felt as a sudden sharp pain within the muscle body.

Treatment of any soft tissue injury is with the RICE principles:

▶ Rest the injured part
▶ Apply Ice/snow or a cold compress (not directly on the skin)
▶ Compress the injury (use a bandage)
▶ Elevate the injured part

All these measures will help to reduce the swelling, bruising and pain, and are best started as early as possible after the injury. Continue with this for 24 to 48 hours or longer if the injury is more severe.

Use an elastic bandage, or a thick layer of padding kept in place with a crepe bandage, to compress the swelling. Check the bandage regularly in case further swelling has made it too tight.

Simple painkillers are useful to ease the discomfort. If the sprain is mild, you may be able to walk on it, perhaps with an improvised crutch to take the weight off it. To prevent further injury, wear boots with good ankle support.

! For severe sprains you will need an X-ray to exclude the possibility of a broken bone, but in the meantime treat as for a broken bone and avoid putting weight on it.

PAINFUL JOINTS

If you're doing any sort of strenuous activity, you're at risk of getting overuse injuries of your joints. Signs are painful, sometimes swollen joints, worse after use.

Treat with rest, a cold compress and anti-inflammatory painkillers like ibuprofen (if you don't have a history of stomach ulcers or indigestion). A support bandage may help, although rest is the most effective measure.

Prevention is the best treatment: make sure you are pre-pared by training well to improve your fitness; remember to warm up and down properly before starting an activity.

MAJOR TRAUMA

INITIAL ASSESSMENT

Accidents can happen anywhere and what you do is deter-mined to some extent by the circumstances you are in and how readily available medical care is. However, remember that emergency services may be very different from what you are used to. They may be very much slower at responding to a call, so you need to be prepared to do at least an initial assessment and to ensure the person comes to no further harm. A basic plan of action is outlined as follows:

▸ keep calm and think through what you need to do
▸ carefully look over the injured person in the position you found them (unless this is hazardous for some reason eg on a cliff edge)
▸ check for heart action (pulses – see diagram), breathing and major blood loss
▸ if necessary, and you know how, start resuscitation – see inside backcover
▸ take immediate steps to control any bleeding by applying direct pressure
▸ check for shock, head injuries, spine and limb injuries, and any other injuries
▸ make the person as comfortable as possible and reassure them
▸ keep the person warm if necessary by insulating them from cold or wet ground (use whatever you have to hand eg a sleeping bag)
▸ don't move the person if a spinal injury is possible
▸ get medical help urgently

HEAD INJURY

Your brain is vital to life and you should do everything you can to prevent injury to it – wear a helmet or hard hat if you are going to do any potentially risky activities. You need to seek medical help for any significant head injury.

Scalp wounds need to be treated like any other wound (see earlier). Serious head injury can occur with little or no signs of external injury. If a person has received an injury to the head, you need to assess whether there has been damage to the brain. You can do this by assessing whether they were unconscious at all (how much damage occurred is related to how long unconsciousness lasted), how they are behaving now, and if they show any signs of deterioration in the hours or days following the accident.

- Dazed but didn't lose consciousness – very little risk of brain damage.
- Unconscious (blacked out) for a few minutes, can't remember accident happening – the person is concussed (ie the brain has been shaken and bruised a bit). They may feel dizzy and nauseated, with mild headache, and memory loss can last for a few hours. Concussion generally doesn't cause any permanent damage, but you need to keep an eye on the person for 24 hours in case they deteriorate. Seek medical help.
- Prolonged unconsciousness of more than 10 minutes (coma) – this usually indicates more serious brain damage, and may be associated with a skull fracture. Put the person into the recovery position (see inside backcover) and get medical help immediately. Evacuation may be necessary.

Signs of a skull fracture include:

- blood coming from nose, mouth or throat not due to external injury
- clear, watery fluid dripping from ear or nose
- a depression or dip in the skull

Anyone who has had a head injury causing unconsciousness, however brief, should be observed for signs of deterioration in the 24 to 48 hours following injury. Head injury can sometimes result in compression of the brain because of bleeding from a damaged blood vessel within the head. This causes blood to accumulate gradually within the closed space of the skull, squashing the brain. Signs of brain compression or severe brain damage include:

- disorientation and confusion
- vomiting
- severe headache
- drowsiness
- irritability or change in personality
- noisy, slow breathing
- unequal or dilated pupils that may not react to light
- weakness down one side of the body

If someone has a head injury but is conscious:

▶ staunch any bleeding
▶ check if they know who and where they are, what the date is etc
▶ check they can move all their limbs and don't have any unusual sensations (eg tingling)
▶ sit them up gradually and then do a test walk to check balance
▶ deal with any external wounds
▶ avoid alcohol and sedatives on the first evening
▶ rest up for a day or two until you're sure the person is back to normal

If the person is concussed (eg keeps asking the same question), keep a close eye on them for the first 24 hours and be ready to get medical help immediately if there is any deterioration in their condition.

Note that sometimes a head injury can occur when someone has lost consciousness from another cause (eg a faint).

NECK & SPINE INJURY

The main worry with any spinal or neck injury is damage to your spinal cord. Apart from supporting your trunk and head, your backbone (spine) provides a protective covering for nerve fibres (the spinal cord) carrying messages from your brain to all parts of your body. If these fibres are partly or completely cut, the damage caused may be permanent. The most vulnerable parts of the spine are your neck and lower back. Causes of spinal injury include falling from a height, diving into a shallow pool and hitting the bottom, a head-on crash in a motor vehicle, and being thrown from a motorbike.

Severe persistent neck or back pain indicate that you may have injured your spine. If you have also damaged the spinal cord, you may not be able to move your limbs, or you may have abnormal or no feelings in your body below the level of the injury (for example tingling or a feeling of heaviness). If the injury is at a high level, breathing difficulties may occur if the nerves to the chest muscles are affected.

The main priority in someone with a spinal injury is to prevent new or further damage to the spinal cord by immobilisation of the spine and extremely careful handling during any evacuation procedure.

If in doubt, eg the person is unconscious, assume there is a spinal injury until proven otherwise.

BROKEN BONES

A break or crack in a bone is called a fracture. Bones are generally tough and you need a pretty forceful injury to break one, although old or diseased bones break more easily. In a simple fracture, the bone breaks in one place and the skin isn't torn. An open fracture is where the broken ends of the bone stick through the skin. You should assume that any fracture associated with a wound near it is an open one, even if you can't see the bone protruding (the broken ends may have come through the skin and gone back).

Any broken bone needs medical attention as it needs to be set properly, and any damage to the surrounding tissues needs to be assessed and treated. Open fractures have the added risk of infection because the bone is exposed, and generally need more urgent treatment.

A broken bone is often obvious because it hurts like hell. Otherwise, indications of a fracture include:

- forceful injury eg a violent blow, a fall or impact with a moving object
- snapping sound as the bone broke
- pain made worse by movement
- tenderness when you press over the bone at the site of injury
- obvious swelling and bruising over the injury site
- pain when you try to use the limb and you can't put your weight on it
- obvious deformity of the limb – twisting, shortening or bending

What you do next will depend to a certain extent on the circumstances you're in and how readily medical help is available. The aim with any type of fracture is to prevent further damage by immobilising the affected part in some way (usually with a splint or sling). Unless the person is in immediate danger where they are, don't move them until the fracture has been supported and immobilised. Painkillers are important but if medical help is close at hand, avoid taking anything by mouth in case an operation is needed to fix the fracture.

Some basic guidelines for a simple fracture are as follows:

- if the affected limb is bent or angled, straighten it by pulling firmly in the line of the bone, but if this causes too much pain, it's OK to leave it
- if you are near medical help, immobilise the limb by bandaging it and support the arm in a sling against your body or bandage the uninjured leg to the injured one

▸ in the field situation, it's worth immobilising the limb in a splint – use plastic air splints or structural aluminium malleable (SAM) splints if you are carrying them, or you can improvise with any piece of equipment you have, but make sure you pad the inside of the splint

Note that simple fractures don't need to be fixed straight away because healing takes several weeks, so if you have a chance to go to a better hospital further away, it would be worthwhile.

With an open fracture, you need to cover the wound and control any bleeding (apply pressure with a clean pad or dressing) before immobilising the limb as for a simple fracture. If no medical help is available within one to two hours, start taking antibiotics (eg cephalexin 500mg four times daily) to prevent infection.

Remember to check that any bandage or splint you've applied is not cutting off the circulation (indicated by numbness, tingling and blue or white colour). Loosen the bandages or splint immediately if necessary.

In cold conditions, frostbite is a particular risk so you need to protect the hand or foot from cold by covering them appropriately.

DISLOCATIONS

This can occur when a bone is wrenched into an abnormal position or because of violent muscle contractions (eg a fit). This displaces the head of a bone from the joint, most commonly the shoulder, thumb, finger and jaw. There can be an associated fracture and there's often damage to the structures surrounding the joint. Don't attempt to replace a dislocation if a fracture is present.

! As a general rule, don't attempt to replace a dislocated joint if medical help is accessible because you can cause permanent damage.

You need to treat dislocations with immobilisation and pain relief as for a simple fracture.

BROKEN RIBS

Flail chest is when a heavy blow fractures several ribs in more than one place. This is an emergency because you will not be able to breathe properly. On inspection, a section of your chest will be moving in the opposite direction to the rest of your chest during breathing. The broken part needs to be splinted immediately by taping a firm bandage over it and supporting your arm in a sling on the injured side.

Otherwise, broken ribs are painful but don't need any specific treatment. Take strong painkillers, such as co-codamol, at the prescribed intervals. If the pain is very severe, or there are multiple fractures, you may need to strap your chest.

! Get help urgently if you experience breathing difficulties or cough up blood.

INTERNAL INJURIES

Some injuries can cause severe internal damage and bleeding without significant external injury. It's easy to control bleeding from external wounds on the skin by applying pressure but you can't do this for internal bleeding.

! Internal injuries are generally caused by considerable violence and always need urgent expert medical care and evacuation if you are in a remote area.

They may not be obvious to begin with, but you need to suspect internal bleeding if there are signs of shock (casualty looks pale, feels dizzy with weak rapid pulse and low blood pressure). Sometimes bleeding in the abdomen can produce a tender, slowly expanding abdomen.

CHOKING

You choke if your airway is completely or partly blocked, for example as a result of swallowing a small bone, eating too quickly or because of vomit, especially if you're drunk. Children often put things in their mouths, and this may result in choking. Small toys, coins and food such as peanuts or boiled sweets are particular risks.

It's usually obvious if a person is choking – they will have difficulty speaking, may gag and usually clutch their throat. A child may make a whistling noise, try to cry but be unable to, or may go blue in the face and collapse.

If an adult or child appears to be choking:

▶ get them to cough – this may bring up the blockage
▶ if this doesn't work, give them four sharp blows between the shoulder blades (ask adults to bend forward; children can be up-ended or bent over your knee)

If this doesn't work, try the following techniques:

▶ child (over one year) – place child on the floor or across your lap and place your hands one on each side of the chest just below the armpits; squeeze the child's chest by giving four sharp thrusts with your hands
▶ adult – lie the casualty down on the floor on their side; place both your hands on the side of their chest, under their armpit, and give four quick downwards thrusts

For babies, you won't be able to get them to cough, so you need to give four sharp slaps between the shoulders to start with – lie the baby face down on your forearm and support their head and shoulders on your hand. If you need to give chest thrusts, lie the baby face down on your lap and give four quick squeezes, as described for a child (but gentler).

! Check to see if the blockage is cleared (remove it from the mouth if necessary) if not, get medical help urgently.

GLOSSARY

acetaminophen – US name for *paracetamol*

acute – describes a brief illness of rapid onset; compare with *chronic*

adrenaline – hormone that prepares the body for flight or fright; it's given by injection to treat severe allergic reactions (such as to bee sting); US term is *epinephrine*

AIDS – acquired immune deficiency syndrome

AMS – acute mountain sickness

antibiotic – drug used to treat bacterial infections

antidiarrhoeals – refers to drugs used to treat the symptoms of diarrhoea ('blockers' or 'stoppers')

Ayurveda – traditional medical system of India and Sri Lanka

bacteria – tiny organisms, some of which can cause diseases that can be treated with *antibiotics*

BCG – stands for bacille Calmette-Guérin; it's the vaccine for tuberculosis

bilharzia – see *schistosomiasis*

booster – dose of vaccine given after a full course to bring protection up to optimum level

bowel – a term for the lower part of the intestinal tract

breakbone fever – old name for dengue fever

CDC – Centers for Disease Control and Prevention (US)

chronic – describes a disease that usually comes on slowly and is prolonged

colic – pain that comes and goes in waves

cutaneous – related to skin

dermatitis – general term for an itchy skin rash

DHF – dengue haemorrhagic fever

diapers – *see* nappies

diuretic – substance (like coffee, alcohol and some therapeutic medicines) that increases the volume of urine lost

drug – any substance used to alleviate symptoms or treat disease; the term is used interchangeably with medicine and medication; also popularly used to describe illegal substances

dysentery – any diarrhoea with blood

eczema – *dermatitis* due to intrinsic causes

415

endemic – describes diseases that occur commonly in people in a particular area

enteric fever – another term for typhoid or paratyphoid fever (enteric means related to the intestine)

epidemic – sudden outbreak of an infectious disease that rapidly affects lots of people

epinephrine – see *adrenaline*

fever – when your body temperature is higher than normal (normal is 37°C or 98.6°F); usually caused by a bacterial or viral infection

generic – used of a drug name, it means the chemical as opposed to the brand name of a drug; by convention brand names are always capitalised

glucose – sugar

haemorrhagic – associated with bleeding

HIV – human immunodeficiency virus

immunisation – production of *immunity*, often through injection of a substance (called a *vaccine*), although oral immunisations are also possible

immunity – protection against disease

Indo-Pacific – relating to the region of the Indian and West Pacific oceans off the coast of South-East Asia

infectious – describes a disease that is caused by a microorganism (bacteria, virus, fungus etc) and can be transmitted from person to person (ie something you can 'catch'), unlike cancer for example

jaundice – yellowing of the skin and whites of the eyes because of the liver not working properly

Lariam – trade name for *mefloquine*

medication – see *drug*

medicine – see *drug*

mefloquine – a drug used in the prevention and treatment of malaria; brand name is *Lariam*

microbe – another term for *microorganism*

microorganism – any organism too small to be visible to the naked eye, includes bacteria, viruses, fungi etc

nappies – called *diapers* in the US

ORS – oral rehydration salts

paracetamol – simple painkiller,

also good for lowering fever; US term is *acetaminophen*

parasite – any living thing (eg a tapeworm) that lives in or on another living thing

pressure bandaging – use of a bandage to apply pressure over a wide area of the limb; used in management of some bites and stings (see also *tourniquet*)

prevalent – widespread, current

prophylaxis – prevention of disease

protozoa – single-celled microorganisms; include malaria parasites and Giardia

resistance – when antibiotics or other drugs are ineffective against a microorganism

schistosomiasis (bilharzia) – parasitic disease caused by a tiny freshwater worm

SPF – sun protection factor

STI – sexually transmitted infection

subcutaneous – describes something (eg an injection, a lump) under the skin

sulpha drugs – a group of antibiotics

TB – tuberculosis

TCM – traditional Chinese medicine

tourniquet – a device used to press on an artery to stop blood flow; use is very restricted, and it's not indicated for treating bites and stings – see *pressure bandaging*

thrush – common name for vaginal candidiasis

topical – term used to describe a treatment that is applied directly to the affected part of the body (such as a cream applied onto a skin rash)

toxin – poison

ulcer – break in the skin (or mucous membrane like the lining of the stomach)

vaccine – preparation that is used to stimulate immunity

vaccination – not exactly synonomous with immunisation, but in this book we have used the terms interchangeably

virus – minute particle; cause many diseases, including colds, flu, hepatitis, AIDS etc

visceral – related to the viscera, or internal organs

WHO – World Health Organization

Colour indicates symptoms
Bold indicates maps

LONELY PLANET PRODUCTS

TRAVEL GUIDEBOOKS

Travel Guides explore a destination in depth, with options to suit a range of budgets. With reliable, practical advice on getting around, restaurants and accommodation, these easy-to-use guides also include numerous detailed maps, colour photographs, extensive background material and coverage of sights both on and off the beaten track.

PHRASEBOOKS

Lonely Planet phrasebooks cover essential words and phrases travellers need to effectively communicate. With colour tabs for quick reference, extensive vocabulary lists, use of local scripts and easy to follow pronunciation keys, these handy, pocket size language guides cover most situations a traveller is likely to encounter.

PISCES BOOKS

Beautifully illustrated with full-colour photos, Lonely Planet's Pisces Books explore the world's best diving and snorkelling areas and prepare divers for what to expect when they get there, both topside and underwater. Dive sites are described in detail with specifics on depths, visibility, level of difficulty, special conditions, underwater photography tips and common and unusual marine life present.

WALKING GUIDEBOOKS

With detailed descriptions ranging from family walks to hard high-level routes, advice on when to and how to do it, detailed and reliable maps and background information, these informative walking guides are an invaluable resource for both independent walkers and those in an organised group - in fact, for anyone who believes that the best way to see the world is on foot.

CITY MAPS

Lonely Planet's City Map series covers the world's great cities, both on and off the beaten track. This full-colour and easy-to-use product contains downtown and metropolitan maps, transit routes, unique walking tours, and essential information (including phone numbers), plus a complete index of streets and sights. The information is up-to-date and accurate, and the maps are plastic-coated for extra durability.

TRAVEL ATLASES

Lonely Planet's Travel Atlases are thoroughly researched and fact-checked by the guidebook authors to ensure they complement the guidebooks. And the booklet format means none of the holes, wrinkles, tears or constant folding and refolding characteristic of large sheet maps.

PLANET TALK

Our FREE quarterly printed newsletter is full of tips from travellers and anecdotes from Lonely Planet guidebook authors. Every issue is packed with up-to-date travel news and advice, and includes a postcard from Lonely Planet co-founder Tony Wheeler, mail from travellers, a look at life on the road through the eyes of a Lonely Planet author, topical health advice, prizes for the best travel yarn, news about forthcoming Lonely Planet events and a complete list of Lonely Planet books and products.

To join our mailing list, residents of the UK, Europe and Africa can email us at go@lonelyplanet.co.uk; residents of North and South America can email us at info@lonelyplanet.com; the rest of the world can email us at talk2us@lonelyplanet.com.au, or contact any Lonely Planet office.

LONELY PLANET PRODUCTS

COMET

Our FREE monthly email newsletter brings you all
the latest travel news, features, interviews, com-
petitions, destination ideas, travellers' tips &
tales, Q&As, raging debates and related links.
Find out what's new on the Lonely Planet Web
site and which books are about to hit the shelves.
Subscribe from your desktop: www.lonelyplanet.com/comet

LONELY PLANET ONLINE

Lonely Planet's award-winning web site has insid-
er info on hundreds of destinations from
Amsterdam to Zimbabwe, complete with interac-
tive maps and colour photographs. You'll also find
the latest travel news, recent reports from travellers on the road, guidebook upgrades and a live-
ly bulletin board where you can meet fellow travellers, swap recommendations and seek advice.
www.lonelyplanet.com or AOL keyword: lp

UPGRADES

Lonely Planet publishes online Upgrades of some of our most popular guidebooks. Upgrades are regular reports from Lonely Planet
authors summarising important information gathered since the
book was published. Designed as supplements to current editions of
selected Lonely Planet guidebooks, Upgrades can be downloaded
for free from the Lonely Planet web site, at:
www.lonelyplanet.com/upgrades

1 Assess the Scene
Is there a danger to yourself, the casualty or others?

- ▶ Yes: if possible remove danger but do not put yourself at risk.
- ▶ No: go to step 2.
- ▶ Have you called for medical assistance?

2 Assess the Casualty
Is casualty conscious? Shake gently and shout for response.

- ▶ Yes: go to step 3.
- ▶ No: place casualty in recovery position (see illustration).

3 Clear Airway & Check Breathing.
Clear and open airway. Remove any objects or vomit.
Check for breathing: is the chest rising and falling?
Can you feel the breath on your cheek? (wait for up to 10 seconds)

- ▶ Yes: place casualty in recovery position and examine for injuries.
- ▶ No: you need to breathe for the casualty: see step 4.

4 Perform Expired Air Resuscitation
Turn the casualty on to their back.

- ▶ Use one hand to gently tilt head back.
- ▶ Pinch nose closed using thumb and index finger of other hand.
- ▶ Open mouth, keeping chin raised.
- ▶ Take a full breath and place your lips on the casualty's mouth
- ▶ Blow steadily into the casualty's mouth for about two seconds.

ADULT
- ▶ Repeat so that you give two effective breaths.

BABY/CHILD
- ▶ Give two effective puffs or light breaths.